OUR LAND
OUR SURVIVAL

OUR LAND OUR SURVIVAL

Vulnerabilization and Decolonial Resistance Through
Communal Land in Puerto Rico and Barbuda

LINE ALGOED

TERRA NOSTRA PRESS

TERRA NOSTRA PRESS

International Center for Community Land Trusts
3146 Buena Vista Street
Madison, Wisconsin, USA 53704

Copyright© 2025 Line Algoed

All rights reserved. No part of this publication may be reproduced, distributed, or transmitted in any form or by any means or stored in a database or retrieval system without the prior written permission of the the International Center for Community Land Trusts, except in the case of brief quotations embedded in critical articles and reviews. For requests for permission to reprint portions of this book, please contact info@TerraNostraPress.org.

The following chapters are reprinted with permission:
Chapter 3, *Radical Housing Journal*, Vol. 1(1), April 2019
Chapter 4, *Avery Review*, No. 61, April 2023
Chapter 6, *International Journal of the Commons*, Vol. 18(1), January 2024

Illustration and graphic design: Maartje Alders

Publisher's Cataloging-in-Publication Data

Names: Algoed, Line, author.
Title: Our land, our survival : vulnerabilization and decolonial resistance through communal land in Puerto Rico and Barbuda / Line Algoed.
Description: Includes bibliographical references. | Madison, WI: Terra Nostra Press (imprint), International Center for Community Land Trusts, 2025.
Identifiers: Library of Congress Control Number: 2025917782
| ISBN: 979-8-9861776-4-9 (paperback) | 979-8-9861776-5-6 (ebook)
Subjects: LCSH Land reform—Puerto Rico. | Land reform—Barbuda. | Land tenure—Puerto Rico—21st century. | Land tenure—Barbuda—21st century. | Community organization—Puerto Rico. | Community organization—Barbuda. | Puerto Rico—Social conditions. | Barbuda—Social conditions. | Puerto Rico—Colonial influence. | Barbuda—Colonial influence. | Decolonization—Puerto Rico. | Decolonization—Barbuda. | BISAC SOCIAL SCIENCE / Activism & Social Justice | POLITICAL SCIENCE / Colonialism & Post-Colonialism | BUSINESS & ECONOMICS / Development / Sustainable Development
Classification: LCC HD1333.P9 .A54 2025 | DDC 333.2—dc

For Caraballo and all the community warriors
in Puerto Rico and Barbuda
¡La Lucha Sigue!

'El territorio es la vida, la vida no se vende, se ama y se defiende.'
"The territory is life, life is not for sale, it is loved and defended"

> Francia Marquez, Vice President of Colombia (2018)

'No puedes comprar mi vida. La tierra no se vende.'
"You can't buy my life. The land is not for sale"

> Calle 13, "Latinoamérica" (2010)

'Our land system is the reason we have survived. As simple as that.'

> John Mussington, marine biologist, Barbuda

CONTENTS

Foreword..xiii

CHAPTER 1
INTRODUCTION 1
   This is Our Land 1
   Land is Life 4
      Research Questions and Research Objectives 6

CHAPTER 2
THE STUDY OF VULNERABILIZATION AND RESISTANCE:
Theories, Cases, and Methods 9
   Literature Review 9
      The Colonial Roots of Contemporary Land Policy......................... 10
      Collective Land Tenure 14
      Disaster Capitalism 19
      Land and Resistance 24
      Global Knowledge Circuits and Decolonial International Solidarity Networks............ 26
   Theoretical Framework 29
      Decolonial Thought 30
      Feminist Research 35
   Positioning Myself in My Research 39
      Case Studies: The Caribbean as the Starting Place........................ 43
      Puerto Rico... 47
      Barbuda 52
      Methodological Approach... 55

CHAPTER 3
THIS LAND IS OURS: Vulnerabilization and Resistance in Informal Settlements in Puerto Rico: Lessons from the Caño Martín Peña Community Land Trust 65
    Introduction 66
    Creation of the Caño Martín Peña Community Land Trust 69
    How the Caño CLT Works *73*
    Hurricane María, Disaster Capitalism and the Response of the Caño Martín Peña Residents 75
        The Response of the Caño Communities to the Hurricane *77*
    A Political Ecological Approach to the Vulnerabilization of Informal Communities 78
        Public Discourse on Housing Informality *80*
        Politics of Unsustainability and Informal Settlements *82*
        Knowledges from the Caño Communities *84*
    Conclusion 86

CHAPTER 4
COMMUNAL LAND AS SURVIVAL: Barbuda's Decolonial World View .. 97
    Barbuda Defies Private Property 88
    "Paradise Found" 90
    Hurricane Irma as Opportunity for "Peace, Love, and Happiness" 91
    Resisting Individual Land Titles 93
    Neocolonial Development and "Sustainability" 94
    Coloniality of Development 99
    Decolonial Resistance for Survival 100

CHAPTER 5
"NEITHER IRMA, NOR MARIA WILL TAKE WHAT'S OURS":
Collective Land Tenure for Just Climate Change Adaptation in Puerto Rico and Barbuda 103
    Introduction 104
    Land Tenure Security and Just Climate Change Adaptation 107
    Research Design and Methodology 110
    Opting for Collective Land Titles: The Caño Martín Peña CLT in San Juan, Puerto Rico 113
        Community Displacements *114*
        The Caño Martín Peña Community Land Trust *116*

    Emphasis on Individual Land Titles and Individual Risk Mitigation
    after Hurricane Maria *118*
  Barbuda's Historic Resistance to Land Privatization 119
    The Barbuda Land Act *120*
    Previous Attempts to Privatize Barbuda's Land *120*
    Land Tenure Reform in Barbuda after Hurricane Irma *121*
  The Benefits of Collective Tenure for Communities Confronting
  Climate Change 113
    The Importance of the Caño CLT in the Face of Climate Change *113*
    The Importance of Barbuda's Communal Land Ownership in the Face
    of Climate Change *127*
  Discussion and Conclusions 130

CHAPTER 6
COMMUNITIES AS GLOBAL ACTORS IN COUNTERHEGEMONIC POLICY MOBILITIES: Lessons from the Community Land Trust Movement 133
  Introduction 134
  Whose Ideas Travel? 136
    The Global CLT Movement as Commons-Based Resistance *137*
    New International Solidarities *139*
    Epistemic Justice and Traveling Knowledges *140*
  Community-Engaged Research 141
  The Community-Driven History of The CLT Movement 143
    The Caño CLT: Born from Community-Driven Mobilities *144*
    The Caño CLT as a Driver for Circulation of CLTs in the Global South ... *145*
    The Relation between Communities and Supporting Organizations *147*
  Conclusion 149

CHAPTER 7
CONCLUSION 153
  Summary of the Findings of the Chapters 155
  Vulnerabilization and Resistance through Communal Land in Puerto Rico
  and Barbuda 158
    Vulnerabilization in Puerto Rico *159*
    Vulnerabilization in Barbuda *162*
    Resistance against Vulnerabilization in Puerto Rico *166*
    Resistance against Vulnerabilization in Barbuda *167*
    Differences Between Communities in Vulnerabilization and Resistance *169*

Implications 178
  Limitations and Research Outlook 180
Our Land, Our Survival 183

Appendix 1: List of Interviews, Observations and Exchanges 185
References 187
Acknowledgements 201
About the Authors 203

FOREWORD

John Emmeus Davis
Editor-in-Chief, Terra Nostra Press

The International Center for Community Land Trusts launched its in-house imprint, Terra Nostra Press, in 2020 with publication of On Common Ground: International Perspectives on the Community Land Trust. Line Algoed co-authored two of its twenty-six chapters and served as one of the book's co-editors.

Over the next five years, all of the books and monographs published by Terra Nostra Press featured the same innovative form of land tenure that had inspired On Common Ground, a social enterprise known as the "community land trust" (CLT). Notably, many of the organizations described in these publications bore only a passing resemblance to the model that had emerged out of the American Civil Rights Movement in the 1970s and been slowly refined over the next two decades. They were variations on a theme of what is known in the United States as the "classic CLT."

These organizational and operational variations multiplied as CLTs continued to spread to other regions of the world. The American "model" remained a touchstone, but the CLT was modified again and again, adapted to fit conditions, priorities, laws, and needs that differed greatly from place to place. Most of the authors published by Terra Nostra Press, accordingly, tended to speak of the CLT rather expansively as a flexible strategy for community-led development on community-owned land of housing (and other land-based assets) that remain permanently affordable. This generic definition has grounded the work of the International Center for Community Land Trusts and guided the selection of manuscripts by Terra Nostra Press.

The portrayal of CLTs in *Our Land Our Survival* is more expansive still. The CLT is viewed by Line—and by the colleagues who joined her in co-authoring the book's middle chapters—not as a singular "model," but as one strategy among several for the "collectivization of land ownership." It can be said, in fact, that the book is not really "about" CLTs, compared to previous publications of Terra Nostra Press.

The regular appearance on stage of the Caño Martín Peña Community Land Trust notwithstanding, the spotlight is usually directed elsewhere. Vulnerabilization and resistance play the starring roles.

Line and her colleagues are less concerned with describing a particular CLT, in other words, than with examining the conditions that make impoverished, place-based communities vulnerable to being displaced when confronted by natural disasters. They look specifically at places in the Caribbean where collective forms of tenure like a CLT have long existed or recently emerged, documenting the ways that collective landholding has served as a "strategy of resistance." It has allowed communities to withstand displacement pressures from land-clearing hurricanes and land-grabbing capitalists who predictably appear in their wake. It has enabled devastated communities to recover more quickly and to develop more equitably.

These findings fly in the face of the dominant development paradigm touted by international agencies, neo-liberal economists, governments at every level, and private investors of every stripe. These global elites are nearly unanimous in proclaiming the privatization of land, individual titling, and an increase in single-family homeownership to be a necessary and superior path to prosperity. This policy trifecta appears in numerous schemes for the rejuvenation of both urban neighborhoods and rural areas, but it is most frequently embedded in programs and plans for the privatization and individualization of customary lands and informal settlements in the Global South, places where generations of people have lived on land or made use of land they neither legally own nor securely lease.

The counter-argument that is forcefully made by Line and her colleagues is that individual titling can actually make it harder for low-income communities to prosper—or even to survive—when battered by extreme weather events. Compiling evidence from the hurricane season of 2017, they show that collective landholding out-performed individual ownership in both Puerto Rico and Barbuda when it came to rebuilding devastated neighborhoods and preventing the displacement of economically disadvantaged residents.

They focus on two islands in the Caribbean, but their analysis is applicable to any vulnerable community impacted by hurricanes, floods, or wildfires, underscoring the potential of collective landholding for climate change adaptation. It is applicable, as well, to any mobilized community whose local leaders are considering whether to adopt a collective form of tenure as a strategy of political resistance and equitable development.

The book is not explicitly "about" CLTs, therefore, but it ends up providing an extremely rich theoretical and practical rationale for why they are needed and what they can do.

The book also deepens the rationale for resident engagement in the management of collective forms of tenure. CLT advocates speak often of the importance of "keeping the 'C' in CLT," meaning that people who live within a CLT's service area should be directly involved in guiding and governing the nonprofit organization that holds the land beneath their feet. Such involvement is said to be good for the organization, contributing to its acceptability, accountability, and productivity. Line and her colleagues make a similar point, extolling the leadership of local residents in organizing and maintaining collective landholding in Puerto Rico and Barbuda. Their analysis of why "community matters" goes further, however, than most of the current CLT literature, for they examine not only how resident engagement strengthens the entity that owns the land, but how it strengthens the community the organization serves.

Their conclusion is that collective ownership in Puerto Rico and Barbuda has delivered a variety of social, political, and pedagogical benefits that accrue to the community as a whole, complementing the benefits that are realized individually by homeowners and renters. Collective forms of tenure have fostered social cohesion and mutual aid. They have given communities the power to confront the state, safeguarding their sovereignty and shaping the trajectory of their own development. They have promoted the participation of residents in the co-creation of ideas and innovations challenging a Western ideology of landownership that views land merely as property, used mainly for the expropriation of resources and the extraction of value.

Notably, these "counter-hegemonic knowledges," as Line Algoed and María E. Hernández Torrales characterize them, tend to travel back and forth across between communities and countries. A countervailing narrative of ownership and stewardship that challenges the orthodoxy of individual landholding in one place inspires critical thinking among local activists in other places. Collective landholding that succeeds in thwarting disaster capitalists in one place incites and informs strategies of resistance elsewhere. Transcending the territorial boundaries of their place of origin, subversive ideas and innovations like these have the potential for forging solidarities and sparking social change on a wider scale.

The transmission of "knowledges" that challenge dominant ideologies and institutions sometimes happens serendipitously, like dandelion seeds carried on the wind. More often, a more conscious, concerted effort is needed to spread the word, bridging geographic, cultural, and linguistic distances between grassroots leaders in different parts of the world. Peer exchanges function especially well in this regard, enabling residents and activists from scattered communities to meet face-to-face, swapping stories and sharing details of insurgent action and collective ownership. Less directly —but no less influentially—ideas and innovations that emerge out of the resistance of beleaguered communities get lifted up for the larger world to see through the published work of engaged scholars like the ones represented in the present volume.

In Line's case, she eschewed the typical academic stance of treating communities as passive subjects of study. She welcomed them, instead, as active collaborators, "engaging these communities at every stage from formulating questions, designing fieldwork, and organizing activities to analyzing findings and writing." Even more, she worked side-by-side with community leaders and allies in Puerto Rico and Barbuda, helping to create the solidarity networks that became the focus of her research.

The book that resulted from this collaborative endeavor breaks new ground. It offers fresh perspectives on the form of tenure featured in all previous publications of Terra Nostra Press. Significantly, it also ventures far afield of the community land trust. Line's book surveys a landscape of theory and practice left largely unexplored heretofore by our other authors, a contested terrain where climate change is found to inflict the greatest damage on communities made vulnerable by a legacy of colonialism, racism, poverty, and land insecurity; where disaster capitalists lurk in the wings, eagerly awaiting an opportunity for quickly acquiring and profitably redeveloping storm-damaged land; where mobilized communities create and share insurgent "knowledges" of property, power, and place, strategies of resistance that are raised on a platform of collective landholding.

These are topics too important to be overlooked by a publisher committed to supporting the worldwide growth of community land trusts and related strategies of community-led development on community-owned land. Terra Nostra Press is proud to add Line's far-reaching, groundbreaking study to our catalogue.

CHAPTER 1
INTRODUCTION

THIS IS OUR LAND

"This is us. This is what we have to show from slavery," Nico Webber Antonio, the owner of a roadside restaurant in Barbuda, told me as I savored her grilled seafood. "By any means necessary, we're going to fight to maintain ownership of this land. It doesn't matter what the government [...] says, or what the [court] says, this is our land." She wore a T-shirt with the inscription: "True Barbudan: one who stands up for Barbuda." This book centers the voices of two Caribbean communities, Barbuda and Puerto Rico, that have been engaged in the struggle of defending their communal land rights. Both communities have endured the profound impacts of the devastating 2017 hurricane season. I situate their experiences with climate-change-induced natural disasters and their not-so-natural aftermath within the ongoing colonial legacies of land as individually held private property.

My research journey started on September 1, 2017, following two years of close collaboration with the Martín Peña communities in Puerto Rico. Originally focused on studying their resistance against gentrification in self-built neighborhoods, my plans abruptly changed when Hurricane Irma struck the Caribbean just five days into my doctoral studies, followed by Hurricane Maria two weeks later. These hurricanes profoundly reshaped the region I had come to love.

The research and published articles that resulted became the core of my doctoral dissertation at the Vrije Universiteit Brussel. They make up the heart of the present volume. Both the dissertation and this book embody a process of engaged scholarship, which evolved drastically from its very start, prompting me to not just to do research, but also to act in other meaningful ways. Both are products of collaborative effort, fueled by the voices and experiences of the communities at the center of this study. The communities under study were not passive research subjects but valued collaborators who are re-centering the relationships of humans with the land and reimagining the significance of collectivity. I coauthored these articles with scholars and practitioners of the region. Beyond mere academic critique, this book traces a path forward as our planet confronts the climate emergency.

This book explores the crucial role of communal land tenure in the fight against the climate crisis, with a focus on Puerto Rico and Barbuda. It scrutinizes the aftermath of the devastating 2017 hurricane season, examining external factors contributing to vulnerabilization within these communities and analyzing their resistance strategies. Emphasizing the prioritization of international capital over local needs, especially evident in coastal areas, the study reveals how this dynamic has spurred land grabbing and displacement. Yet, communal land systems empower communities to mobilize collective responses, protect their rights, and conserve their natural environment. By shielding communities against post-disaster displacements driven by foreign capital, this research highlights how communal land ensures continuity and fosters deeper cohesion. It serves as a foundation for mutual aid initiatives, enhances political influence, and fosters international solidarity.

This study underscores how communal land embodies an ethos of interconnectedness between humans and nature, nurturing counterhegemonic 'epistemologies of the land' that challenge dominant colonial and patriarchal narratives of property. By advocating for a reevaluation of property notions through tenure plurality, it underscores the necessity of amplifying local voices and countervailing knowledges to effectively confront the climate emergency. Centering Caribbean communities, this study unveils the interconnectedness between land tenure systems and global crises, advocating for a paradigm shift away from viewing land as mere property towards a holistic understanding of human-earth relations. It reframes these communities not as passive victims but as proactive agents crafting essential counterhegemonic knowledges to inform global responses, thereby paving the way for sustainable land use and equitable development.

Figure 1: Aerial view of Codrington and Codrington Lagoon, Barbuda. Source: Google Images

Figure 2: Aerial view of the Martín Peña communities. Source: Corporación del Proyecto ENLACE del Caño Martín Peña

LAND IS LIFE

For Caribbean communities land has always been a contest for life itself (Wolfe, 2006). The principles that historically pushed colonialism, from seizing land and uprooting populations to endangering life-worlds, persist in the contemporary Caribbean landscape. Presently, this manifests as real-estate interests staking claims on land, often leveraging juridical measures, favoring global financial elites and disadvantaging local communities. Efforts to increase land tenure security for disenfranchised communities, especially in areas with highly valuable natural resources and in self-built and self-organized urban settings, have been focused on private land ownership. A global scan of literature shows that in such settings, regularizing land through individual property titles is ineffective in halting displacements and dispossessions (e.g. Dyal-Chand, 2010; Rakodi et al., 2009; Clichevsky, 2003; Connolly, 2013; Varley, 2017). Instead, these land titling programs promote integration of land into the global land market, contributing to the global rush on land—a key component of neoliberal globalization. These processes have been accelerated after several disasters have struck the region over the past decade, ranging from economic collapse, hurricanes, earthquakes, and the recent COVID-19 pandemic, leaving local communities in distress.

The emphasis on private land property is rooted in colonial history. The colonial ideology of land improvement based on Western cultivation forms remains entrenched today, invalidating any other understanding of land (Bhandar, 2018). This continued 'colonial inhabitation' (Ferdinand, 2022)—a way of inhabiting the earth where some appropriate and exploit land for the benefit of only a small group—further produces vulnerability. As a resistant response, residents from these communities organize to defend their land through collective forms of land tenure. Collective land tenure functions as a powerful counterforce against vulnerabilization, defined as processes whereby populations are made and kept vulnerable, giving rise to a transformative political conception of 'property.' Scholars have stated that there is an urgent need to grasp other ways of relating to land, ways that have been obscured by imperial modes of ownership (Bhandar, 2018; Escobar, 2016). By relating to the land in a nonextractive way (Klein, 2007), these communities challenge the core tenets of Enlightenment thought, which made us believe that humans are separate from and superior to nature—a division that ultimately led to the current climate crisis (Crichlow et al., n.d.).

This research delves into the intricate interplay of land policy, colonial legacies, and climate change within the Caribbean, specifically focusing on climate-change-affected Puerto Rico and Barbuda. In Barbuda, residents fiercely defend a centuries-old collective land ownership system crucial for preserving their beaches and wetlands—vital ecosystems for survival (Figure 1). In Puerto Rico, residents have established a community land trust (CLT) in the Caño Martín Peña area to formalize land ownership and prevent displacement following the ecological restoration of a heavily polluted waterway (Figure 2). Both communities, severely impacted by hurricanes Irma and Maria in 2017, had to navigate past radical neoliberal reforms imposed by governments and financial partners. These reforms that had already started before the hurricanes, but were intensified after they struck the islands. Climate change increases the frequency, intensity, and severity of hurricanes, due to the warming up of the oceans.

Informed by literature on contemporary land policy, communal land tenure, disaster capitalism, decolonial resistance and policy mobilities, I scrutinize the tension between vulnerabilization processes and the local communities' resistance against these processes. Specifically, I look at how the interests, policies, and discourse of political and economic elites perpetuate the vulnerability of residents in environmentally fragile areas (vulnerabilization). I also investigate how communal land tenure[1] allows communities to resist vulnerabilization through land-use control and protection of the environment, while building international alliances, strengthening themselves to face climate change and to have greater sovereignty over their recovery from climate-change-induced disasters and subsequent forms of disaster capitalism (resistance).

Grounded in decolonial thought and feminist research, this study explores the ongoing characterization of communities as 'uncivilized' or, in contemporary terms, 'underdeveloped,' due to their ways of relating to the land, reminiscent of historical depictions of native peoples during colonial invasions (Bhandar, 2018). The research scrutinizes how communal land tenure systems and the related grassroots community development processes challenge prevailing modern, colonial, capitalist, and patriarchal

---

1   By *communal land tenure,* I refer broadly to systems in which land is held in common by a place-based community. In this book, I use the term to denote both Barbuda's traditional collective land tenure system—where land is held by the Barbudan community as a whole—and a more contemporary adaptation of that same principle, in which land is owned by a non-governmental organization on behalf of a geographically defined community, such as in the case of the Caño Martín Peña CLT. While I recognize that related terms such as "common land," "collective land tenure," "shared land ownership," and "cooperative land ownership" each carry specific legal and historical meanings, I use communal land tenure as an umbrella term that centers the principle of place-based, community control over land, across both customary and institutional forms.

ideologies (Lugones, 2010). Patriarchy, in this context, is conceptualized as an enduring ontology that perpetuates principles of separation, hierarchy, appropriation, domination, and violence (Escobar, 2023) that lie at the basis of colonial inhabitation, and the transformation of land into 'property.' The Cartesian dualism that separates humans from non-humans, also associated men with culture and women with nature, reflecting analogous dichotomies for black and native people, who were historically depicted as closer to the 'state of nature' (Connell, 2017, p. 169), and deemed unfit to own property, a privilege reserved solely for White men (Bhandar, 2018; Wynter, 1982). In this context, decolonial feminism emerges as an invaluable framework for understanding land not merely as property or a commodity, but as a nurturing force for life and the reproduction of a common shared by all (Escobar, 2023). I understand the story of resistance of these two communities against private property as a fight for sovereignty and survival facing neoliberal globalization and its global land grab; survival not only of its people and environment, but also of knowledge-practices that view land as necessary for life.[2]

Research Questions and Research Objectives

This research examines how communal land tenure systems respond to crises induced by climate change amidst power struggles between elite interests and vulnerable communities. The central research question is: **In what ways do these communities use communal land tenure to resist against the consequences of climate change and the vulnerabilization imposed by political and economic elites?**

The research objectives are listed as follows:

1. **VULNERABILIZATION**: Investigate and elucidate the events that occurred in the aftermath of the hurricanes in 2017 in the Caño Martín Peña area and Barbuda. Explore how the events preceding and succeeding these natural disasters can be comprehended as processes of vulnerabilization; a term I conceptualize as those processes that produce and perpetuate vulnerability. Unpack the ways in which political and economic elites contribute to vulnerabilization within these communities. What specific instruments, interests, and hegemonic knowledges are mobilized to vulnerabilize communities?

---

2   Throughout this work, "private property" refers specifically to individually titled ownership (i.e., "privately titled property"). This excludes collectively governed forms such as CLTs and cooperatives, which are also forms of private property in a broader legal sense.

2. **RESISTANCE:** Provide a detailed description of how these communities leverage their communal land tenure systems to resist external pressures. Resistance is understood as the strategies and mechanisms employed by communities to counter the processes of vulnerabilization, particularly through their control of development facilitated by communal land tenure systems. Investigate the significance of their local knowledge in the broader context of global struggles against climate injustices and epistemic extractivism. Analyze why and in what ways these locally produced knowledges are crucial for understanding and confronting systemic injustices on a global scale, yielding a counterhegemonic worldview, conceptualized by Gramsci (1995) as the way people formulate ideas and discourse to contest prevailing assumptions, beliefs, and normalized behavioral norms. Analyze how these knowledges travel globally. What specific instruments, interests, and counterhegemonic knowledges are mobilized to resist vulnerabilization?

To achieve these research goals, I formulated the following research sub questions:

- In what ways are these communities being vulnerabilized through land encroachment?
- How are these communities resisting this vulnerabilization, mobilizing their communal land tenure systems to halt the encroachment?
- How do these Caribbean land struggles shape emerging decolonial epistemologies on land property, fueling a counterhegemonic worldview?

To answer these research questions, this book is divided into seven chapters. The second chapter gives an overview of the literature this study builds on and describes the theoretical lens through which the study was conducted, with an emphasis on Caribbean literatures. Chapters Three and Four detail the processes of vulnerabilization and resistance in Puerto Rico and Barbuda, respectively. Chapter Five addresses the main research question and investigates the myriad ways through which these two communities use communal land tenure to protect themselves from the consequences of climate change and counter the vulnerabilization imposed by (local) political and (global) financial elites. Chapter Six examines how knowledges produced in the struggles for the defense of communal land ownership travel across the world, shedding light on how historically marginalized communities serve as a frequently overlooked actor in the realm of policy mobilities. Finally, in Chapter Seven, I bring together the main insights derived from this exploration, offering a concise answer to the research questions and a reflection on the implications and limitations of this research.

Chapters Three through Six are composed of articles that have been previously published, three as peer-reviewed academic articles and one as an online journal article. All of these articles have been co-authored. The names and positions of my co-authors are mentioned at the start of each chapter.

CHAPTER 2

THE STUDY OF VULNERABILIZATION AND RESISTANCE

THEORIES, CASES, AND METHODS

LITERATURE REVIEW

The literature that informed and guided my research addresses the central role of land in both the vulnerabilization of communities and their resistant responses to such vulnerabilization. First, I examine literature on the historical origins of land policy, emphasizing its colonial roots as well as the contemporary manifestations of these colonial legacies. Then, I explore the history of collective land tenure and contemporary forms such as community land trusts. Following this, I examine literature on disaster capitalism and the coloniality of disaster, focusing on the impacts of these processes on land. Subsequently, I discuss literature on movements advocating for decolonization through land. Finally, I analyze literature on the significance of the knowledges generated within these resistance movements for its impact on global policy circuits.

The Colonial Roots of Contemporary Land Policy

Land has been a site of conflict in the Caribbean region since the European conquest of 1492. Following the conquest, a "half millennium of land grabs and one-cent treaty sales" ensued (Harjo, 1991, cited in Wynter, 1995, p. 6). Sailing west rather than east, as he was instructed, the Italian navigator Christopher Columbus initially arrived in the northern Caribbean islands of the Bahamas, paving the way for European colonization. Subsequent European invaders invoked the then prevailing legal tool, the 'doctrine of discovery,'[3] to assert rights over the lands they had "discovered," especially those not inhabited by Christians. These lands were deemed "discoverable," i.e. empty, *terra nullius* or wastelands, disregarding the obvious presence of large Indigenous populations (and their empires, economic organization, scientific sophistication, etc.) The doctrine of *terra nullius* became ingrained in public international law. Property law played a pivotal role in the colonial accumulation of land, a process delineated by Brenna Bhandar (2018) in her seminal book *Colonial Lives of Property: Law, Land, and Racial Regimes of Ownership*. The dominance of private property ownership persists to this day and continues to overshadow Indigenous and alternative approaches to land and resources.

Let us go back in time and look briefly at the origins of private property. How did this principle become so ingrained in Western culture? The origins of private property can be traced back to classical Roman law. The Romans introduced the principle of *dominium*, recognizing the rights and powers of the current possessor over a thing (Seipp, 1994). This evolution continued in twelfth-century England, when feudal lords started granting specific land rights to tenants. However, these rights were not equal with those of the lords, and property rights were not absolute. The contemporary understanding of private property as we know it today, one that allows for the unfettered enclosing, buying, selling, and renting of land, emerged between the sixteenth and seventeenth centuries (Encylopedia.com, n.d.) with colonialism and the ensuing expansion of capitalism.

John Locke, an English philosopher, played a pivotal role in shaping the concept of private property. His ideas, articulated in *Two Treatises of Government* (1690), had a profound impact on the justification and comprehension of private property rights. Locke's labor theory of property installed an ideology of "improvement" that privileges

---

3 Only in 2023, the Vatican repudiated the 'doctrine of discovery' (Lalji & Hancheroff, 2023).

European forms of cultivation up until today. A man obtains a right over land, Locke asserts with this theory, once he mixes his labor with it and thus "improves" it. Locke writes: "Land that is left wholly to Nature, that hath no improvement of Pasturage, Tillage, or Planting, is called, as indeed it is, wast [sic]" (Locke, 1690, cited in Bhandar, 2018, p. 48). According to him, any man (only men) who takes land out of common ownership and appropriates it to himself to "improve" it has given something to humanity, not taken it away (Meiskins Wood, 1999, p. 111). This theory emerged as the dominant framework for understanding land ownership, yet it was selectively applied. Enslaved people who worked the land were excluded from ownership rights. Ellen Meiskins Wood highlights a critical nuance in the relationship between labor and property rights, pointing out that it is possible for one man to claim property rights using the labor of another man (1999, p. 111).[4]

Millions of Indigenous peoples held a perspective on land ownership that is divergent from that of European colonists. The European concept of slicing up land, handing out legal titles, and granting exclusive domain, known as "enclosures," often involved violently seizing the land on which others had depended for livelihoods, and using it as the foundation for exclusive and private wealth. These ideologies and practices have ingrained private land ownership into one of the world's dominant and least contested doctrines. Private land property is now considered essential for personal advancement and national development, not only by governments, but also by most individuals. In this study, however, I contend that private property should neither be treated as the default, nor as a natural state or a universality. Today, up to 2.5 billion people rely on Indigenous and community lands, which means these communities collectively hold, manage or use just over half of the planet's land, representing a tenure plurality that is central to this study. Legally, only one-fifth of communal land is recognized, leaving the remaining lands in an ambiguous and confused state, exposed and susceptible to land grabs by powerful entities such as governments and corporations (Oxfam et al., 2016).

The colonial concept of enclosing, parceling, and dividing land is evident in land policies such as the General (or Dawes) Allotment Act of 1887 in the United States. In *Settler Memory*, Kevin Bruyneel (2021) describes how the Dawes Act carved up Indigenous lands and distributed individual plots of land to Indigenous male heads of

---

4   The novel *Crooked Plow* (Vieira Junior, 2023) by Brazilian geographer Itamar Vieira Junior beautifully describes the struggles of those who have labored for large landowners for decades and rightfully deserve land ownership.

households, while selling the remaining plots to white settlers. Simultaneously, the U.S. federal government enacted the "Peace Policy," which aimed to confine Indigenous peoples to reservations and assigned missionaries to enforce Euro-American customs of clothing, agriculture, and Christianity, including heteropatriarchal family structures and gender roles. Property and patriarchy, as Bruyneel (2021) argues, were "twin pillars of settler colonial rule" (p.51). In her article "Whiteness as Property," Cheryl Harris (1993, p. 1722) discusses how land allotment was essentially an assimilation program aimed to make Indigenous people "citizens" and coerce them into relinquishing their lands (also cited in Bhandar, 2018, p. 7). Native Americans were seen as "primitive" due to their ways of holding the land. To remain on the land under the Land Allotment program, Native Americans had to accept individual land grants that later were seized by land speculators.[5]

Bhandar (2018) contends that institutions like the World Bank and the IMF and some governments have continued these colonial practices by advocating for land titling programs. For her, these programs represent a contemporary manifestation of a legal device with a long and pivotal role in appropriating and transforming Indigenous lands into individually held private property (Bhandar, 2018, p. 78). The enforcement of private titles, Bhandar argues, still represents the legal manifestation of an economic system and philosophical perspective that asserts individual private property ownership as an essential prerequisite for individual and national advancement and prosperity. This practice, rooted in Lockean philosophy, is influenced by the Peruvian neoliberal economist Hernando de Soto (2000) who argues that poverty in the global south can only be reduced by replacing customary land tenure (in rural and urban areas) with individual property rights.

A substantial body of literature has criticized this theory (Dyal-Chand, 2010; Rakodi et al., 2009; Clichevsky, 2003; Varley, 2017). These scholars argue that property titles have minimal impact on tenure security, access to credit, and poverty reduction. Rashmi Dyal-Chand details how titling programs in many global-south cities led,

---

[5] The Land Allotment program is depicted in the 2023 Hollywood film "Killers of the Flower Moon," featuring Robert De Niro. The film is about the Native American Osage, who were forcedly resettled from Kansas to an area in Oklahoma where later oil was found and made the Osage the richest people per capita on earth. The Land Allotment program pressured the Osage to subdivide their reservation into individual allotments and introduced the "head rights" system, granting quarterly funds derived from the Osage Mineral Estate. These head rights could not be bought or sold, only inherited. Some non-Osage men, marrying into such families, resorted to horrific acts, including murdering their Osage wives, to secure ownership (Bahr, 2023).

reminiscent of the Land Allotment program, to land speculation and a surge in housing prices, disadvantaging low-income owners (2010, cited in Bhandar, 2018, p. 77). A growing body of evidence sheds light on why specifically residents in self-built and self-organized urban areas[6] in the global south choose to reject land titles. For instance, Octifanny et al. (2022) shows how residents in Indonesian self-built urban areas reject titles because of distrust in government-provided public services and fear for interference from illicit activities. In Brazilian favelas, often located near tourist areas offering spectacular views, state governments distributed land titles, invested in policing and public services, forced community businesses to formalize, which initiated the early stages of gentrification (Fidalgo Ribeiro et al., 2020).

This study builds on the notion that land titling programs are a contemporary manifestation of colonial land policy and contribute to ongoing global land grab. The global land grab started with the European conquest of the Caribbean and is today as present as ever. After the European invasion, a "half millennium of land grabs and one-cent treaty sales" ensued, as Susan Shown Harjo's quote at the beginning of this chapter indicated. The term land grab refers to the capturing of power to control land and other associated resources like water, minerals or forests, in order to control the benefits of its use. The global land grab is the project "to fix or consolidate forms of access to land-based wealth" (TNI, 2013, p. 3). This happens often, but not only, in countries in the global south, by governments, corporations, or foreign investors. The purpose of these rushes on land may include agricultural production, mining, or other large-scale development projects.

Aligned with this perspective, Jamaican scholar Jean Besson (2015) articulates how the promotion of individual land ownership in mining regions within the Caribbean, coupled with measures facilitating land division, titling, sale, and taxation, mirrors a broader global movement aimed at expanding land markets—an essential facet of neoliberal globalization. Legal land tenure expert Liz Alden Wily characterizes the global land grab as a "permanent condition" (Terra Nostra Press, 2020), highlighting the plight of rural communities inhabiting customary lands across Africa, Asia, and

---

[6] In the course of my research, inspired by my collaborators, I stopped using the term "informal" settlements, for several reasons: 1) residents of these neighborhoods often perceive it as derogatory; 2) it fails to acknowledge that these areas were frequently established with government support; 3) alternative terms like *comunidades autogestionadas* (self-built and self-managed communities) more explicitly convey the level of agency exercised by the residents in the development process.

Latin America, where evictions, displacements, and disruptions to livelihoods are increasingly common. These predominantly forested or rural lands are systematically transferred in large-scale transactions by governments to foreign entities, primarily multinational corporations and investment firms (Alden Wily, 2012; Bogaert, 2023, p. 117).

This study underscores a resurgence in global land grabs, linking this trend to its specific ramifications in regions targeted for tourism and urban development, where land grabs often facilitate extractive economic models. My research explores the potential of communal land systems to mitigate these trends. Colonial legacies persist within the context of neoliberal globalization, perpetuating historical patterns of exploitation and dependency. Postcolonial and contemporary colonial nations grapple with economic underdevelopment, burdened by enduring debt that maintains ties to former colonial powers. Land grabbing, the colonial legacy of study in this study, remains rampant under neoliberalism as corporations appropriate land for extractive industries, displacing local communities and echoing past injustices.

Collective Land Tenure

Despite the prevalence of individualized private property as the dominant paradigm, collective land tenure comprises more than half of the world's surface. A substantial body of literature describes the many different forms of communal land tenure that continue to exist and their importance for Indigenous and local communities. Notably, Jean Besson and Janet Momsen, in their significant contribution on land and development in the Caribbean (1987, 2007), explore the various forms of communal land tenure that persist in the region, many as *de facto* possession.

In the Caribbean, local communities (many Maroon and other Afro-descendant groups) collectively own an estimated 100,000 hectares of land. However, only 2% of the lands occupied by these communities and groups are formally recognized (Rights and Resources Initiative, 2015, p. 4). Following the phases of the abolition of slavery in the Caribbean, many liberated formerly enslaved people found themselves part of a landless proletariat that relied on large plantation holders who continued to control most of the agricultural land. Some managed to join Maroon communities, establishing so-called "family lands." These small plots of land, widespread across the Caribbean, are considered the inalienable property of all descendants of the ancestor who obtained the land (Besson and Momsen, 1987, p. 13). Crucial for my research is Besson and Momsen's (1987, p. 18) argument that these landholding forms represent more than a cultural survival of ancestral African cultures, but rather, what they call a "resistant response" against the locally established unequal societies.

The first CLT that originated with New Communities Inc. in Georgia in the United States in 1969 has roots in a similar resistance. CLTs, as discussed in this book, are nonprofit organizations that hold land on behalf of a place-based community, while serving as the long-term steward of land on behalf of that community (CLT Center, n.d.-b). In Albany, Georgia, landless peasants, affiliated with the Civil Rights Movement, aimed to break free from economic reliance on White landowners. To achieve this economic emancipation, they jointly acquired 6,000 hectares, blending communal land ownership, individual home ownership, and cooperative agricultural organization. They established the first CLT as we know it today.[7]

New Communities' founders drew inspiration from communities around the world engaged in various forms of collective land holding, including Indigenous peoples' communal lands, Mexico's *ejidos* (communal lands still comprise 55% of Mexico's land), Ujamaa Villages in Tanzania, and Gramdan Villages in India. The last emerged out of India's "land gift movement," when affluent individuals were persuaded by followers of Gandhi to donate land to impoverished groups.

The founders of New Communities were *also* influenced by the *moshav ovdim*, cooperative communities (similar to the Kibbutz) that were established by labor-Zionist settlers on Palestinian land in the early 20th century. The Moshavim are worker cooperative agricultural settlements that combine collective cultivation with independent household management. Labor-Zionism, predating Zionism as a political movement, played a pivotal role in Israel's pre-state land settlement, leading to the vast loss of Palestinian land. The moshav ovdim embodied labor-Zionist ideals of shared public assets, mutual aid, credit provisions, and self-governance through a general assembly and various committees (Willner, 1965, p. 67).

---

7   The classic 1937 novel *Of Mice and Men* by John Steinbeck beautifully explores the theme of land as a symbol of emancipation, telling the story of American migrant workers who dream of owning a piece of land as a means of self-determination and an escape from harsh labor conditions.

In my work with the CLT movement, I have argued for the need to acknowledge CLTs' complex histories, rooted in *both* struggles for liberation and emancipation from (neo-)colonial oppression and in neoliberal globalization and settler-colonial histories of land grabbing in Palestine. This complex history is often, forgotten. I have been critical about how policymakers have erased the roots of CLTs as resistance responses; CLTs are often presented merely as technical solutions, with policymakers seeing them as "quick fixes" to deeply entrenched structural problems (despite recognizing the slow and complex processes of creating a CLT). Instead of acknowledging CLTs as expressions of resistance and fights for liberation by marginalized communities, policymakers often portray them as "models" that can be implemented from above. Conferences on CLTs frequently lack resident representations,[8] illustrating top-down implementation. Recognizing the roots of CLTs in land grabbing has become even more important amidst events like the ongoing genocide in Gaza tied to the violent land grabs in Palestine.[9] It is crucial to acknowledge that part of the historical pedigree of CLTs lies in self-organized, "sustainable" communities that were established on land violently seized from Palestinians, akin to histories of settler colonialism described above. The African American civil rights leaders who toured Israel in 1968 and then returned to Georgia to found New Communities, however, were profoundly aware of the expropriation of Palestinian lands. They were impressed with the moshavim, but at the same time they were deeply disturbed by the discrimination they saw being inflicted on the Palestinians, which they recognized as similar to the discrimination they were suffering at home (Terra Nostra Press, n.d.-a).

The point is, even CLTs can participate in land grabbing or perpetuating settler colonial practices, and the movement needs to be aware of this to prevent such practices. Additionally, CLTs remain within the private property regime, installing a heavy bureaucratic burden on communities, many of whom may have a historical or Indigenous claim to and relationship with the land. This is for example the case for the Tongva Taraxat Paxaava Conservancy, a CLT on occupied Tongva territory (Los Angeles). CLTs are property schemes, whereas for many of these communities traditionally the relationship with the land goes beyond that of a property relationship. Still, a growing number of CLTs are acknowledging the land grabs in their histories

---

8   This was the case in the *4èmes Journées des Organismes de Foncier Solidaire* on the French version of CLTs held in Paris, France, in December 2022.

9   The genocide in Gaza coincided with the final writing stages of my dissertation, filling me with a terror that inevitably slips into this text.

and Indigenous groups across the Americas are turning to CLTs as strategies for decolonization and a return to communal land ownership.

The reader will therefore not find as much literature about CLTs as one might anticipate in a book featuring a particular CLT, the Caño Martín Peña CLT. Recognizing the resistance of communities, such as those in Barbuda and the Caño Martín Peña area in Puerto Rico as struggles for the territory by Indigenous and local communities, I align the Caño more closely with the struggle in Barbuda than with the CLT movement in the USA or Europe. The Caño CLT, like the communal land system in Barbuda represents a resistant response by a group of people striving to liberate themselves from the colonial and hyper-capitalist global land grab, re-establishing a relationship with the land that goes beyond that of mere property.

This is also why I anchor this study in the foundations of Indigenous struggles for the defense of the territory rather than in burgeoning bodies of literature on the commons that seems to mostly focus on Europe. While commons scholars explore the "remarkable growth of commons initiatives and the multitude and heterogeneity of the new initiatives, which through self-organization [...] meet social needs in non-market ways" (Kukh et al., 2018, p. 13, *own translation*), I do not share the same enthusiasm. This study tries to understand the context in which resistance emerges, and this context is a remarkable new wave of enclosures. As Escobar puts it: "We are witnessing a renewed attack on everything collective; land grabbing and the privatization of the commons (including sea, land, even the atmosphere through carbon markets) are a sign of this attack" (Escobar, 2016, p. 23).

This study explores the land conflicts within Caribbean communities through the insights of Indigenous scholars such as Eve Tuck and her (non-Indigenous) colleague Wayne Yang. In their essay, "Decolonization is not a Metaphor," they contend that efforts to claim land for the Commons erase "existing, prior, and future Native land rights, decolonial leadership, and forms of self-government" (Tuck & Yang, 2012, p. 28). Practices like urban homesteading, an American lifestyle reminiscent of the Israeli moshav ovdim or Kibbutz, established on appropriated Palestinian territory, are similar to "re-settling urban land in the fashion of self-styled pioneers in a mythical frontier [...] while evading Indigenous sovereignty and the modern presence of actual urban Native peoples" (Tuck & Yang, 2012, p. 28). My intention is not to discredit the Commons movement; this growing movement has played a vital role in challenging, from the grassroots, the "empire of finance," in which as Raquel Rolnik

(2019) illustrates, financialization has seized the control of urban areas and housing systems globally and led to homelessness and dispossession, despite promises of universal homeownership. In the (neo-)colonial context of the Caribbean, however, the predominantly European literature on the Commons provides limited insights into comprehending the circumstances wherein vulnerabilization and resistance arise due to ongoing power dynamics between (neo-)colonizers and the colonized. Many of the authors I cite in this book have written about the Commons (e.g. Gibson-Graham, Oliver-Smith), however, I choose to not deploy the term as an analytical category in my analysis.

The role of communal land in the context of climate change is central to this study. A mounting body of evidence underscores the significance of communal land tenure in the context of global change, most importantly for climate change adaptation and environmental protection. An analysis conducted by the Rights and Resources Initiative, Woods Hole Research Center, and World Resources Institute reveals the contributions of Indigenous peoples and local communities to climate change mitigation. The report found that these communities oversee a minimum of 24% of the total aboveground carbon stored in the world's tropical forests—an amount exceeding 250 times the carbon dioxide emitted by global air travel in 2015 (Rights and Resources Initiative, 2016). Protecting communal land, therefore, is a crucial element in addressing our climate emergency.

In their study on the decolonial resistance of the Maya land struggle against foreign logging corporations in Toledo District in Belize, Filiberto Penados et al. (2023) detail how "securing land tenure for Indigenous people and peasant communities is one of the most effective ways to mitigate climate breakdown and stave off the collapse of the planet (p. 4). Linda Shi et al. (2018) examine the role of collective land tenure in urban resilience in China's urban villages and connect the benefits of collective land tenure to current climate change debates. They argue that collective property increases the adaptive capacity of vulnerable communities confronted by climate change; the community governance linked to collective land tenure empowers communities to transform their shared land ownership into physical and social improvements.

While this study builds on the abovementioned research, it diverges from the concept of "resilience," a term frowned on by my research collaborators. This study centers on resistance rather than resilience. For this position, it builds on the critique of Ingelford Blühdorn, who writes about the "politics of unsustainability," denoting political decisions that merely manage the social and ecological consequences of unsustainability, rather than trying to tackle its causes. "Its main preoccupation is to promote societal adaptation and resilience to sustained unsustainability" Blühdorn writes (2013, p. 21). Feminist scholar Sara Ahmed (2017, p. 236) criticizes the way in which "we are asked to become resilient, so we can take more (more oppression, more pressure)." The Native American novelist Tommy Orange (2018) echoes this sentiment in *There There*. "Don't make the mistake of calling us resilient. To not have been destroyed, to not have given up, to have survived, is no badge of honor" (p.137). A popular social media meme reads: "Instead of praising people for being 'resilient,' change the systems that make them vulnerable."

Disaster Capitalism

Vulnerability does not inherently characterize human nature; rather, it is a result of intricate political and economic processes that are intensified after disasters strike. My co-author for two of the chapters that follow, María E. Hernández Torrales, and I term this phenomenon "vulnerabilization" to indicate how communities are made and kept vulnerable. This process clearly emerged in the aftermath of Hurricane Maria in Puerto Rico's Martín Peña area, where the need for risk mitigation in self-built neighborhoods was ignored and displacement in the name of safety was endorsed. Similarly, in Barbuda, environmental engineering practices (excavating sand, replacing dunes, destroying mangroves, flattening beaches, etc.) to develop a coastal real-estate market (Hassan, 2018) after Hurricane Irma are exacerbating damage and further vulnerabilizing the local population. My research seeks to comprehend how collective land tenure responds to disaster shocks and their aftermath, and whether this type of land tenure can counter these vulnerabilization processes.

The literature on disaster capitalism is central to understanding vulnerabilization and the role of land in these processes. Naomi Klein (2007), in her celebrated book *The Shock Doctrine*, describes disaster capitalism as the "orchestrated raids on the public sphere in the wake of catastrophic events, combined with the treatment of disasters as exciting market opportunities" (p.6). "Only a great rupture—a flood, a war, a terrorist attack," Klein writes, "can generate the kind of vast, clean canvases [disaster capitalists] crave. It is in these malleable moments, when we are psychologically unmoored and physically uprooted, that these artists of the real plunge in their hands and begin their work of remaking the world" (p.21).

A large body of Caribbean literature has followed these ideas after the devastating hurricane season in 2017. These authors have significantly contributed to debates on disaster capitalism, making the important link between climate disasters and the region's (neo-)colonial histories and presents. In "The Making of Caribbean Not-so-Natural Disasters," Cruz-Martínez et al. (2018, p. 5) contend that no event is strictly or exclusively natural. They assert that historical or contemporary colonialism underlies the heightened inequality and incomplete recoveries in the Caribbean and increases the region's susceptibility to disasters. The authors elucidate how the legacies of Western powers' occupations persistently impact the islands' governance, shaping the social geography and concentrating lower-income residents in disaster-prone areas.

In a *Special Issue* entitled "The Caribbean after Irma and Maria: Climate, Development & the Post-Hurricane Context," Jeff Popke and Jamaican scholar Kevon Rhiney (2019) focus on various Caribbean islands, including Barbuda, Puerto Rico, and Sint Maarten. They note that in each of these case studies, rebuilding efforts prioritize the interests of foreign capital rather than addressing local needs. The papers shed light on the challenges of "building back better" (a phrase often used after the hurricanes) in a Caribbean region marked by a history of dependent development. For Rhiney (2019) these papers reinforce the need to rethink "the historical, ethical, and (geo) political relevance of this [...] moment" (p. 9). In parallel, a statement in an exhibition I visited in the Belgian town of Hasselt in which Caribbean, mostly Puerto Rican artists explored the impact of the 2017 hurricanes, read: "A storm never comes alone. They're accompanied by political and economic storms, the origins of which can be traced to the colonial past" (Z33, 2021).

Puerto Rican scholar Yarimar Bonilla extensively explores how catastrophic events such as hurricanes, earthquakes, and various forms of political and economic crises unfold along the fault lines of long-standing racial and colonial histories and exacerbate existing inequalities (2020, p. 1). Bonilla terms this process "the coloniality of disaster," drawing parallels to Anibal Quijano's concept of the "coloniality of power," which describes structures of power and control emerging from the conquest of the Americas to the present. Puerto Rican decolonial scholar Nelson Maldonado Torres (2018) suggests viewing colonialism itself as a form of disaster (cited in Bonilla, 2020).

This prompts inquiries into the intricate relationship between colonialism and capitalism and the question of which one emerged first. The term "disaster capitalism" may imply that capitalism becomes disastrous only in the aftermath of calamities, or that capitalism is established (or expanded) solely after such disasters occur. Rosa Luxemburg's capitalist catastrophe theory sheds light on how catastrophes have always been an integral aspect of capitalism, particularly in colonized nations. Luxemburg describes capitalism for people in colonized countries "as a sudden catastrophe, an unspeakable misfortune fraught with frightful suffering" (Luxemburg, 1925, p. 133, *own translation*). Capitalism, according to Luxemburg, relies on colonialism and imperialism to defer the eventually inevitable standstill of accumulation. Luxemburg writes:

> The development of capitalism has been possible only through constant expansion into new domains of production and new countries. But the global drive to expand leads to a collision between capital and pre-capitalist forms of society, resulting in violence, war, revolution: in brief, catastrophes from start to finish, the vital element of capitalism (1921).

Raj Patel and Jason W. Moore also write about this constant expansion of capitalism, using the term "colonial frontiers" to refer to the official borders that marked the progressing limits of colonial encroachment of the lands allocated for settlement. For them, capitalism "creates an ecology that expands over the planet through its frontiers, driven by forces of endless accumulation" (Patel & Moore, 2018, p. 49). This accumulation necessitates constant expansion into new territories, requiring ever more land. Marxist geographer David Harvey (2004, p. 65) employs the term "spatio-temporal fixes" as a metaphor for resolving capitalist crises through geographical expansion.

Harvey's (2003) term "accumulation by dispossession" builds on Marx' notion of "primitive accumulation" to describe the process whereby over-accumulated capital seizes hold of assets and turns them to profitable use. Primitive accumulation "entailed taking land, say, enclosing it, and expelling a resident population to create a landless proletariat, and then releasing the land into the privatized mainstream of capital accumulation" (Harvey, 2003, p. 149). The increase of global land grabs demonstrates that the process of primitive accumulation is not something of the past but continues today. As mentioned earlier, a third of the world population still lives on communal lands, whose tenure is often unrecognized, and who are severely affected by this accumulation. Although hegemonic, privately held property is not a universal reality. This has also been stressed by feminist Commons scholars Gibson-Graham in their book *The End of Capitalism (As We Knew It)*. They criticize positioning capitalism as the universal form or model of economy to which other forms of economy must aspire, calling this "capitalocentrism"—an analogy with phallocentric discourse in which woman is always compared to man ("the same, the opposite, or the complement of man"). Non-capitalist forms of economy, they argue, are also positioned as the opposites, the subordinates, the unimaginable others of capitalism (Gibson-Graham, 2006, p. 35). But these forms are more than just alternatives to the norm. Communal land, comprising still more than half of the world's surface, is one such form.

This research does not specifically draw on Marxist literature to explore the crises of capital over-accumulation and its constant need for new lands, nor does it draw on neo-Marxian concepts such as dependency theory, uneven development, or subordinate financialization. While these frameworks are instrumental in dissecting the roots of inequality, foundational to the global land grab in the context of neoliberal globalization, they do not specifically address the disparities in knowledge production—who decides what becomes the "norm"?— in fully empowering those entangled in these struggles. Instead, this study aligns with decolonial thinkers, all of whom draw from Marxist traditions yet argue that capitalism cannot alone account for the colonial matrix. Leading in the development of this argument is the Jamaican thinker, Sylvia Wynter. Her work, navigating through, beyond, and in opposition to Marxism (Sorentino, 2022), posits that the capitalist mode of production is subordinate to racial domination. Similarly, Indian writer Amitav Ghosh (2021) critiques the Western intellectual and academic tendency to view capitalism as the prime mover of modern history. Such an approach abstracts capitalism from broader geopolitical contexts. He references decolonial scholars like W.E.B. Du Bois who argues that the colonial conquest of land, slavery, and race were crucial to the emergence of capitalism as a system (Ghosh, 2021, p. 117). Citing Cedric Robinson, Ghosh suggests that the fixation of Western radicalism with capitalism as a system is a way of evading the real "nastiness" (2021, p. 119). It becomes more convenient to discuss abstract economic systems than to address racism, imperialism, and the structures of organized violence sustaining global power hierarchies. Similarly, Cornel West asserts that racism predates capitalism, finding its roots "in the early encounter between civilizations in Europe, Africa, and Asia, encounters which occurred long before the rise of modern capitalism" (cited in Bhandar, 2018, p. 6). These debates matter for this study as it contends that contemporary land struggles in (neo-)colonial contexts transcend mere anti-capitalist sentiment; they are also about the fight for sovereignty—a struggle that started half a millennium ago.

Bhandar (2018) discusses how ideologies of European racial superiority, along with legal narratives that equated civilized life with English property concepts justified the colonial appropriation of Indigenous lands. The invaded spaces were deemed lacking civilized inhabitants, therefore considered "empty and ripe for appropriation" (Bhandar, 2018, p. 4). Whether people were deemed capable of appropriation depended on prevailing racial difference concepts. Indigenous and colonized populations were depicted as outside history, lacking cultural practices, thought habits, and economic organization to be considered sovereign and rational economic subject, deemed unfit to own property (2018, p. 3). Bhandar writes: "Those communities who lived as rational, productive economic actors, evidenced by particular forms of cultivation, were deemed to be proper subjects of law and history; those who did not were deemed to be in need of improvement as much as their waste lands were" (2018, p. 8). Tuck and Yang echo this, saying that "epistemological, ontological, and cosmological relationships to land are made pre-modern, backward, savage" (2012, p. 5).

Caribbean communities who are survivors of centuries of slavery are now confronted with the catastrophic threats of hyper-capitalism (Connell, 2017, p. xi), caused by the ongoing global land grab. This study examines how this land grab unfolds after disasters. How are disasters used to rebuild societies on a free-market model by way of continuous land enclosures and emphasis on land titling programs? In *The Shock Doctrine*, Klein (2007, p. 507) illustrates this point in her chapter "Blanking the Beach." After the 2004 tsunami, the Maldives government, as Klein reports, declared many islands "unsafe and unsuitable for habitation," initiating a more aggressive relocation program than ever before. A similar situation unfolded in Puerto Rico and Barbuda. "All these coastal areas are now open land!" Klein cites locals, linking it to the colonial doctrine of *terra nullius*. "If the land was declared empty or 'wasted,' it could be seized, and its people eliminated without remorse," she writes (2007, p. 508). The notion of wasteland has legally justified the dispossession of Indigenous peoples since the European invasion to this day.

Anthropologist and disaster scholar Anthony Oliver-Smith (2005) notes that removing people from familiar environments after disasters severs their connection to the material and cultural resource base essential for individual and communal life. Locals' resistance to resettlement, he argues, underscores the importance of a sense of place in creating an "environment of trust," linking space, kin relations, local communities, cosmology, and traditions (Oliver-Smith, 2005, p. 48). That attachment to the land, especially after disasters, is central in this study. Land, in the words of the Indigenous scientist and thinker Max Liboiron, is "the unique entity that is the combined living spirit of plants, animals, water, humans, histories, and events" (cited in Ghosh, 2021, p. 36).

Land and Resistance

Vulnerabilized communities have long used land to resist oppression. "Land is necessary for life. Thus, contests for land can be—indeed, often are—contests for life," asserts Patrick Wolfe (2006, p. 387) in his important essay "Settler Colonialism and the Elimination of the Native." "Land is what is most valuable, contested, and required," echo Tuck and Yang (2012, p. 5). Globally, communities have mobilized to defend their territories and life-worlds against dispossession driven by the global land grab. In the USA, notable instances include the Dakota Access Pipeline Protests, where grassroots Native American movements opposed the pipeline's construction in 2016, and the Landback movement that advocates for the return of communal lands to Native Americans. In Mexico, the Zapatista Army of National Liberation battles against land reforms that would privatize the ejidos. In Ecuador, the Siekopai Indigenous community won a trial in 2023 through which they reclaimed communal land in the ancestral Pë'këya territory in the Ecuadorian Amazon and regained control over its natural resources to protect them from exploitation. These are just a few examples of the global resistance against dispossession.

I position the struggle of Caribbean communities within these contemporary struggles for the protection of collective land rights and natural resources. As Escobar (2016, p. 13) notes, these struggles "are best understood as ontological struggles and as struggles over a world where many worlds fit, as the Zapatista put it; they aim to foster the pluriverse." The pluriversal vision of a world in which many worlds fit challenges the supposed universality of capitalist property norms (Bhandar, 2018, p. 78). It challenges the view of the Earth as desacralized and inanimate and "Nature" as a mere resource repository (Ghosh, 2021, p. 37) and the way land is transformed into property, limiting human relationships with land to the owner's connection with their property (Tuck & Yang, 2012, p. 5). Ghosh (2021) traces the roots of "world-as-resource" concept to colonialists such as the Dutch VOC Jan Coen, suggesting that in that time they also served as highly influential philosophers. The colonial violence towards "natives" and the landscapes they inhabited laid the foundations for mechanistic philosophies that would later inspire contemporaries like Descartes (Ghosh, 2021, p. 37). A pluriversal world, sought by those engaged in land struggles, embraces Indigenous approaches to land and resources, in which land is central to survival and nature is inseparable from humans.

Contemporary land struggles trace their roots to historical battles against slavery. Maroon communities, for example, formed by those who escaped slavery, those who not only resisted enslavement but also cultivated a distinctive relationship with the Earth and non-humans (Chaillou et al., 2020). In his doctoral dissertation, African American studies scholar Robert Justin Connell (2017) depicts the Maroon history of resistance as a struggle to preserve land and autonomy from the encroachments of capital and the state. According to Connell, the Maroons possess a spiritually grounded preservationist ethos towards nature. Unlike Western preservationism, which Connell describes as biocentric for viewing Nature as external to humans, the Maroon variant explicitly integrates the use of the land, avoiding the removal of humans from the landscape and allowing the forest to be utilized (but not over-utilized) for human needs (Connell, 2017, p. 164). The ongoing survival and spirituality of the Maroons are intrinsically linked to the well-being of the forest. In the National Geographic documentary *The Territory* (Pritz, 2022), a Brazilian Indigenous youth echoes this sentiment: "Non-Indigenous people always say the same: 'Indigenous people have too much land, you need to clear the trees and raise cattle.' But I don't agree. The forest and its rivers are our home, they support us."

These struggles are historically connected to resistance against the continuation of the plantation system even post-abolition. Post-abolition resistance was also the impulse behind New Communities. In the words of Mtamanike Youngblood, captured in the film, *Arc of Justice*, "the idea behind New Communities was to take civil rights one step further in economic independence and economic rights." More than anything else, New Communities was seen by the African Americans who founded it to be a platform for consolidating the gains of struggle for political and legal rights, creating an island of security and dignity for a racially oppressed people amidst a sea of white supremacy. In his book *The Haitians: A Decolonial History*, Haitian scholar Jean Casimir (2020) explains how formerly enslaved Caribbean communities rejected integration and assimilation into commodity-producing plantations. Instead, they withdrew to their plots, focusing on subsistence agriculture—a concept Casimir terms the "counter-plantation system." This was not merely a counter-reaction but originated from a parallel knowledge system (Bogaert, 2023, p. 261) that emphasized equal gender relations, indivisible collective property, and Lakou housing—clusters of homes surrounding a central courtyard, fostering solidarity among extended families to safeguard against the plantation's return (Haiti Lab, 2012).

Similarly, Sylvia Wynter (1971, pp. 99-100, also cited in Bogaert, 2023, p. 207) writes about 'the plot system,' referring to the small plots of land that enslavers would give to enslaved people to grow their own food to feed themselves (cheaper for the enslavers). On these plots Africans could practice the values of traditional African societies. Here, "the land remained the Earth—and the Earth was a goddess" Wynter says. With the discovery of the New World, and its vast exploitable lands, she writes, new societies were created for the market, where Man was reduced to labor, and Nature to Land. The plot system was a folk culture that became a source of cultural guerilla resistance to the plantation system. The plot also hints at the intrigues, conspiracies, and other subversive actions that were conceived and planned on that piece of land while growing essential food for survival. Although the plot was inextricably linked to the plantation, it was also a dynamic space of resistance against the continuation of the plantation system that became the dominant paradigm for how the Earth and most of its populations are treated (Bogaert, 2023, p. 207).

The chapters that follow explore how the Caribbean communities centered in this research are using communal land to resist vulnerabilization, and doing so, how they are decolonizing the concept of property and relations between humans and the Earth, grounded in historical struggles. It scrutinizes how these resistance narratives endure today amid the ongoing global land grab, particularly in urban and tourist-targeted areas, areas that are understudied in this field.

Global Knowledge Circuits and Decolonial International Solidarity Networks

The forms of knowledge generated through land struggles have profound implications. The study presented in the pages that follow posits a more explicit examination of the mobility of these knowledge forms and their impact on global policy circuits. Doreen Massey's concepts of "relationality" and "territoriality" in policy circulation (Massey, 2011) are useful to build the argument that the interconnectedness between communities—their "relationality"—is consistently undervalued and understudied, while their "territoriality" is disproportionately emphasized, perpetuating the misconception that these communities only exert influence at a local level.

Important contributors to policy mobility studies, such as Eugene McCann and Kevin Ward, define policy actors as "politicians, policy professionals, practitioners, activists, and consultants." They describe how these actors shuttle policies and knowledge globally through various means such as conferences, fact-finding study trips, and consultancy work (McCann & Ward, 2011, p. xiv). Yet, many of these studies focus on policies "from above" and fail, at least explicitly, to incorporate the perspectives of the people directly affected by these mobile policies, specifically those of low-income communities in urban settings. I argue, in contrast, that these communities are active participants in these global circuits; their ideas travel too and influence policy "from below" during those trajectories.

If more attention is spent on the knowledges produced by low-income communities involved in social struggles, it may lead to more effective policies. This assertion draws on the insights of decolonial scholars Walter Mignolo and Arturo Escobar, who highlight the significance of knowledges emerging from historically marginalized spaces that have been silenced and devalued by prevailing modern epistemologies, politics, and economies (Mignolo & Escobar, 2010, cited in Ferdinand, 2022). Escobar contends that these forms of knowledge are more appropriate to understand social transformation than most academic knowledge, as they offer a more farsighted approach to modern challenges, one that is "uniquely attuned to the needs of the Earth" (Escobar, 2016, p. 14). Françoise Vergès (2021, p. 16) further underscores this perspective; he emphasizes the dangers of ignorance surrounding the circulation of people, ideas, and emancipatory practices within global south and highlights the imperative of acknowledging south–south exchanges to challenge the hegemony of the north–south axis. Rosalba Icaza and Rolando Vasquez (2013), in their paper "Social Struggles as Epistemic Struggles," contend that social struggles have the capacity to generate knowledges and reveal the limits of our academic frameworks. Social struggles are therefore to be considered "theoretical revolutions." Ideas travel among historically silenced communities, influencing policies during this mobility, and this demands a more specific focus.

The significance of acknowledging the interconnectedness of social struggles is evident in Angela Davis' use of the term "collective liberation."[10] In *Freedom is a Constant Struggle*, Davis (2016) explores how liberation from systemic oppression can only be attained when all oppressed groups work together. Emphasizing the

---

10   I am reminded of the posters I see daily on my way to the university in Brussels that say, "Palestinian liberation is collective liberation."

intersectionality of struggles against repression, poverty, racism, sexism, homophobia, and transphobia, Davis also highlights the struggle for land justice in Palestine. Meaningful victories in the fight for justice can only be realized when we comprehend the interrelated nature of these struggles. "Local issues have global ramifications," she writes (Davis, 2016, p. 95).

Ultimately, the land struggles under study in this book are about collective liberation and they can be seen as a continuation of a struggle that started 500 years ago. Along these lines, this research approaches the international solidarity between the Caribbean communities under study and other communities facing similar circumstances as "theoretical revolutions," integral to these global social struggles for collective liberation. This solidarity manifested not only in the support received after the hurricane season in 2017 and its devastating aftermaths but also in the expressions of support these communities extend to other oppressed groups worldwide.

This study contends that internationalism is a sine qua non for decolonization. Decolonization is necessary for collective liberation and challenging the supposed necessity of private property is a crucial step in decolonization. This is in line with Kevin Bruyneel's assertion that centering land, and the relationship people have with land has the potential to offer liberating alternatives for how to live in relation to one another and to land (2021, p. 59). According to Frantz Fanon, decolonization is not possible without international solidarity, with a vital role for the European working classes. In *The Wretched of the Earth*, Fanon (1963) emphasizes that

> [t]his huge task [...] will be carried out with the indispensable help of the European peoples [...]. To achieve this, the European peoples must first decide to wake up and shake themselves, use their brains, and stop playing the stupid game of the Sleeping Beauty. (p. 106)

Tuck and Yang (2012) stress that decolonization is not a metaphor; it demands the actual repatriation of land to Indigenous peoples, which necessitates the abolition of settler property rights and sovereignty. Decolonization, according to them, requires "the abolition of land as property and upholds the sovereignty of Native land and people" (2012, p. 26). They argue that genuine opportunities for solidarity arise only when the "incommensurable" aspects of social struggles are recognized rather than the commonalities.

I shall argue in the pages that follow that decolonization is also necessary to fight against the climate emergency. Central to this argument is the advocacy for safeguarding or reinstating communal land tenure for historically marginalized communities. The literature reviewed above underscores that the trajectory of European colonialism, initiated with the conquest of the Caribbean, significantly accelerated environmental degradation. Lingering colonial legacies, particularly the insistence on private property in land, intensify the region's vulnerability to disasters. Communal land ownership emerges as a crucial factor in combating the climate emergency.

Expanding on the existing literature, this book investigates the specific dynamics of Caribbean communities grappling with communal land ownership in the not-so-natural aftermaths of climate-change-induced disasters. Notably, one such community, the Martín Peña community, is situated in an urban setting which is understudied in literature on communal land that is often focused on rural or forest areas. Meanwhile, the other community under study, Barbuda, actively resists urbanization, striving to preserve its natural coastal areas from large-scale tourism-targeted development as a strategic defense against the repercussions of climate change, which also remains understudied in the literature on the global land grab. This research provides ethnographic insights into the functioning of communal land ownership within Caribbean communities grappling with the aftermath of climate-related disasters and sheds light on how their land systems serve as a protective barrier against vulnerabilization.

THEORETICAL FRAMEWORK

The theoretical assumptions that have guided my research, as well as the theoretical gaps identified in the literature review, can be summarized as follows. Firstly, the literature lacks specificity regarding the struggles for land in urban and tourism-targeted areas and reveals a gap in understanding CLTs as rooted in resistance in line with the origins of other forms of communal land. I emphasize the need to explicitly foreground land in discussions on the links between disaster capitalism and its inherent connections to historical and current injustices. The current literature also lacks specificity regarding the mobility of the knowledges produced within these struggles and their importance in combatting the consequences of climate change.

To address these gaps, I propose a theoretical framework to position myself in these debates on the intricate interplay of land policy, colonial legacies, and climate change in the Caribbean. This section unveils the assumptions and orientations that have guided me as an engaged decolonial feminist researcher. The section is organized in two parts. First, I will discuss how decolonial theory can help us think through two themes: how the epistemologies of the land challenge hegemonic Western knowledges, and, how decolonial theory can help us understand the colonial roots of the climate crisis. Secondly, I will discuss the feminist research approach I have taken in this study.

Decolonial Thought

The Caribbean is a region steeped in the history of colonialism, postcolonialism, and neocolonialism, as well as in a history of continual anti- and decolonial struggles since the European conquest in 1492. Persistent land conflicts resulting from this history underscore the importance of examining these issues through a decolonial lens. The Puerto Rican scholar Nelson Maldonado Torres (2018) describes decolonial thinking as a critical approach that posits colonialism as a fundamental problem, one that continues to influence contemporary practices, ideas, and structures associated with Western forms of modernity (Maldonado Torres, 2018, p. 800). This book foregrounds the enduring dominance of private land ownership as one of those key practices perpetuated by colonial legacies. The decolonial turn, as Maldonado Torres puts it (2018, p. 800), signifies a shift in the attitude of the colonized, who actively engage in questioning, problem identification, and utilizing lived experiences and knowledge to address prevailing issues. This book interprets the ongoing struggles in the Caribbean to regain or sustain collective land as a manifestation of this decolonial turn.

Decolonial thought consciously diverges from and criticizes postcolonial studies, considering the latter a depoliticized approach associated with multiculturalism in the so-called peaceful, postcolonial era, rather than acknowledging historical continuities. "Naming the world as 'post-colonial' is to name colonialism as finished business," as Linda Tuhiwai Smith puts it (1999, p. 98). The Peruvian decolonial sociologist Aníbal Quijano (1998) introduced the term "coloniality of power" to illustrate that colonial power relations extend beyond economic-political and legal-administrative realms to include an epistemic and cultural dimension (Quijano, 1998, p. 19, cited in Verschuur

& Destremau, 2012, p. ii). This concept encapsulates how legacies, hierarchies, and knowledge-practices imposed by colonial institutions persist even after formal decolonization and reinforced by those in power. The coloniality of power is the basis for the success of neocolonialism. *Neocolonialism* is characterized by foreign economic actors exploiting and destroying natural resources under the guise of 'development,' disregarding local inhabitants, a core tenet of contemporary neoliberal globalization. Combating neocolonialism involves an *anticolonial* struggle rooted in concrete political practices such as juridical efforts. Countering coloniality constitutes a *decolonial* struggle aimed at transforming hegemonic ideas and established narratives. I interpret the struggles of the two central Caribbean communities in this study as both anticolonial and decolonial.

Decolonial struggle involves actively seeking knowledges that offer alternative and oppositional interpretations of our world and social realities. This is what George J. Sefa Dei and Cristina Sherry Jaimungal (2018) describe in *Indigeneity and Decolonial Resistance*: colonial thinking originates from the oppositional emancipatory struggles of colonized subjects worldwide, as Melissa Weiner and Antonio Carmona Báez articulate (2018). These resistance movements, they argue, persisted from the era of slavery through the 'postcolonial' period, up to the present (2018, p. xiv). This underscores the emphasis of this book on the importance of the knowledges produced by these movements.

These reflections draw inspiration from the critical insights of two Caribbean thinkers, the Trinidadian historian CLR James in *Black Jacobins* (1938) and the Martinican psychiatrist Frantz Fanon in *The Wretched of the Earth* (1963). Both scholars place the colonized, marginalized by the colonial order, at the very heart of world history (Bogaert, 2023, p. 175). Similarly, Haitian scholar Jean Casimir (2020) draws upon the wisdom of Argentine decolonial feminist María Lugones, who asserts,

> If we conceive of oppressed individuals not only as enduring oppression but also as actively resisting or subverting a system intent on shaping, diminishing, violating, or eradicating them, then we simultaneously perceive at least two realities: one characterized by the logic of resistance and transformation, the other by the logic of oppression. (Lugones, 2003: 12, cited in Casimir, 2020, p. 3)

This oppositional logic of resistance and oppression is at the core of this study. Decolonization, therefore, entails acknowledging the significance of these counter-narratives that emerge from resistance. These epistemes provide an alternative perspective through which to interpret our social realities. It is through these epistemes that I approach the struggle for collective land rights within the two Caribbean communities central to this study. These communities not only endure oppression—over a long time and now worsened by climate change—but actively resist it, while producing knowledges that destabilize dominant paradigms.

Frantz Fanon underscored the pivotal role of land for colonized peoples, emphasizing, "For a colonized people, the most essential value, because the most concrete, is first and foremost the land: the land which will bring them bread and, above all, dignity" (1963, p. 44). In colonial contexts, land transcends mere property; it carries a deeper significance, highlighting the inseparable connection of populations to their physical environments. In a recent lecture, Arturo Escobar echoed this sentiment in reference to defenders of the River Atrato in Colombia's Chocó region against gold mining industries, echoing this sentiment: "We cannot live without the mountain, without the lake because we are the lake, we are the forest, we are the river" (Escobar, 2023). This profound connection to the land, as noted by Amitav Ghosh (2021, p. 212), is attributed to the survival of Indigenous Peoples, especially in the face of extermination. George J. Sefa Dei (2022, p. 113) has labeled these perspectives 'land as Indigenous epistemology,' or what I call epistemologies of the land. For Indigenous peoples, Dei explains, the concept of 'Land' extends beyond physical boundaries to encompass the universe, including water, rivers, seas, sky, plants, animals, rocks, and all living and non-living entities. In this worldview, all these possess life. The interconnection between land and life is therefore absolute; without land, there is no life.

Upon their arrival, colonialists perceived the lands as devoid of all such meaning and of civilized inhabitants, rendering them ripe for appropriation and the imposition of European cultivation methods (Bhandar, 2018; Ghosh, 2021). In doing so, they laid the foundation for a fundamentally new conceptualization of the Earth, one that has persisted to the present day—a disconnection between land and humans, between nature and humans. These mechanistic ideologies profoundly influenced Enlightenment thinkers such as René Descartes (Ghosh, 2021: 37), who promoted the necessity to dominate and transform nature as a central tenet of liberal Enlightenment. From then on, embracing "civilization" entailed accepting the Earth as inert and machine-like, with no aspect of it able to elude human comprehension. A distinctive feature of "savagery" was the acknowledgment of the vitality of natural and celestial entities (Ghosh, 2021, p. 87). This perspective established a hierarchy in which natives were positioned as "naive savages" who require rescue, education, and development to conform to production methods that benefited the colonizer.

The European colonization of the Americas violently imposed a specific approach to inhabiting the Earth. Settlers' relationship to land as property owners was based on a system of patriarchy, extraction, and commodification, directly at odds with Indigenous practices based on the relationality with territory and life (Bruyneel, 2021, p. 71). Malcom Ferdinand termed this way of relating to the land "colonial inhabitation" which became the one way of inhabiting the world, subjugating lands, humans, and non-humans to the desires of the colonizer (Chaillou et al., 2020; Ferdinand, 2022). Central to colonial inhabitation was the introduction of private land ownership, where plots were allocated to individuals—men only—for cultivation, facilitating export and trade with the metropoles. This introduced the idea that some were entitled to appropriate the Earth for the benefit of just a few people (idem), an idea that lingers on and brought us where we are today.

"The West thinks of itself as the world," Arturo Escobar said (2023). It absorbs and obliterates any alternative worldviews that do not align with its own. Settler colonialists universalized Western systems, as articulated by Fanon: "The settler makes history. He is the absolute beginning" (Fanon, 1963: 51). Tuck and Yang make a similar observation: "Settlers become the law, supplanting Indigenous laws and epistemologies." That the West thinks of itself as the world becomes evident in the persistent hegemony of Western knowledge production. Linda Tuhiwai Smith (1999: 63) observes that the globalization of knowledge and Western culture perpetuates the West as the center of legitimate knowledge, acting as the authority on what constitutes 'universal' knowledge, marginalizing alternative ways of knowing.

However, within the framework of neoliberal globalization, the concept of "the West" itself becomes diffuse. For instance, one might question whether China's significant influence on the postcolonial world perpetuates hegemonic ideologies from the West or if it represents something entirely distinct. Ghosh (2021, p. 196) illustrates how, in appalling imitations of the settler-colonial mistreatment of Indigenous populations, an increasing number of forest lands in India, for example, have been exploited for mining and tourism purposes, sometimes with the backing of exclusionary conservationists who advocate for the displacement of forest-dwellers under the guise of environmental conservation. The sacred mountains of forest-dwelling communities have been desecrated, their lands inundated by dams, and their spiritual beliefs and practices denigrated as "primitive superstitions"—echoing the very language employed by colonial administrators, scientists, and missionaries. Similar dynamics can be observed across the global south, including the countries central to this research.

This study foregrounds the alternative ways of knowing that persist until this day and sheds a spotlight on the perspectives of those who use collective land as resistance against the endurance of mechanistic views of Nature, against the ongoing global land grab, and against ongoing vulnerabilization brought about by climate change. I view these communities not as victims of natural disasters, poverty, or dispossession; rather as agents of resistance who have actively used the struggles against these forces to construct forms of counterhegemonic knowledge[11] that offer crucial insights for navigating through the challenges posed by the climate emergency. The significance of these epistemologies of the land extends beyond local, place-based struggles; they become pivotal in addressing the planetary crisis.

Decolonial thinking serves as a useful framework for clarifying the connections between the enduring impact of centuries-long European colonization, starting with the conquest of the Caribbean, and the ongoing climate emergency. Belgian decolonial scholar Koen Bogaert contends that colonial projects played a pivotal role in shaping an economic system that consumes ever more natural resources, exacerbating climate destruction while relying on the exploitation of inexpensive lives, land, and labor (2023, p. 122). In an article about post-Irma Barbuda, West Indian scholars Baptiste and Devonish state that those who "caused climate change are now reaping the benefits of the disasters caused by that same changing climate while those who did not cause climate change are having what little they did have before the climate change effects confiscated" (Baptiste & Devonish, 2019, p. 15). Similarly, Ghosh recounts how ecological interventions were not mere byproducts of European settlement in the Americas; rather, they were a central aspect of the project (2021, p. 63). The explicit goal was to transform perceived wastelands into territories aligned with a European conception of productive land that entailed the destruction of ecosystems. Ghosh persuasively argues "[w]hat seems unlikely today is

---

11   Counterhegemony, conceptualized by Antonio Gramsci (1995), refers to the manner in which people formulate ideas and discourse to contest prevailing assumptions, beliefs, and entrenched behavioral norms.

that transformations of such magnitude could have occurred without any planetary consequences" (2021, p. 52).

Ghosh underscores that Indigenous peoples have been saying that the current phase of the planetary crisis is not new but rather a manifestation of the Earth's response to the far-reaching ecological transformations initiated by European colonization worldwide (Ghosh, 2021, p. 167) and ongoing until the present day. In many places, European colonizers destroyed the entire web of nonhuman connections that sustained a certain way of life. The concept of Nature as an inert entity, separate from humans, is therefore an essential element of Western modernity, which has become hegemonic among the global elite. Seeing natural elements, such as rivers, beaches, waterways, volcanoes, and forests as meaningful actors in history is dismissed as either delusional or a "primitive superstition" (Ghosh, 2021, p. 39). Describing their lab on Climate Change, Decolonization, and Global Blackness at Duke University, African American Studies scholar Michaeline Crichlow and Brazilian critical race theory philosopher Denise Ferreira da Silva underscore that the contemporary threats face by the planet and its inhabitants can be traced back to the genocidal global development project that was colonialism. They emphasize how the global south has felt the disproportionate impact of this project and arguing that climate justice initiatives must recognize the enduring impact of historical operations and racial disparities, which have imposed an unequal burden on formerly colonized regions and their inhabitants. Only this approach will guide us towards a path of systemic and equitable transformation (Crichlow et al., n.d.).

Earlier, I outlined how authors have drawn connections between climate change and the colonization of the Americas. I explored the links established by authors between communal land tenure and its significance for communities grappling with climate change. I will next consolidate these three themes and investigate the ways in which communal land tenure, emerging as a resistant response to colonial legacies, serves to protect communities from the consequences of climate change.

Feminist Research

As a feminist, all research I conduct is feminist, both theoretically and methodologically. As discussed earlier, property and patriarchy are both foundational and intertwined elements of colonial rule (Bruyneel, 2021, p. 51). Turning land into 'property' is a patriarchal and colonial construct. Patriarchy is not only understood as the domination of women by men, but also, as Arturo Escobar puts it (2023), the broader, enduring values of separation, control, hierarchy, and appropriation. Decolonization, therefore, he says, needs depatriarchization. Decolonial feminism then emerges as a way of life centered on nurturing life and fostering the reproduction of what is common to all. Thinking within this framework, I concur that adopting a feminist lens helps us comprehend the importance of communal land tenure in addressing the planetary crisis.

The introduction of private property has historically played a crucial role in the oppression of women, as Friedrich Engels argued in his seminal 1884 work, *The Origin of the Family, Private Property and the State*. Engels highlighted that the erosion of matrilineal inheritance, or "the overthrow of mother-right," marked the "world historical defeat of the female sex" (Engels, 1884) and instituted the first division between men and women (Ferrars, 2024). In the realm of modern property law, women were denied ownership of landed property until the late 19th century (University of Nottingham, n.d.), with male relatives controlling any allotted property.[12] Notably, even when women gained property rights, these privileges were initially limited to White women. Brenna Bhandar exposes how the appropriation of land under Lockean philosophy became a perceived "God-given, natural right of men" (2018, p. 49). She describes how this appropriative behavior served as the ideal archetype of the settler, whom she terms the "self-possessive individual." This was juxtaposed against figures like the "Savage," "Indian," women and children, all deemed lacking the capacity for self-possession. The racial and gendered ontology of the self-possessive subject shaped the juridical category of the "Indian" as one who is unfit to own property and who is not a proper subject of law. This relegated them to reserves outside the mainstream market economy.

Sylvia Wynter calls this self-possessive subject simply "Man," asserting that our conception of humanity is overly associated with this figure, which "overrepresents itself as if it were the human itself" (Wynter, 2003, p. 260). Wynter's insights reveal how property ownership achieved universality under Western knowledge hegemony, aligning it with natural reason and positioning "men of property as men of reason" (Wynter, 1995, p. 66). "Degrees of Natural Reason allotted by Nature came to be 'signified' by specific indicia, the central one of which was the degree of property

---

12   A topic amply studied by the Victorian novelist Jane Austen. For example, in her celebrated novel *Pride and Prejudice*, she focuses on a family solely made up of daughters who could not inherit their father's property and therefore had to find a man (Johnson Lewis, 2019).

owned," she writes (1982, p. 6). This perspective perpetuated a classification of "natural difference," where women, excluded from property ownership, were deemed "the classificatory principle of connaturality" (1982, p. 8). This sixteenth-century concept of Man, shaped in Western Europe, prioritized reason and intellect, with non-reason personified in marginalized groups. The historical perception of Nature as an inherently feminine domain of disorder led to efforts to conquer, subjugate, and appropriate it (Ghosh, 2021, p. 255). This mindset extended to all groups associated with Nature, excluding them from civilization, including racialized peoples, justifying their domination and dispossession. Bhandar elaborates on colonial representations of Indigenous land as feminized, available for appropriation, or as wasteland awaiting fertility through European cultivation practices (2018, p. 30).

This follows the logic of the Cartesian dualism discussed earlier that entails the conceptual separation of humanity from the natural environment and gave rise to oppositional binaries between Men and Women. Men became associated with culture and reason, while Women were linked to Nature.[13] This division spawned additional binaries, such as reason/emotion, production/reproduction, active/passive, and order/chaos (Connell, 2017, p. 168). Consequently, this framework not only fostered a notion society detached from the interconnected web of life, but also relegated most women, Indigenous peoples, enslaved peoples, and colonized communities to a status of not being fully human, positioned them outside the realm of full societal membership, and perceived them as part of Nature, treated as social outcasts (Patel & Moore, 2018, p. 35). During my research, I attended an exhibition at the Barbican Centre in London, entitled RE/SISTERS: A Lens on Gender and Ecology. This exhibition highlighted the impact of colonialism, revealing the shift it installed from a woman-centered view of Nature to a mechanistic, patriarchal system primarily concerned with exploiting natural resources. The exhibition featured the efforts of activists who emphasize the pivotal role women play in advocating for and nurturing the planet. In the exhibition catalog, the curator discussed how the exhibition counters the perception that women are merely synonymous with Nature and viewed as "objects, subjects, and products to be dominated by the heteropatriarchal gaze" (Barbican, 2023, p. 15).

---

13 In her book *Empusion*, Nobel Prize-winning novelist Olga Tokarczuk offers a feminist response to Thomas Mann's *The Magic Mountain*. She uses quotes from men like William Shakespeare and Charles Darwin to explore women's perceived closeness to nature: "Their unbridled biologism, their unsettling proximity to nature, presented a factor that destabilized the social order. Yes, they should be completely hidden away in the private sphere, from where they would no longer threaten the world order" (Tokarczuk, 2023, p. 236, *own translation*).

Positioning this study within feminist research does not mean my research solely focuses on women or gender. Nor does this work use 'race' as an analytical category. Instead, I adopt a decolonial feminist approach to land and property that recognizes their pivotal roles in oppressing women and marginalized groups of color within a persistent logic of coloniality. In this context, the research resonates with the perspectives of Rosalba Icaza Garza (2023) who urges us to recognize the coloniality of gender and its potential to constrain the breadth of various social movements. A singular focus on gender, she says, can inadvertently perpetuate systems of dominance. This concept, the coloniality of gender, was originally proposed by María Lugones (2016) to help us understand the influence of European colonialism on contemporary gender structures. The concept is useful as it helps dissect the struggle against patriarchy. That struggle was central to my research, which looked at how oppressed individuals are using countervailing practices to challenge dominant modern, colonial, capitalist, and patriarchal ideologies (Lugones, 2010).

My research is also built on the insights of Angela Davis who emphasizes that feminism extends beyond advocating for gender equality (Davis, 2016, p. 110). Feminism demands not only a consciousness of patriarchy, but also of how patriarchy needs racism, capitalism, and colonialism to function. Davis contends that feminist methodologies have provided us with epistemological and organizational tools to explore connections that may not be immediately evident. Decolonial feminism encourages modes of thought and action that prompt us to consider interconnected aspects and to dissect seemingly natural associations. This study employs those epistemological tools to examine associations between private property and "progress," and how countervailing land practices challenge these dominant modern, colonial, capitalist, and patriarchal ideologies (Lugones, 2010).

I have specifically adopted a feminist political geography approach, a strand of political geography that distinguishes itself by deviating from an orthodox state-centric focus (Flint & Taylor, 2018, p. 83). Feminist geographers advocate for an examination of how everyday life is structured by institutions like the household, or in the case of this research, by private/communal land ownership and the struggles for land rights. Feminist political geographers thus position groups that are historically marginalized by the colonial order at the very heart of the world system and its history. As a feminist geographer, I shift from the state-centric "from above" perspective to a view "from below", delving into the ordinary everyday dynamics in people's households, streets, neighborhoods, and communities. This approach centers the perspectives of those affected by climate change and the ongoing global land grab, with a special focus on the Caribbean as a locus of political change. This perspective again diverges from orthodox Marxism, which identifies the most industrialized parts of the world as the primary sites for socialist revolution (Flint & Taylor, 2018, p. 121). Feminist political geography, like all feminist research, assumes a political stance that extends beyond academic critique. This book is the result of such engaged scholarship. Indeed, academics are activists, who "truly work for change rather than merely indulge in academic rhetoric," as Audre Lorde put it (1981). Research, like teaching, is therefore a political act (Flint & Taylor, 2018, p. 83). This approach requires fully integrating the body—with all its emotions, imperfections, tensions, and contradictions—into the research and into academia. Ultimately, this study interprets the struggles for communal land as a fight for the return of a woman-centered view of land that is common to all and necessary for life, employing feminist methodologies and approaches.

POSTIONING MYSELF IN MY RESEARCH

I entered this research with previously established professional and emotional connections with residents, community leaders, and staff at the Caño Martín Peña CLT. My initial encounter with them happened two years before starting my research during my role as an evaluator for the World Habitat Awards. Throughout those two years, I stayed in Puerto Rico, actively collaborating with the Caño, assisting them with the increased visibility and international outreach resulting from the Award. This experience allowed me to personally witness the significance of collective land tenure for historically marginalized communities within the context of present-day US colonialism. Additionally, during my doctoral research, I spent 10 months on the Caribbean Island of St Martin where my Puerto Rican partner serves as the President of the local university and conducts research on climate change challenges in the region. Like Puerto Rico and Barbuda, St Martin was heavily affected by the 2017 hurricane season. The island is an air- and sea-route hub for people migrating among the Lesser Antilles, as well as for populations from the global north engaging in tourism. During the months I spent on the island I observed how life was interrupted for the transient and vulnerabilized Caribbean peoples after the hurricane and during the pandemic. In acknowledging my pre-existing convictions, engagement, and personal relations with the region, I clarify that my approach to this research adopts an "embodied objectivity" (Haraway, 1988). From the start, I have used this research to further explore something I was already convinced of. My research questions do not seek to inquire *whether* collective land tenure helps marginalized communities in resisting vulnerabilization; rather, they aim to explore *in what ways* this happens, and how these forms of knowledge produced by communities—"from below"—help address the consequences of climate change.

One of the epistemological tools offered by feminist methodologies is the shift away from the pursuit of objectivity and neutrality in research. Cheryl Harris, citing the feminist legal scholar, Katharine T. Bartlett, articulates the concept of positionality as a theory of knowledge, challenging the idea of objective, neutral truths in favor of a truth that is situated and partial, emerging from individual involvements and relationships (Harris, 1993: 1727). Donna Haraway similarly advocates for knowledge that is situated and embodied, challenging forms of irresponsibly "unlocatable" knowledge claims. Haraway argues for the "view from the body, always a complex, contradictory, structuring and structured body" critiquing the conventional understanding of objectivity as a "view from above, from nowhere" (Haraway, 1988, p. 589). This view "from nowhere" hides a very specific position (usually male, White, heterosexual, human) and therefore falsely presenting it as universal (Rogowska-Stangret, 2018). Haraway labels this perspective the "god trick," an ideological standpoint used to justify an oppressive and masculinist form of objectivity that renders alternative positions invalid (idem). "Many currents in feminism attempt to theorize grounds for trusting especially the vantage points of the subjugated," Haraway writes. "There is good reason to believe vision is better from below the brilliant space platforms of the powerful" (1988, p. 583). Here, I explicitly adopt a feminist geographical locatable view from below. 'From below' is translated in Spanish as *desde abajo*, a phrase frequently used by my research collaborators in Puerto Rico when emphasizing the importance of communities in generating genuine lasting social change.

In an exploration of "the engaged turn" in research, Sherry Ortner (2019) argues that researchers are starting to do more than just offering academic critique. Engaged scholarship, she says, requires allowing 'affect' into research. Emotions contribute to a fuller understanding of research topics, forming an integral part of the engagement inherent in all research. My research revolves around land, symbolizing life, and the communities I collaborate with are engaged in a struggle for survival. Consequently, addressing this topic solely from a rational standpoint is insufficient; rather, it necessitates the inclusion of our anger, sadness, passion, hopes, joy, and love. Accordingly, I acknowledge that my body is not a machine-like instrument that

I can reset every time I enter the "field."[14] Ortner argues that an engaged feminist stance does not impede a commitment to the "principles of accuracy, evidentiary support, and truth," the foundation of all scientific work. The crucial distinction lies in engaged researchers openly acknowledging emotional, personal, and political biases, whereas non-engaged work tends to conceal those biases. This approach, far from compromising data accuracy, fosters trust—an essential element in research— and therefore brings more intimate insights. Adopting an engaged stance requires acknowledging the inherent contradictions within my position throughout the complexities of the research process. Feminist scholars stress that research inherently embodies micro power relations that are mirrored and encapsulated within the broader processes we aim to transform (Mora, 2017, p. 48). As a White, able-bodied, middle-class woman affiliated with a European university, I recognize these contradictions and power relations. My multiple travels to the Caribbean, facilitated by a European salary and research grant, underscore this privilege. During each of these journeys, my institution assured me of repatriation in the event of a hurricane or other natural disasters, despite the exorbitant flight prices driven by disaster capitalism during such events.

Another contradiction revolves around "epistemic extractivism." The staff and community leaders of the Caño Martín Peña consistently expressed their opposition to this type of extractivism, condemning the tendency of individuals to come and study their community organization processes and subsequently claim them as their own. Linda Tuhiwai Smith aptly encapsulated this phenomenon with the subtitle *They Came, They Saw, They Named, They Claimed* in her book *Decolonizing Methodologies* (1999, p. 80); she highlights the Western inclination to assert ownership over knowledge and the research process itself, often neglecting its reciprocal nature (Tuhiwai Smith, 1999, p. 176). Despite being acutely aware of these tensions and historical complexities, I engaged in the collection of knowledge to bring it back to Europe and publish it under my name—a trajectory that brought me on a path to promotion in the academic world (even though a Ph.D. is by no means a guarantee for employment in academia). Therefore, I conducted this research with a profound sense of humility, recognizing and acknowledging the power differences at play. Eager to listen and learn, I addressed these dynamics with the intention of fostering a genuine knowledge exchange.

---

14   I am reminded of a befriended researcher in St Martin who criticizes the notion of "entering the field" by underlining the inseparability between her and her research: "The field is *in* me. I don't go there. I am there" (Lysanne Charles, personal conversation, 2021).

A member of a Mapuche community expressed this perspective on Facebook, denouncing the practice of epistemic extractivism and calling for engaged scholarship. They criticized individuals who investigate Mapuche, and other Native peoples' lives without maintaining a genuine political commitment to the ongoing struggles of these communities.

> Against those who fatten libraries and raise discourse and knowledge that remains locked in the bubble of the academy. Against all those who do not maintain any kind of political commitment to our people who are fighting, against those who do not flinch from the hunger strikes of our people. What do I do with your thesis, what do I do with your paper when the [police] come to pave me, when they jail me for defending my mapu?

In her book *Kuxlejal Politics*, Mariana Mora (2017) echoes this sentiment, questioning the purpose of academic work. She invites us to consider whether academic contributions serve merely to create aesthetically pleasing books, secure employment, and find a place in libraries, or if their purpose extends to meaningful action. These perspectives underscore the disparity between academic pursuits and the urgent, real-world struggles faced by historically marginalized communities (2017, p. 25). In his article "Insurgent Research," Adam Gaudry argues that insurgent researcher recognize that their primary responsibility is not to the academy, but to the communities they work with (2011, p. 123). Gaudry writes:

> A central part of articulating a liberatory praxis is developing a realizable alternative to the oppressive and exploitative colonial status quo. While many researchers have become quite adept at critiquing the imperial situation, many fail to articulate meaningful alternatives outside of the colonial system (2011, p. 133).

When arguing for greater attention to non-extractive ways of relating to Land, this book simultaneously argues for non-extractive ways of doing research. To address the complexities (and contradictions) that arise with that endeavor, and in line with feminist researchers, I advocate for a shift towards speaking *with* rather than speaking *for* those who struggle, and for a collaborative rather than exploitative relationship (Flint & Taylor, 2018, p. 84). Rather than just offering a critique, I advocate for meaningful action, carving an alternative path forward outside of the colonial system, based on the knowledges of the communities at the center of this study, to whom this study is accountable.

Case Studies: The Caribbean as the Starting Place

The Caribbean is the ideal geography from where to examine the intricate interplay between land policy, colonial legacies, and their enduring ecological consequences. In my view, it is the world's most "geographic" yet paradoxically "ungeographic" region. It is of the highest geographic importance because it is the "starting place," as Malcom Ferdinand puts it (2021, p. 20), from where the world was globalized. This cradle of modernity gave rise to engrained institutions, with private property at the center. When the "Old World" invaded the "New World," it conceptualized Earth as a totality, enabling the envisioning of finite resources (Ferdinand, 2022, p. 12). Sylvia Wynter (1995) elaborates on this geographic transformation in her essay "1492: A New World View" noting that prior to Columbus' Caribbean journey, the world was perceived as divided into two zones: the European 'temperate' zone and the 'torrid' zone. The temperate zone was deemed "rational," while the torrid zone was "wild" and uninhabitable, its "wastelands" devoid of "civilized" people due to their "primitive" notions of the land. The introduction of Western land-holding forms, central to the appropriation of land and the domination of its peoples, rendered the world a geographically homogeneous entity, transforming the 'torrid zone' into a 'real geography' no longer deemed uninhabitable.

Simultaneously, the Caribbean remains one of the world's most "ungeographic" regions. Frequently mistaken for "paradise," it is misconstrued for the benefit of a privileged few at the expense of many.[15] The Caribbean is viewed as "a series of landscapes to be mined for their wealth or enjoyed for their beauty by outsiders" (Besson & Momsen, 1987, p. 39). The history of its people has been relegated to the background and their contributions have been made invisible (Ferdinand, 2021, p. 20) despite their importance in shaping today's world. Its global image has been appropriated by external forces—colonialists, real-estate investors, tourists, shell companies, and remote workers—who have flocked to the region in different stages of history. The narrative surrounding the Caribbean seems to belong to everyone except its own people, perpetuating a perspective that the land is up for grabs.

---

15 As a European conducting research in the Caribbean, I frequently heard the joke that my work likely involved sipping Piña Coladas in a hammock on the beach.

A very different narrative emerges when we center the perspectives of Caribbean populations, and when we posit colonialism as a fundamental problem. For centuries, these communities have stood at the forefront of global processes. Situated at the birthplace of globalization, they have confronted the enduring impacts of historical and contemporary colonialism, postcolonialism, coloniality and neocolonialism; global processes that have continuously vulnerabilized them, a process now worsened by climate change. Concurrently, the same populations have actively engaged in anticolonial and decolonial resistance ever since the first arrival of the conquistadores, notably exemplified by transformative insurgencies like the Haitian Revolution that altered the world order. Thinking from these Caribbean perspectives provide crucial insights into the dynamics between vulnerabilization and resistance, which is the core objective of this study. As previously discussed, the profound transformations associated with European settlement, particularly in the Caribbean, had far-reaching consequences on a planetary scale. The Caribbean therefore is uniquely positioned for an exploration of the roots of contemporary global crises. By doing so, we can untangle the connections between climate change and colonialism, specifically related to land tenure systems, offering insights that can guide us toward a more sustainable future. Countervailing and oppositional Caribbean perspectives on land ownership and ecological thinking can help us chart this course, prompting a paradigm shift away from land as property and toward collectively held land. This approach recognizes the interconnectedness of communities with the land and all its facets.

In the past decade, the consequences of climate change have intensified, coinciding with a global surge in land rushes. This phenomenon has occurred around the world, for example, the land grabs in Sri Lanka and The Maldives following the 2004 tsunami, as Naomi Klein vividly described *The Shock Doctrine* (2007). The 2017 Atlantic hurricane season served as a turning point in the Caribbean, not only because it ranked among the most severe on record,[16] but also because it sparked a heightened awareness of the intrinsic links between climate change and colonial legacies. Terming it 'the hurricane moment,' Sir Hillary Beckles, the Barbadian vice-chancellor of the University of the West Indies, wondered "how these ill-winds so precisely trace the journeys of the deadly European slave ships that crossed the middle passage" (cited in Popke & Rhiney, 2019, p. 2). Acknowledging and building upon these perspectives

---

16   This season produced 17 named storms of which 10 became hurricanes including six major hurricanes (Category 3, 4 or 5) (NOAA, 2017).

helps as we collectively move towards social and environmental justice in the face of the climate emergency.

As described in the opening sentences of this book, my doctoral studies started on September 1, 2017. I had just begun drafting a research design based on what lessons could be drawn from the Caño Martín Peña CLT in fighting gentrification in self-built neighborhoods. Five days later, Hurricane Irma happened, and Hurricane Maria two weeks afterward. The initial weeks, if not months, of my doctoral studies, were consumed by a deep sense of sadness and terror induced by the devastation, leading me to engage in international solidarity efforts. During this tumultuous period, an accidental encounter with a social media article drew my attention to Barbuda's situation in the aftermath of Hurricane Irma. Despite being forcedly evacuated off the island, the islanders now confronted the impending privatization of their centuries-old communal land tenure system. Much like Puerto Rico, they observed a prioritization of international capital interests over local needs in the recovery process. The focal point of these foreign elites' attention was undeniably the land, particularly the coastal areas of the two islands. The hurricanes served as a catalyst, exacerbating pre-existing issues in Puerto Rico and Barbuda. At this point, I decided to concentrate my research on the difference that communal land ownership could make for the two communities facing similar challenges. I was fascinated by the historical and contemporary connections between the communities, as well as their differences. In Puerto Rico, the communal land system developed as a reaction to 'informal', self-organized land use resulting from colonial planning decisions, whereas in Barbuda, it arose in response to the colonial slave regime and functioned as a self-organized system until it was ratified in the Barbuda Land Act in 2007. Furthermore, self-built neighborhoods like the Martín Peña communities exist due to forced displacements from areas like Barbuda, a process exacerbated by climate disasters and their not-so-natural consequences. Both communities are deeply influenced by the colonial concept of property and their resistance to it.

Puerto Rico and Barbuda are indeed very different Caribbean Islands, varying greatly in size, population, and GDP. Beyond these quantitative dissimilarities, their colonial histories also diverge significantly. Puerto Rico, having been a former Spanish colony, is presently a US colony, officially designated as an "Estado Libre Asociado" or an unincorporated US territory. In contrast, Barbuda is part of the twin-state Antigua and Barbuda, a sovereign nation that became independent in 1981 after enduring 349 years of British colonial rule, while Barbuda contested the joining of the two islands on account of the contrasting land holding systems. Due to these diverging colonial histories the legal systems are different. Puerto Rico has a legal system that is based both on the Spanish civil law and the Anglosaxon common law systems. The Spanish Civil Code of 1890 represented a key moment for the hegemony of the modern concept of private property in Puerto Rico, after decades of practicing Spanish Crown concessions as conditional authorizations for land occupation (Fontánez Torres, 2008, pp. 6-7). Antigua and Barbuda is a common law jurisdiction, and as a Commonwealth country still falls under the Judicial Committee of the Privy Council in London. Additionally, the Martín Peña communities, situated in a central part of the Puerto Rican capital, are highly dense, urban, self-built ("informal") neighborhoods. They are extremely diverse and transitory, serving as arrival neighborhoods for people migrating from other Caribbean islands (Haiti, Dominican Republic, Jamaica, etc.) or Latin America (Venezuela, Colombia, etc.). On the other hand, Barbuda has a very low density and a small population, located in a predominantly rural environment. The community is tight knit with intricate family ties. Most Barbudans have descendants who were brought by force to the Caribbean through the transatlantic slave trade. A lot of Barbudans currently live outside of the island, predominantly in Antigua, the US or in Leicester (UK), but may return after retiring. A large part of the Barbudan diaspora is actively involved with current affairs on the island.

A comparative overview of these islands' features is provided in Table 1. There are compelling reasons that support the decision to bring together these two Caribbean communities in this research. The convergence of shared experiences is what encouraged me to do a comparative analysis. This convergence can be summarized as follows:

- Both communities had robust communal land systems at the time of the 2017 hurricane season, located in environmentally vulnerable, yet geographically valuable areas, rich in natural resources.
- Both communities found themselves in contemporary colonial and neocolonial situations, navigating the dynamics of external influences.
- Both underwent significant reforms in the aftermath of this season, observing that recovery efforts centered foreign capital rather than local needs.

Table 1: Data on Puerto Rico and Antigua and Barbuda

Island	Population	Population density	Surface	GDP per capita	Poverty index
Puerto Rico	3.264 million	368 per km²	8,870 km²	32,640.71 USD	41.7%
Caño Martin Peña District	11,939	15,984 per sq mile (6,148 per km²)	1.8 km²	Not available	60.1%
Antigua & Barbuda	93,219	214 per km²	440 km²	15,781.40 USD	18% (not official data)
Barbuda	1,634	10.2 per km²	160 km²	Not available	Not available[17]

Sources: World Bank, Census Reporter, US Census Bureau, UNDP.

Puerto Rico

Caño Martín Peña Community Land Trust. The first case that I selected for this research is the Caño Martín Peña CLT, known as Fideicomiso de la Tierra del Caño Martín Peña. Prior to starting this study, I had already been actively engaged with this CLT; I had advocated for its recognition and suggested it as the winner to the judges of the World Habitat Award in 2015. My decision to select this case originates from my motivation to comprehend its significance in the context of global crises.

Established in 2004, the Caño CLT emerged as a result of the collective mobilization of thousands of residents inhabiting seven neighborhoods in central San Juan. These historic, self-built communities surround a heavily polluted mangrove waterway. The following chapters of this book elaborate extensively on how residents inventively constructed this CLT by modifying elements from existing CLTs and introduced new features to address the challenges posed by residing on land without acknowledged ownership. The primary goal of the CLT is to collectively regularize the residents' relationship with the land they have been inhabited for decades, protecting them against the inevitable displacement that would result from the dredging of the waterway for ecological restoration and the subsequent surge in land prices. The demand for dredging of the waterway, campaigned for by the surrounding communities, aims to restore the ecological value and natural beauty of the mangrove waterway and

---

17   Although there are no official figures for poverty on Barbuda, members of the Barbuda Council have stated that there is no homelessness and that no one is in significant household debt (D. Warner, personal conversation).

to reconnect several lagoons and channels. Dredging makes the communities' prime location attractive to real-estate developers and causes land values to escalate. The residents established the CLT during a period when awareness of the limitations of private property titles was growing. Titles were being sold to speculators, displacing significant portions of the communities. Historical displacements had occurred earlier due to the US government-sponsored Eradication of Slums Act of 1945.

The Caño CLT spans 280 acres across the Caño Martín Peña Special Planning District, which itself covers a total of 450 acres. Crucially, the lands under the CLT are inalienable and cannot be sold; this ensures that these communities are protected from involuntary displacement for generations to come. Established as a non-profit, private organization, the CLT has perpetual existence and independent legal status. It operates as a membership organization capable of acquiring new land, selling, and reacquiring structures with priority when the owners decide to sell. The CLT also has the authority to design a resale formula to ensure housing affordability in perpetuity. The Board of Trustees governs the CLT and includes representatives from the community, private sector, and government sector, with a majority being community residents. The eleven-member board comprises four members residing on the CLT land, two delegates from the G-8 community organization, two non-resident experts chosen by the board, and three representatives from government institutions: one from the ENLACE Project Corporation, one from the Municipality of San Juan appointed by its mayor, and one appointed by the governor of Puerto Rico.

The ENLACE Caño Martín Peña Project Corporation (Corporación del Proyecto ENLACE del Caño Martín Peña, hereafter ENLACE or the Corporation), a public entity, supports the CLT. ENLACE is tasked with implementing the community-designed District Plan over a 25-year period, with significant resident participation and collaboration with public and private sectors. The Corporation's Board of Directors, designed by the community, ensures project continuity despite governmental changes, with a majority of community leaders appointed by the governor and the mayor of San Juan from a shortlist submitted by the G-8, the Group of the Eight Communities Along the Caño Martín Peña, Inc. (*Grupo de las Ocho Comunidades Aledañas al Caño Martín Peña, Inc.*). The G-8 is a community-based, non-profit organization that unites 12 community organizations surrounding the Martín Peña waterway, including neighborhood resident associations, councils, and a youth association, Young Leaders in Action (*Líderes Jóvenes en Acción* or LIJAC).[18] Neighborhood councils, led by bi-annually elected community leaders (see Figure 4), represent the residents. The G-8's board is composed of community leaders who are elected bi-annually by residents; the board governs the organization and ensures that decision-making is democratic and that community interests are effectively represented and upheld.

Figure 4: Community members in an election of a neighborhood council in April 2019. Source: Line Algoed

Colonial Context. Puerto Rico has been a colony of the United States since Spain was defeated in the Spanish-American war in 1898. As an unincorporated territory of the United States, the island is controlled by the US government. Puerto Ricans are US Citizens, but they cannot vote for the US President, nor do they have representation in the US Congress. For the colonized, second-class citizens of Puerto Rico, life can be harsh on the island. Around 41% of Puerto Ricans live in poverty, exacerbated by consumer prices higher than those in the US; this is a consequence of the colonial Jones Act that mandates all goods to pass through a US harbor.

Even before Hurricane Maria hit Puerto Rico, the nation was declared bankrupt in 2017, burdened by a USD $73+ billion public debt (Heath & Newmyer, 2017). This debt, a disaster for most, became an alluring investment opportunity for some. Then President Barack Obama established a non-elected Financial Oversight and

---

18 A full list of the 12 organizations that comprise the G-8 can be found on the website: https://g8pr.org/conocenos/organizacionesmiembro/

Management Board through the Puerto Rico Oversight Management and Economic Stability Act (PROMESA), effectively dismantling the country's fragile fiscal autonomy. Empowered by the territorial clause of the US Constitution, the Board wields authority over Puerto Rico's financial planning, laws, budgets, and regulations. Austerity measures have been imposed on the population to repay bondholders, a significant proportion of whom are vulture funds, specializing in investing in high-risk, weak debt. Notably, Puerto Rico's public debt has never undergone an audit. Few Puerto Ricans resonate with the narrative of having lived "beyond their means."[19]

Disaster Recovery Focusing on Foreign Capital. On September 20, 2017, Hurricane Maria ravaged Puerto Rico. The storm was characterized by local scholars as an "unnatural disaster resulting from a long history of colonial subjugation, economic hardship, environmental injustice, infrastructural neglect, and […] a broken rule of law" (Lloréns et al., 2018). In its aftermath, Puerto Rico became a textbook example of disaster capitalism, marked by accelerated privatization and brutal austerity measures. Hundreds of operational public schools were closed, and the education system underwent semi-privatization through the introduction of charter schools and private school voucher; this was a widely unpopular policy reform that was spearheaded by then Secretary for Education in the Puerto Rican government, the American-born Julia Keleher, who later faced FBI indictment for using school land for personal gain (Wyss, 2020). Simultaneously, the privatization of the electric power grid—and its sale to the Canadian company LUMA Energy—resulted in persistent blackouts, leaving an infrastructure that has not yet fully recovered from the hurricane's impact and remains heavily reliant on fossil fuels.

Amidst this crisis and facilitated by the Puerto Rican government's tax incentives, outside investors seized opportunities to acquire land, particularly in coastal areas, driving up prices and gentrifying the island (Marcos & Mazzei, 2022). The controversial Law 22-2012 (now a component of Law 60-2019) grants full tax exemption on US federal income taxes, Puerto Rico income taxes on dividends, interests, capital gains, and 75% exemption on real and personal property taxes for properties used in export, promotion, and trade services. Importantly, the law requires beneficiaries to purchase property in Puerto Rico. Almost half of these real-estate transactions fell within

---

19 A common fallacy of equating public debt with private debt was exploited to justify brutal austerity measures in the aftermath of the global financial crisis. While principles like balanced budgets, savings, and living "within one's means" hold validity at the household level, applying them on a macroeconomic scale is misguided. In fact, abstaining from deficit spending and investments on a macrolevel can ultimately have detrimental effects on everyone's well-being.

a price range accessible to local workers (Sutter & Sosa Pascual, 2018). Investors started exploiting these incentives, buying up affordable housing, hoarding extensive property holdings, escalating rents, and displacing residents in neighborhoods across the island (Santiago-Bartolomei et al., 2022). Numerous properties were transformed into short-term rentals (Figure 5) to cater to tourists or other visitors—a consequence of a policy emphasis on promoting the "visitor economy" championed by key disaster recovery players like the Foundation for Puerto Rico (Foundation for Puerto Rico, n.d.). According to a study conducted by the Puerto Rican Center for a New Economy, the surge in short-term rentals was disaster-driven, with an increase up to 31% in average daily Airbnb listings since Hurricane Maria. Disasters, the report's authors argued, create the ideal conditions for investors to exploit short-term drops in housing prices, acquiring properties for conversion into highly profitable short-term rentals (Santiago-Bartolomei, 2022).

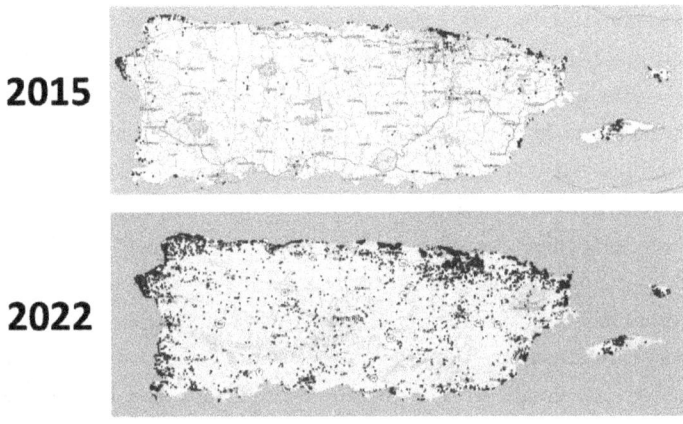

Figure 5: Localization of properties listed as short-term rentals. Source: Rosa Rosa et al., 2023.

Meanwhile, Puerto Ricans are leaving the island, grappling with escalating land and housing prices, and dwindling employment prospects. According to US Census Bureau (2018), 130,000 people permanently departed the island. Puerto Ricans are witnessing a population replacement. As a coastal area resident put it: "We will be a Puerto Rico without Puerto Ricans" (Graulau, 2021). Conversely, Edwin Miranda, a government official, part of the controversial Telegram group of elected officials that was leaked, blatantly remarked, "I saw the future […] is wooooonderful […] there are no puertorricans" (sic) (Valentín Ortiz & Minet, 2019)[20] confirming the suspicion of many Puerto Ricans that these policies are directed at their departure. Situated adjacent to San Juan's Central Business District, and close to major public transportation hubs, the corporate interests in the lands of the Martín Peña communities are significant.

Barbuda

Barbuda's Unique Communal Land Ownership System. The second case chosen for this study is Barbuda (Figure 6). Barbuda is part of the sovereign state of Antigua and Barbuda situated in the Leeward Islands of the Lesser Antilles. The nation comprises two main islands of Antigua and Barbuda that are separated by approximately 40km, along with several smaller islands. Barbuda is the only island in the world where the whole land is collectively owned. The land is not considered state property, and there is no private ownership; consequently, the land cannot be sold. This distinctive communal landholding system has persisted since the island's initial habitation, spanning colonial eras and persisting into its current "postcolonial" state. It has allowed Barbudans to stop developments that do not benefit the community, and to continue to fish and hunt, and grow most of their food, like they always have. Barbuda's centuries-old communal land system now faces threats. Following Hurricane Irma, the Central Government of Antigua and Barbuda, headquartered in Antigua, and their economic allies, have been taking advantage of the island's pristine condition. They initiated policy changes and promoted luxury real-estate projects, jeopardizing the communal land system. This aggressive move to exploit the island's unspoiled state is met with resistance from its small population, who staunchly contest this encroachment on their unique way of life and consider it a way to dispossess them of their land and resources.

After enduring centuries of slavery followed by de facto possession of the land, Barbudans were officially granted legal status as lawful tenants with communal possession rights through a colonial enactment in 1904 by the British Crown. This communal tenure persisted throughout the twentieth century and underwent further refinement and ratification in the Barbuda Land Act of 2007. This legislation states that the island is collectively owned by the people of Barbuda and each Barbudan is entitled to three plots of land: one for housing, another for agriculture, and a third

---

20   This message can be found on page 868 of the 889 pages of Telegram messages that were published by Puerto Rico's *Centro de Periodismo Investigativo*. This publication led in summer of 2019 to the biggest anti-government protests in Puerto Rican history, eventually ousting the then Governor Ricardo Rosselló.

one for business. While the Crown maintains symbolic ownership of the land, the legal administration is entrusted to the Barbuda Council. Comprising nine directly elected members and two ex officio members serving four-year terms, the Council possesses the authority to allocate and lease plots of land. Certain plots may be leased to international investors for a limited period, but any substantial development requires explicit and informed approval from a majority of Barbudans. These individuals must be fully informed of comprehensive plans during village meetings that are conducted regularly and as needed.

Figure 6: Barbudans at a Homecoming event in July 2018. Source: Line Algoed

Colonial Context. The island's initial inhabitants were the Kalinago, who named it Wa'Omoni, meaning the "Island of Herons." The Kalinago fiercely defended their land against European settlers. In 1628, King Charles II claimed the island as his personal property and later leased it to the Codrington family in 1685, who stayed for nearly two centuries. Barbuda's dry land was unsuitable for large-scale sugarcane production and served as housing for enslavers, while enslaved Africans worked to supply livestock and food staples to the Codrington's Antigua estates. When the Codrington family finally left in 1870, Barbudans refused to pay rent to the British Crown. This defiance contributed to the legal acknowledgment of communal tenure and solidified their de facto ownership through uninterrupted inhabitation.

On November 1, 1981, Antigua and Barbuda gained independence from Britain, a development contested by Barbudans who feared the imposition of Antigua's freehold system on their communal land tenure. As articulated by Baptiste and Devonish (2019, p. 2), the creation of this small island, bi-nation, Caribbean state is a consequence of the European colonial invasion of the Caribbean spanning from the fifteenth century onward, as they were forced into this union with Antigua. Despite persistent dependence on Antigua for essential public services, many Barbudans have continued to call for secession, particularly due to land issues (Lightfoot, 2020, p. 137), highlighting the ongoing tensions within this delicate twin-state relationship.

Disaster Recovery Focusing on Foreign Capital. On the night of September 5-6, 2017, Hurricane Irma struck Barbuda with an unprecedented force and devastated the island. In its aftermath, Prime Minister Gaston Browne of the twin state's Labor Party, a former Antiguan banker, justified the evacuation of the population, citing the impending threat of another storm. Similar to what the Maldives government did after the tsunami, as described by Naomi Klein, Browne called Barbuda unsafe and unsuitable for habitation ("barely habitable" in his words). Despite the passing of this subsequent storm without making landfall, Barbudans were forcibly kept away for 30 days. Critical institutions such as schools, the bank, and the hospital remained shuttered for months longer, while the restoration of electricity and communication services also lagged. Exploiting the chaos, the Central Government engaged in a classic example of disaster capitalism, initiating the construction of a new international airport during the enforced evacuation. This move lacked approval from the Barbudan people or the Council, and an environmental impact assessment was not presented. The construction was a fulfillment of promises made to luxury real-estate developers.

For example, under a ninety-nine-year land lease deal with "Peace, Love and Happiness" (PLH), the Central Government gave greenlight to the development of a lavish $2 billion residential community in the post-disaster period. Teaming up with Discovery Land Company, DeJoria and partners, the government started construction of 450 exclusive residences for the ultrawealthy on the island's pristine beaches of Coco Point and Palmetto Point—the latter being protected by the Ramsar Convention on Wetlands. Earlier, in 2015, the American actor Robert De Niro disclosed his intentions to transform an abandoned resort into a Nobu luxury residential community, calling it "Paradise Found," offering to pay a meager annual lease of $62,000 USD for the land (Frank, 2015). To facilitate De Niro's project, the Prime Minister introduced the Paradise Found Act in 2015, bypassing the community approval sections of the 2007 Barbuda Land Act. Despite vehement local opposition, the Act was enacted, securing approval for the controversial project. After the hurricane, De Niro ardently claimed to be helping Barbudans, while working behind the scenes to change its communal land system (Klein & Brown, 2018).[21]

Methodological Approach

As discussed earlier, my research started in the same month that hurricanes Irma and Maria hit the Caribbean region in September 2017. This means my research sites were in constant development from the very beginning up until writing these pages. Additionally, I actively contributed to creating the solidarity networks that have served as sites of research. I have indeed taken an engaged stance and endeavored to speak *with* the movement, rather than *for* the movement. I do not study these communities, I work alongside them.[22] The process was long and messy, and therefore hard to write down. My methodological approach aligns with participatory action research (PAR) that involves the participation and leadership of the communities affected by the issues under study, the coproduction of knowledge, and the collective work towards emancipatory social change (Cornish et al., 2023, p. 1).

My commitment is towards the communities I work with, and it is to them that this work is accountable, more than to academia. Adam Gaudry identifies this approach as essential to "insurgent research"—research dedicated to challenging oppressive and colonial structures. He emphasizes the responsibility researchers have to avoid misrepresentation and distortion of the communities they study and instead to speak with these communities (2011, pp. 123, 134). I term my approach "insurgent PAR." Doing so, I want to highlight that while not all PAR is insurgent, all research that is committed to decolonization, especially when working with vulnerabilized, oppressed communities, must involve PAR; this means engaging these communities at every stage from formulating questions, designing fieldwork, and organizing activities to analyzing findings and writing. Without this level of community involvement, we would risk doing extractive research that serves academia and not the communities itself.

---

21   In "Killers of the Flower Moon" Robert De Niro plays an uncannily similar character, claiming to help the Osage community while being after their land and resources.

22   "*Lxs acompaño*"—I accompany them. In the Spanish-speaking Caribbean, social scientists use the term "*acompañar*," walking alongside the communities.

In this study, this insurgent collaborative research project is reflected in several key actions. First and foremost, I have been engaged in continuous solidarity work that includes fundraising for disaster responses and for Barbuda's legal battles, turning up for meetings, showing support, and staying in touch. Secondly, I coauthored all my articles with people from the Caribbean and shared all writing with my key contacts in the communities before their publication, acknowledging that no amount of fieldwork will ever be sufficient to claim full knowledge over a subject, particularly one in constant development. Additionally, I have actively sought to share speaking invitations, whenever possible, extending the platform to include community residents or staff.

Figure 7: Community-to-community exchange hosted by the Caño CLT in May 2019. Source: Line Algoed

Another important element of my Insurgent PAR was "learning by working." In his dissertation about Maroon communities, Robert Connell (2017, p. 31) posits that "learning by working" is a highly engaged variant of participant observation, where the researcher participates in the community's daily work with the aim to generate trust and gain intimate knowledge of the less obvious aspects of the community, while reciprocally, community members will have a much clearer idea of who the researcher is and what their intentions are, rendering the research process more transparent. This is what I did when I continued the work that predates my doctoral research, generating activities and new networks that served as sites for this research. In this framework, I helped organize three community-to-community exchanges, two in person and one online. The first in-person exchange took place in Rio de Janeiro in August 2018, for which I helped secure funding from the Lincoln Institute of Land Policy (LILP), a think-tank based in Cambridge, Massachusetts (USA). Using these funds, I collaborated with the Caño CLT and the Brazilian non-profit Catalytic Communities in a research project to study the feasibility of establishing similar CLTs in Brazilian favelas. The second in-person exchange took place in the Martín Peña area in May 2019 (Figure 7). The preparatory meetings for this exchange happened during my fieldwork in Puerto Rico, leading me to spend a significant amount of time in the Proyecto ENLACE offices, working daily alongside staff and community leaders. Funded by the Ford Foundation, 49 community leaders and professionals from supporting organizations traveled to Puerto Rico from 17 different countries in the Caribbean, Latin America, Africa, Asia, Europe, and the USA, funded by the Ford Foundation. I kept notes during these exchanges and conducted in-depth interviews with participants and community leaders that I have used for this research.

I also actively helped compose and participated in two transnational networks. These networks became circuits for this research and helped me gain valuable firsthand insights into transnational knowledge circuits and solidarity. First, I helped establish the International Center for CLTs ("the CLT Center"), an organization with the aim to support CLTs and similar strategies of community-led development on community-owned land in countries throughout the world. I served on the Executive Committee and Governing Board of the CLT Center alongside Caño CLT staff and Board members, participating in the daily functioning of the Center and organizing events to bring together practitioners from CLTs worldwide. I coedited the first book published by the Center's imprint, Terra Nostra Press, entitled *On Common Ground: International Perspectives on the Community Land Trust* (Davis et al., 2020). Finally, I helped convene and participated in a research project entitled Food, Land, and Climate Justice in the Caribbean, funded by the UK Global Challenges Research Fund (GCRF), with participation of community leaders and scholars from Barbuda, Belize, Jamaica, Puerto Rico, and Providencia (Colombia). The network around this project later turned into the Stronger Caribbean Together network with six more Caribbean islands and countries joining. As part of this network I attended monthly online meetings between mid 2019 and mid 2022 and helped organize three webinars on the following topics: Hunger, Covid-19, Resistance and farmer-based solutions (held on 1 May 2020); Capitalism of Disaster in the Caribbean: Tourism, Development and Displacement of Local Communities (held on 21 June 2021); and finally, Climate Change and Land Tenure in the Caribbean (held on 24 March 2022). These network engagements were integral to my research, providing me with a more purposeful experience and resulting in deeper insights.

The Insurgent PAR process became a cyclical approach of *reflection-research-action-reflection* (Herrador Valencia et al., 2012), akin to the Caño CLT community organization methodology of 'planning-action-reflection' discussed in Chapter Three. In my research, community-to-community exchanges played a pivotal role as spaces of reflection, driving the research that then led to various actions. These actions included establishing CLTs in Rio's favelas, exploring communal land systems in other areas, and enhancing community organization tools in existing communal land systems. Each action spurred further reflection, some of them manifesting as new exchanges. Typically, PAR is initiated by researchers (Herrador Valencia et al., 2012, p. 48), but in my case, it was a collaborative effort with the Caño CLT. By applying for the World Habitat Award, they had already embarked on a journey of reflection, international outreach and solidarity building, a process I supported by playing an active role in it. This assistance aligns with the insurgent process, emphasizing that liberation must arise from the grassroots, from below—not from the researcher's own interests, regardless how well intended they may be. Insurgent PAR, as developed through historical and ongoing liberation struggles (Glassman & Erdem, 2014), is indeed unapologetically liberatory in its orientation (Gaudry, 2011, p. 133).

Despite these commitments, the reality remains that I advance professionally by employing the knowledge generated in a struggle to which I feel deeply connected and believe is crucial for collective liberation, but that is not my own. I continually grapple with the question of how my academic research can effectively make visible the practices and knowledges of these communities without perpetuating imbalanced power relations. These uncertainties extend beyond my personal position to broader academic practices, but I carry a responsibility as an academic. Ultimately, this research positions itself as imperfect yet socially committed, with the aim of contributing to the work of the communities, that is to make visible the struggles of these residents and the worldwide significance of the knowledges produced in these struggles. This contribution is made within the framework of solidarity work, an essential aspect of decolonization.

To study the fundamental dynamics of vulnerabilization and resistance within these communities, my research concentrated on understanding the tactics and systems utilized by political and economic elites in both producing and capitalizing on the vulnerability of these communities. Concurrently, I tried to comprehend the strategies and mechanisms deployed by inhabitants of communal lands in their acts of resistance. To gain nuanced insights into the organization of this struggle, my ethnographic research deliberately centered on the experiences of the "vulnerabilized" rather than on the "vulnerabilizers."

Data Collection Methods. I relied on multiple methods and data sources, predominantly rooted in my anthropological training that convinced me of the necessity to spend as much time as possible near the communities central to this research. I cannot claim to have done a full ethnographic study, which would have required my participation in the daily life of these communities over a longer period. Funding restraints, teaching responsibilities in Brussels, and the COVID-19 pandemic prevented this. Instead, I present this research as a "multisited and fragmented ethnography," spanning seven years, from September 2017 to September 2024. This approach involved alternating periods spent on the islands and in Brussels, where I maintained close contact with both communities through personal and group WhatsApp communications, solidarity work, meetings and webinars, and collaborative article writing. These periods spent away from the islands were as important for this research as the actual fieldwork, as the research happened in a growing framework of international solidarity.

Ethnographic Fieldwork. Engaging in ethnographic fieldwork within the communities helped me immerse myself in their social fabric following the hurricanes. I obtained a deep understanding and acquired firsthand insights into the dynamics of post-disaster social life and the complex processes underpinning life on communal land. In total, I spent 21 weeks in Puerto Rico and Barbuda. My first visit to the Martín Peña area in Puerto Rico in the frame of my research was in March 2018 (6 months after hurricane Maria), with subsequent visits from February to May 2019 and in February 2022. My first visit to Barbuda was in July 2018 (10 months after hurricane Irma), with subsequent visits from January to February 2020 and in February 2023.

During these visits, I conducted 58 semi-structured, in-depth interviews to obtain firsthand accounts of the events and processes under study. The interviews that I conducted early in my research also helped me finetune the focus of this research. I recorded and transcribed most of these interviews. In Puerto Rico, I conducted interviews with residents, community leaders engaged with *G-8 Grupo de las Ocho Comunidades Aledañas al Caño Martín Peña, Inc.* (the umbrella organization of community initiatives in the area), staff at the Caño Martín Peña CLT and Proyecto ENLACE del Caño Martín Peña, members of the Board of the CLT and Proyecto ENLACE, as well as with scholars associated with the work of the Martín Peña communities and officials involved in disaster recovery. In Barbuda, I conducted interviews with residents, community leaders, members of the Barbuda Council, members of the political party Barbuda People's Movement, as well as officials involved in disaster recovery based in Antigua. Additionally, during these visits I conducted participant observation at public meetings. Appendix 1 provides a complete overview of the interviews and the participant observation activities I conducted for this research.

Actively engaging in the events organized by my research respondents allowed me to gain insights that were not easily accessible through interviews alone, such as understanding the nuances of social interactions and group dynamics. This helped me gain valuable insights about the organizational processes at the basis of communal land. In the Martín Peña area, these were Community Council meetings where daily concerns in the different Martín Peña neighborhoods were discussed among residents and community council members. I also observed community council elections, when members are elected for a period of two years. I attended G-8 meetings and G-8 elections, when the G-8 community leaders were elected for a period of three years. I attended numerous Proyecto ENLACE and CLT staff meetings and a few advisory council meetings and disaster recovery community meetings, at which the consequences of Hurricane María were discussed. I was invited to come along on several community and staff excursions outside of San Juan. I participated in anticolonial protests and marches for Puerto Rican political causes in which Caño residents participated, such as the protests against the Financial Oversight and Management Board (Junta de Control Fiscal, or "La Junta")—the unelected Board composed of Wall Street members—or the student protests against the austerity measures imposed by that Board. Finally, I attended public events organized by Foundation for Puerto Rico, the main and controversial recipient of disaster recovery funds from the US government.

In Barbuda, where I spent less time than in Puerto Rico, I attended the following activities: the homecoming events in July 2018 that brought together Barbudans from around the world to visit the island and support the community in the aftermath of the hurricane; village meetings at which community concerns are discussed; church services, where people come together to pray, sing and eat; community walks and activities such as street cleaning; and meetings of the political party Barbuda People's Movement. I also observed the Privy Council hearing for the case two Barbudans against the Central Government of Antigua and Barbuda held in London in November 2023.

An important aspect of ethnographic fieldwork is "deep hanging out" (Geertz, 1998). This method is crucial as it recognizes that everything is data, not just the formal discussions with research respondents. It made clear to everyone involved what the researcher's role is. This method recognizes that social research takes time and is a social interaction based on trust, which is not only built up during formal research moments. The fact that residents saw me hanging out on the porch of a small neighborhood pub in Codrington's main street chatting with village elders, or in the Martín Peña monthly artisanal market, or at community field trips deeply impacted my relationships with them. It clarified I was not only there to extract knowledge, but that I was participating in daily life, connecting with residents in whose lives I was genuinely interested, beyond my research. This method recognizes that people are not simply "knowable;" what they say depends on context and personal relationships like it does in any other interaction. This method recognizes that we enter as humans, and not as machine-like instruments in our research.

Document Analysis. To understand how policymakers justify their decisions and shape public opinion, I analyzed post-disaster government documents, campaign documents, laws, as well as recorded interviews with politicians and developers. To understand how economic elites participate in the production of vulnerability I studied leases, archives of tourism brochures, and environmental impact assessments. To gain insights into how the communities organized resistance, I studied internal governance documents, community meeting recordings, as well as recorded interviews with community leaders.

For Puerto Rico, these documents include internal governance documents; letters from ENLACE to Puerto Rican politicians; fact sheet from ENLACE on Maximizing CDBG-DR funds; popular education materials; laws; PR Disaster Recovery Action Plan for the Use of CDBG-DR Funds in Response to 2017 Hurricanes Irma and Maria; and finally, media articles following Hurricane Maria. For Antigua and Barbuda, these documents include Barbuda Channel footage of village meetings and interviews conducted with politicians and investors; archival research of deeds in Antigua and Barbuda national archives; commercial brochures of former and future real-estate projects; Barbuda Council press releases; laws; Peace, Love, and Happiness Leases; Environmental Impact Assessment prepared for PLH/Discovery Land Company; Antigua and Barbuda Department of Environment (DoE) Review on PLH development; John Mussington's comments on DoE review; Global Coral

Reef Alliance's comments on PLH development; Global Action Lawyers Network (GLAN) rebuttal to PLH; and finally media articles following Hurricane Irma.

Discourse Analysis. My fieldwork and interviews focused on residents, community leaders and staff closely involved in the land struggles and communities. Despite numerous attempts, I could not secure interviews with leaders of the Puerto Rican government or the Central government of Antigua and Barbuda, or with the investors involved in the luxury real estate developments on Barbuda. Addressing this limitation, I analyzed discourses these political and economic elites employ during media interviews, as well as documents such as brochures, websites, publicity campaigns, and the Environmental Impact Assessments (sponsored by the developers). In this analysis, I focused on the way language and communication are used to justify the policies and practices my respondents observed.

Autoethnography. I used autoethnography, a method that systematically analyzes personal experiences. I critically analyzed experiences, events, and partnerships in which I have been closely involved, using emails, WhatsApp exchanges and personal journal notes as data. This method was necessary in this research as the topic and the networks that served as sites of analysis were in constant development.

Visual Methods. In collaboration with a Belgian journalist, I coproduced a short documentary about the land struggle in Barbuda, funded by the Fonds Pascal Decroos for investigative journalism in Belgium and the Flemish public broadcaster, VRT. The documentary centers the perspectives of Barbudan activists and their reasons for fighting to protect communal land ownership. We interviewed 16 Barbudans (included in the overall count of interviews for this research) and captured daily life on the island. It is an important output of my research, as some aspects of these communities can only be told with the help of images, such as the natural beauty of Barbuda. In this documentary, I intentionally diverged from an "objective" stance, openly expressing my support for the Barbudan struggle. I consciously chose to avoid presenting "both sides" of the conflict, unlike other reporters in Barbuda or similar sites of conflict. Journalistic norms typically value "the right of reply" for those accused of something. While we did attempt to interview proponents of land privatization in Barbuda, including the Prime Minister and developers at the Discovery Land Company, they declined (or simply ignored us). Though there are tensions within the Barbudan community, I chose not to sensationalize these conflicts. Instead, I focused on the shared goal that unites most Barbudans: preserving their communal land ownership. This aligns with my research approach, emphasizing the broader communal consensus over internal divisions.

Data Analysis. Recognizing the innate storytelling nature of human beings, I used narrative analysis as my primary lens for data interpretation. The first-person accounts of experiences shared by my respondents served as core material for my analysis. Russell Bernard, author of the book *Research Methods in Anthropology*—a book my anthropology professors used to call "the Methods Bible"—highlights that narratives often revolve around recounting events: "What happened? How did it happen? Why did it happen? What was the result?" (2011, p. 416). These questions help to uncover recurring themes and structures within the narratives. Embracing this methodology, I asked exactly those questions, and subsequently went deeper into the themes that would emerge during the interviews. During the initial lockdowns in 2020, I transcribed most interviews almost verbatim. In the interpretation phase, I employed thematic analysis to further decipher the narratives, aiming to identify patterns and categorize the responses based on the emerging themes. An overview of the predominant themes, alongside a selection of subthemes used to organize the answers and formulate conclusions, is presented in Table 2.

Table 2: Overview of the predominant themes and subthemes used for thematic analysis

Main themes	Selection of subthemes
Vulnerabilization	"recovery funds," "displacement mechanism," "exhaustion," "government mistrust," "individual titles," "climate change," "disaster/hurricane"
Resistance	"elite interests," "community organization," "legal strategies" "the land is ours"
Benefits of communal land	"sovereignty," "solidarity," "unity," "protection," "sense of belonging," "peace of mind." "community consciousness," "right to return"
Recovery	"Maria/Irma revealed," "disaster capitalism," "recovery actors," "recovery funds"
Community control	"disaster preparedness," "climate adaptation," "real participation,""collective intelligence"
Decolonial feminism	"every day life in the (neo-)colony," "patriarchy," "relationship with land,""epistemologies"

Subsequently, I used triangulation to cross-verify the validity of the responses through the convergence of information from different sources. In social science, triangulation refers to the integration of different data types or methodologies to collect varied perspectives on a particular subject (Olsen, 2004). Cross-verifying what residents told me with media interviews with political and economic elites and published documents helped confirm the validity of the data.

CHAPTER 3

THIS LAND IS OURS

Vulnerabilization and Resistance in Informal Settlements in Puerto Rico: Lessons from the Caño Martín Peña Community Land Trust[23]

Authors: Line Algoed, María E. Hernández Torrales[24]

Abstract

Between 2002 and 2004, residents from seven informal settlements located along the Caño Martín Peña, a highly polluted channel in San Juan, Puerto Rico, established a community land trust to regularize land tenure and protect the historically marginalized barrios against the threat of displacement, as an unintended consequence of the ecological restoration of the channel. This article looks at the Fideicomiso de la Tierra del Caño Martín Peña (the Caño Martín Peña Community Land Trust or Caño CLT) from a political ecological perspective, as it aims to identify how the interests, policies and discourse of political and economic elites function to perpetuate the vulnerability of residents in unplanned settlements, and how the Caño CLT is an effective instrument to counter this process. The Caño CLT supports on-site rehabilitation by taking land out of a hostile market, reinforcing solidarity networks, and democratizing sustainable planning through ongoing participatory planning-action-reflection

---

23 This article is published in Radical Housing Journal: Algoed, L., & Hernández Torrales, M. E. (2019). The Land is Ours. Vulnerabilization and resistance in informal settlements in Puerto Rico: Lessons from the Caño Martín Peña Community Land Trust. *Radical Housing Journal,* 1(1), 29–47. DOI: *https://doi.org/10.54825/MOVK2096*

24 María E. Hernández Torrales is Adjunct Professor at the Legal Aid Clinic at the University of Puerto Rico Law School and Former Chair of the Board of Trustees, Fideicomiso de la Tierra del Caño Martín Peña.

processes. It is a critical piece of the wider comprehensive development ENLACE Caño Martín Peña Project, whose benefits include reducing the risk of flooding and restoring the environmental qualities of the mangrove channel. The article considers that informal settlements like those in the Martín Peña area are often located in a city's most environmentally vulnerable, yet ecologically and geographically valuable areas, prone to land grabs after disasters. By looking at public discourse in Puerto Rico and the U.S. in the aftermath of the devastating hurricanes that struck the island in 2017, we analyze the assumed links between informality and vulnerability and how these assumptions are used to spur public support for displacements. The article argues that documenting and theorizing the knowledges produced by the enduring resistance of the Martín Peña communities can support residents in unplanned settlements in the Global South to come together and create mechanisms that protect land and counter vulnerabilization.

Keywords
Community Land Trusts, informal settlements, political ecology, vulnerability, land rights.

> *In Puerto Rico you had a big curtain, hiding everything. And Hurricane María took care of that. So the people could see what was really happening on our island (UNC, 2018).*
> —José Caraballo Pagán, Caño Martín Peña resident

INTRODUCTION

Puerto Rico, a non-incorporated territory of the U.S., has been in a severe economic crisis since 2006, facing an unaudited public debt of USD $73 billion. The situation worsened after Hurricanes Irma and María hit in September 2017. Thousands of people died in the aftermath, mainly due to the lack of electricity, communication, food, and clean water. Different Puerto Rican activist groups are advocating transitions to other societal models to move away from what caused these crises. The case of the barrios along the Martin Peña estuarine tidal channel (*caño* in Spanish), located at the heart of the San Juan Metropolitan Area, presents an example of such an alternative approach. For decades, residents have struggled for community land ownership, the right to the city in decent, equitable conditions, and environmental justice. These communities are among many that were established 'informally'—

that is without formal ownership of the land, without building permits or without following building codes—on ecologically vulnerable public lands along the Martín Peña channel. During the process of modern industrialization in the 1930's and 1940's, impoverished peasants migrated mainly to San Juan, the capital of Puerto Rico, and built makeshift wooden and tin homes on the wetlands along the channel, using debris and vegetation as fill materials. As time passed, residents went through on-site rehabilitation, land regularization through individual land titling, and the implementation of several housing policies that eventually led to evictions and the displacement of half of the settlements.

In the early 2000's, thousands of residents participated in the planning-action-reflection process that led to the establishment of the first Community Land Trust (CLT) in an informal settlement in Latin America and the Caribbean. The Fideicomiso de la Tierra del Caño Martín Peña (the Caño Martín Peña Community Land Trust; hereafter the Caño CLT) is an instrument to regularize land tenure through collective land ownership and individual surface rights. It was conceived to avoid gentrification under the assumption that once the channel is dredged–a demand of the surrounding communities– several inland lagoons and channels would be reconnected, and thus the privileged location of the communities would attract developers and land values would increase. Different from individual land titles, with the Caño CLT the land can never be sold, protecting the communities for generations to come from involuntary displacements, such as those that could occur as an unintended consequence of the urban reform and ecosystem restoration project that residents have been fighting for to improve living conditions. The Caño CLT has been internationally recognized by a World Habitat Award for its potential to inspire other land rights struggles.

This article describes how the economic crisis in Puerto Rico and the aftermath of Hurricanes Irma and María have led to massive migration to the United States, lowered land prices, and how poor communities are becoming a target for displacement due to policies that highlight their vulnerability to disasters and discard the potential for on-site risk mitigation and equitable recovery. For the Government of Puerto Rico, regularizing land tenure has become a priority. Nevertheless, it is well known that individual land titles will expose informal settlements in privileged locations to a hostile real estate market that might lead to displacement. We argue that, although designed to protect informal settlements from increases in land value, the Caño CLT is also effective against displacement in the current landscape. The Caño Martín Peña communities (hereafter the Caño communities) are located in one of the city's most ecologically and geographically valuable, yet environmentally vulnerable areas. These areas are the most in need after disasters, but because of the value of their location, they become prone to land grabs and other forms of disaster capitalism, thereby supporting the continued vulnerabilization of informal communities. We argue that the Caño CLT and the wider ENLACE Caño Martín Peña Project provide a counter mechanism to this, by taking the land out of a hostile market, strengthening their communities through on-site rehabilitation and equitable, just recovery, reducing the risk of flooding and restoring the environmental qualities of the mangrove channel. Moreover, reinforcing solidarity networks, democratizing sustainable planning processes, and garnering political power will be key to counter disaster recovery housing policies that promote displacement.

The article is organized into three sections. First, we introduce the Caño CLT, how it was created and how it functions. Then we describe the disaster capitalism that followed Hurricane María, how the policies to address the financial and climate crises can lead to displacement and how the Caño communities have responded. In the final section, we use literature on political ecology to consider the knowledges of the Caño communities and why they can help other resistances worldwide.

The authors of this article have been involved directly from academic and professional perspectives, collaborating with the community leadership, and helping in the development and advancement of the instruments created by them to attain their collective goals. Together with the community leadership and supporters we conduct ongoing long-term action research. After Hurricane María, continuous exchanges with community leadership and with staff of the ENLACE Caño Martín Peña Project Corporation through meetings and direct conversations have provided valuable information on how they have grown to a next level, facing the most pressing priorities imposed by the emergency, like repairing, building and providing roofs for the most vulnerable residents, while at the same time they continue focused on their mission remaining on the solid foothold created within the communities, the Caño CLT. This article is based on those constant exchanges. In addition, it is based on in-depth unstructured and semi-structured interviews with community leaders and members of the CLT before and after Hurricanes Irma and María, as well as discourse analysis of government and media discourse on housing informality following the hurricanes.

CREATION OF THE CAÑO MARTÍN PEÑA COMMUNITY LAND TRUST

Puerto Rico's rapid industrialization process led to the establishment of unplanned communities in coastal cities across the island. In the developmental discourse of the succeeding governments, these settlements were declared unfit for human habitation and portrayed as a threat to health, security, and wellbeing of all citizens of Puerto Rico. The Puerto Rico Eradication of Slums Act of 1945 spurred support for clearances, sponsored by U.S. federal government, which only resulted in the relocation of clusters of poverty to other areas. Many families were forced to move to public housing projects, but as the government would not provide housing for everyone, the existence of informal settlements was mostly tolerated.

Today, thousands of people still live in these communities. Approximately 25,000 people live in the Caño area, in eight communities located along the Martín Peña tidal channel. Paved roads, electricity and running water are now available, but most homes still lack proper storm water drainage and a sanitary sewage system, and sewage still flows directly into the channel. The channel is blocked and frequent floods with contaminated water affects 70 percent of the communities. A strong sense of attachment to the land, persistent deprivation and fear of displacement led the residents of seven of the eight Martín Peña communities to create the Caño Martín Peña CLT as a practical solution to address structural problems that reproduce poverty and marginalization.

Due to its national significance, the U.S. Environmental Protection Agency (EPA) chose the San Juan Bay Estuary, where the channel is located, to become part of its National Estuary Program. The San Juan Bay Estuary Comprehensive Conservation Management plan, adopted in the late 1990's, included the dredging of the environmentally degraded Caño Martín Peña and addressing infrastructure challenges in the adjacent communities as the main actions required to uplift the ecosystem. In the early 2000's, the Government of Puerto Rico converted the dredging into a strategic project and assigned it to the Puerto Rico Highway and Transportation Authority (PRHTA), a public corporation under the Department of Transportation and Public Works.

Employees of PRHTA took a completely different approach to the involvement of the communities along the tidal channel (Algoed et al., 2018, p. 13). The team, initially composed of planners and community social workers, implemented a methodology that was new to the PRHTA. Rather than reducing citizen participation to public hearings after the planning stage of a project is almost finalized, they assembled the community leadership, helped strengthen grassroots organizing, and started planning not only the dredging of the channel, but rather the comprehensive development of the affected communities. Residents were invited to think critically about their living conditions and started conveying their distrust in government in relation to the displacement of families to public housing. They questioned who the beneficiaries of the proposed strategic infrastructure project would be, and whether it would lead to further displacements, knowing the value of their centrally located lands. They expressed their strong desire to remain in the community, as well as their fear of displacements.

The communities embarked upon a comprehensive planning, action, and reflection process, that during the first two years included organizing more than 700 community meetings and outreach activities. This process transformed the infrastructure project into a comprehensive development project known as Proyecto ENLACE del Caño Martín Peña (ENLACE Project). Building trust between the Authority's personnel and the community, fundamental to fostering participation, took time. The leadership of the communities created the grassroots nonprofit organization, the Group of the Eight Communities Along the Caño Martín Peña, Inc. (G-8), which brought together all the grassroots organizations. The dialogue among communities led to a greater understanding of the problems they had in common, rather than the differences. As Juanita Otero, one of the community leaders involved in the process from the beginning, described it: "The greatest achievement is for the eight communities to speak the same language. We were close physically and, despite having so many things in common, we were not working together. Now we can support each other." (Hernández Torrales, 2007, p. 794).

The participatory planning process resulted in several instruments, designed from the bottom up. The first was a Comprehensive Development and Land Use Plan for the Caño Martín Peña Special Planning District (District Plan), conceived with the residents of the communities, which envisioned "a united, safe and prosperous community, model of coexistence in the heart of San Juan." The District Plan contains strategies to tackle the conditions of marginalization and integrate the communities with the rest of the city, to rehabilitate the channel and provide infrastructure with the least possible number of relocations, provide rehousing options for affected families within their communities, and ensure that public and private investment in the area is channeled to community businesses to strengthen the neighborhood economy.

The process also led to a new legislation: Law 489, enacted by the Government of Puerto Rico on September 24, 2004. As the electoral process of 2004 approached, community leaders expressed their concern that, with a change of government, the work would be lost. With the support of lawyers and external advisors, and learning from prior experiences, a bill was prepared and discussed extensively to ensure that it was consistent with the decisions made by the communities. After significant community lobbying and strategizing, the bill was finally passed into law. The law recognized the G-8 as the representative entity of the Caño communities. It also created two additional instruments that were to promote equitable, participatory, and sustainable development in the area. The first one is the Corporación del Proyecto ENLACE del Caño Martín Peña (ENLACE Caño Martín Peña Project Corporation), a public corporation with the mandate to implement the District Plan, with government resources assigned for a limited period of 20 to 25 years, with the participation of residents and in partnership with public and private sectors. The Board of Directors of ENLACE was designed by the community, ensuring the continuity of the ENLACE Project despite changes in government. ENLACE's design effectively placed governmental instruments and resources in the hands of the community. It achieved the democratization of planning for social and ecological sustainability.

Finally, the Law also created the Fideicomiso de la Tierra del Caño Martín Peña or Caño CLT. The ownership of the land on which the communities had lived for over 70 years, previously in ownership of different public agencies, was transferred, first to ENLACE and then, to the Caño CLT. The land was kept out of the real estate market in perpetuity.

Previously, community land trusts were mostly found in the U.S. and in European countries, where they tackle the growing lack of affordable housing in cities with rising housing costs by taking land out of the market and putting it into nonprofit trusts for collective land ownership. More recently, CLTs are being created in the Global South as a tool to regularize land tenure and mitigate the historical causes of poverty, and the Caño CLT is leading as an example. The community land trusts movement, as it is known today, is described by CLT practitioner and scholar John E. Davis (2010, p. 3) as profoundly "rooted in a fertile seedbed of theoretical ideas, political movements, and social experiments that had been laid down over a span of many decades." The model as implemented in the U.S. is distinguished by three clusters of characteristics: ownership, organization and operation. In this approach, land is treated as a common heritage, not as an individual possession; land is permanently taken out of the market; individual owners own all structural improvements (the houses and other buildings) separately from the land; and a long-term ground lease gives the owners of the structures the exclusive use of the land beneath their buildings. When we delve into these characteristics, we can find an ethic of stewardship defined as "land treated as a common heritage: encouraging ownership only by those who are willing to live on the land and to use the land, not accumulating more than they need; emphasizing right use and smart development; capturing socially created gains in the value of land for the common good" (Davis, 2010, p. 4).

Figure 8: "And for the first time, we the residents became actors of our future." Members of the Caño CLT in front of one of the murals in the area. Source: Line Algoed

The Caño CLT was inspired by the principles of U.S. CLTs, but the instrument was recreated by residents to serve their particular needs, adding their own legal figures, such as surface rights, which we will describe below. Community organizing processes that promote critical and autonomous thinking, the equitable exchange of knowledge and popular education techniques resulted in residents designing their own CLT, and thus, fully owning it (Figure 8).

How the Caño CLT Works

Today, the Caño CLT gives almost 2,000 low-income families collective land ownership of 78 hectares of land in a privileged area of San Juan (Figure 9). The deliberative process of selecting and adapting this new land tenure mechanism in Puerto Rico deepened community cohesion and brought the communities together to protect the land their parents and grandparents "created" (by filling it with debris) (Fuller Marvel, 2008: 112), as well as restore the environmental qualities of the tidal channel.

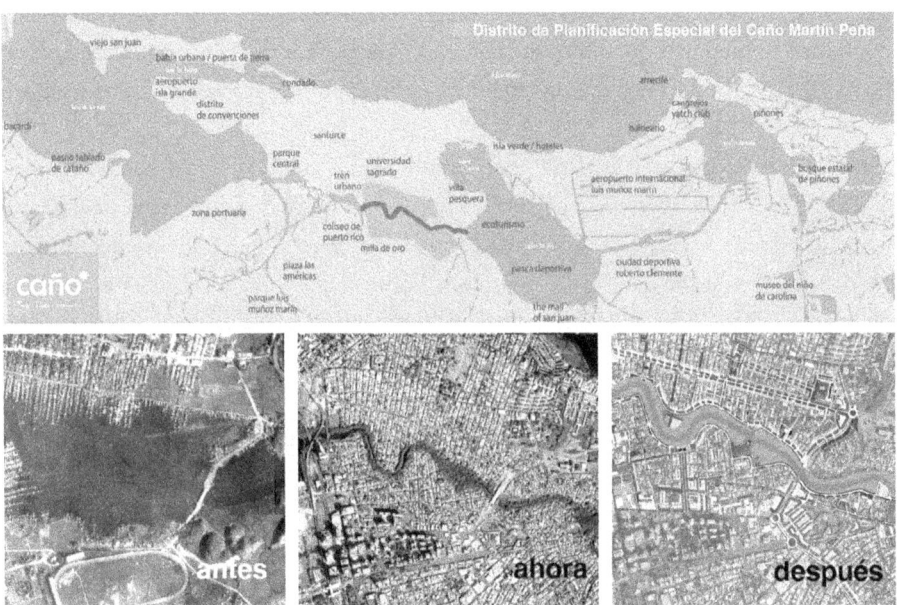

Figure 9: Location of the Caño Martín Peña Special Planning District in San Juan, the evolution of the Martín Peña tidal channel and the proposed dredging. Source: Corporación del Proyecto del Caño Martín Peña

The Caño CLT regularizes land tenure within the Caño Martín Peña Special Planning District, ensuring permanently affordable housing and preventing involuntary displacement and gentrification as an unintended result of the much-needed Caño Martín Peña Ecosystem Restoration Project. The CLT is a nonprofit organization governed by a majority of community residents. The Board is comprised of eleven trustees, six of which are residents from the Special Planning District communities appointed by the Caño CLT member assembly or the G-8, and two others are selected by the board. The other three trustees are representatives of the state and local governments (one from the board of directors of ENLACE, one appointed by the governor and one appointed by the mayor of San Juan). The composition of this board was designed by the residents, and it allows the community to maintain control of the land and the assets that were transferred to the Caño CLT via legislation or later acquired. The trustees establish the administrative policy of the CLT and ensure that land serves the best interest of both the larger community and the households who live on the CLT's land, especially those who have to be relocated as part of the implementation of the District Plan. This board of trustees is accountable to the Caño CLT's membership comprised of those individuals and families living on the collectively owned land (the beneficiaries). The assembly of members collectively makes important decisions about the land and other assets. No land within the Special Planning District can been cumbered without the expressed consent of the assembly.

The relationship between the collective landowner and the individual homeowners is regularized via the conveyance of surface rights. This right to use the plot of the land where the home is located is confirmed and evidenced through a notary deed that is executed between the Caño CLT and each homeowner and recorded as a property separate from the land with the Puerto Rico Property and Real Estate Registry. The content of the deed is fully transparent, and all the terms and conditions are discussed and revisited during the signing process. The surface rights deed recognizes the separate individual property of the structural improvements (i.e. the house). For the first time, the homeowner will see their house—often built by the family throughout several decades, but never legally owned—recorded officially under their name within the government records. By regularizing land tenure, residents also gain access to other legal protections available in Puerto Rico. For example, in the surface right deed the homeowner can claim the protection of the family home against non-mortgage related debt claims.

Surface rights can be inherited, sold, and mortgaged, giving families formal access to this type of credit. The Caño CLT, however, retains the first right of refusal. Similar to the U.S. CLTs, when the Caño CLT sells a surface right or a housing unit it owns, and particularly when such property was developed with subsidies, the deed also includes a resale formula that limits equity. As another important and fair component of the terms and conditions included in the surface rights deed, the resale formula ensures that subsidies invested in developing the housing unit last longer, secures a fair return on the seller's investment and creates the opportunity for another low-income family or individual to enjoy adequate affordable housing in the city (Algoed et al., 2018, p. 24).

Through the Caño CLT, the residents of the Special Planning District are now among the largest landowners in San Juan. The G-8, as the institutional expression of the organized Caño communities, has garnered a strong voice able to influence politics. During election campaigns, for example, the G-8 invites political candidates to sign an agreement with the commitments made to advance the implementation of the Comprehensive Development Plan, including the ecosystem restoration of the Martín Peña tidal channel and other critical housing and infrastructure works. Such commitments are published, and compliance is reported in the G-8 newspaper *Raíces* ('Roots' in English).

HURRICANE MARÍA, DISASTER CAPITALISM AND THE RESPONSE OF THE CAÑO MARTÍN PEÑA RESIDENTS

Hurricane María was the most destructive disaster in a century in Puerto Rico. It is estimated that at least 2,975 people died. Regardless, many political leaders and economic elites have described the hurricanes as a unique opportunity to restructure Puerto Rico. "It's a tough time, but it's also an opportunity to start anew, to execute proper reforms–like energy reform, regulation reforms, tax reform, education reform, and health care reforms," Governor Rosselló stated (O'Leary & Chiriguayo, 2018). While dealing with the recovery process, the government has been pushing through an agenda of drastic social and economic reforms that were planned prior to the hurricanes, mostly as part of the austerity measures to address the massive public debt. Overwhelmed, Puerto Ricans still recovering from the effects of Irma and María and trying to rebuild their lives are also dealing with school closures, changes in the government pension system and labor laws, limited access to healthcare, among others.

Puerto Rico has become a textbook example of 'disaster capitalism', in which collective trauma is exploited to implement, more rapidly, extreme austerity and structural reforms that were already planned before the disaster. It also embodies what Mutter (2015, p. 158-9) discusses: "natural disasters make the rich richer and the poor even poorer." Disasters and the influx of money that follow are a temptation for many in power. It is a situation that is ripe for manipulation for social, political, and financial gains.

The unprecedented economic crisis of the last decade, a disaster for most, has equally become an opportunity for a small group of people who benefit from crises. Puerto Rican debt became a highly profitable asset to invest in. The U.S. imposed and non-elected Financial Oversight and Management Board, through the Puerto Rico Oversight Management and Economic Stability Act (PROMESA), put an end to the country's already fragile fiscal autonomy. Supported by the territorial clause of the U.S. Constitution, the Board has the power to decide over the country's financial planning, laws, budget, and regulations to be imposed on the population to repay bondholders, a significant proportion being vulture funds, i.e. funds that invest in debt that is considered very weak and risky. Puerto Rico's USD $74+ billion public debt has never been audited and few Puerto Ricans can identify with the discourse of having lived beyond their means.

Only a crisis—actual or perceived—produces real change, according to Milton Friedman (Klein, 2007: 20). The Government of Puerto Rico and the Fiscal Oversight Board are indeed using these economic and climate crises to produce real change through a complete restructuring of society, by selling off public assets and installing brutal austerity.

Desperate to improve their conditions, an estimated 400,000 Puerto Ricans left the island between October 2017 and February 2018 (Echenique & Melgar, 2018), on top of the estimated 500,000 Puerto Ricans that had already left before the hurricanes since the economic crisis started in 2006 (IEPR, 2016). Simultaneously, the Government of Puerto Rico is attracting wealthy foreigners to relocate to the island with a 4 percent corporate tax approved in 2012, as opposed to the 21 percent corporate tax that they would pay in the U.S. These tax exemptions do not apply to Puerto Ricans already living on the island. Puerto Rico is experiencing a population swap that is in line with earlier policies of poverty deconcentration at the start of the 20th Century, when it was said that there are too many poor people in Puerto Rico and that it needs more "men with capital, energy and enterprise" (Whalen, 2005: 7). As Oliver-Smith (2005: 58) puts it: "What nature has started, the government would finish."

The Response of the Caño Communities to the Hurricane

On September 20, 2017, two weeks after Hurricane Irma, Hurricane María took its toll in Puerto Rico. In the Caño area, over 75 families were left homeless, approximately 1,200 roofs lost or severely damaged, and 70 percent of the community land flooded with contaminated water. Nonetheless, the organized community, their collaborators and in total more than 700 volunteers responded swiftly to assess the damages and provided first aid and relief. The grassroots organizing, and a strong institutional framework comprised by the G-8 and its member organizations, ENLACE and the Caño CLT, facilitated recovery in the area.

The lack of electricity and communications led many residents to leave Puerto Rico and find support with families in the U.S. Some of these families and individuals were denied individual assistance by FEMA and instead urged to abandon the island as part of their relief policies. But the largest part of the community residents had the chance to stay and start anew. The communities responded immediately to the crisis situation, knowing that waiting for government for help would take too long. In the month after María, 800+ tarps were delivered by the U.S. Army Corps and distributed by ENLACE, families had access to food, water, medical care, and even cash. Vegetative material and debris were collected, and kits to address the mosquito and rat plagues were distributed. Residents became actors instead of disaster victims, which according to Oliver-Smith (2005: 53) is essential for communities to recover after catastrophes. Together with donations from local and U.S. foundations, over 45 new partnerships, and 700+ external volunteers contributed to the effort. The G-8 selected the most vulnerable residents to help with the construction of permanent roofs, an ongoing activity as this article is being written. With assistance from professional organizations, three model resistant homes will be built.

The Caño communities have been pointing out that implementing the District Plan is key to reducing flood risks in the District and the San Juan Metropolitan Area, and that the ENLACE Project has the potential of becoming an example of just, equitable, and participatory recovery. Although included in the Government of Puerto Rico's request for Federal assistance, the USD $215M Ecosystem Restoration of the Caño was not chosen among the projects to be funded with the $15B in recovery funds assigned to the U.S. Army Corps of Engineers under the Bipartisan Budget Act of 2018 (BBA). The U.S. Department of Housing and Urban Development (HUD) allocated

$20B in Community Development Block Grant—Disaster Recovery (CDBG-DR) funds to Puerto Rico, whose use will be determined by the Government of Puerto Rico as per HUD regulations. Such funds present an opportunity to fully fund the main aspects of the District Plan. However, the Action Plan presented for the first $8.3B lays out strategies that promote displacement of vulnerable communities, even where on-site risk mitigation is feasible. For example, the housing strategy focuses on providing individual families options to relocate outside the floodplain and prohibits reconstruction and rehabilitation within the floodplain. In communities such as Martín Peña, where flood reduction is feasible, denying the possibility to build in the current floodplain above the flood level can have the effect to displace families in need. As both the governor and the housing secretary have recently expressed, the new public policy about communities in sensitive areas is *"se acabó el ay bendito"* (good will is over). However, it seems that this policy will only target low-income communities, as on-site reconstruction is available to others that can afford it. Despite all the efforts of Caño residents to stop displacements from their communities, the damage to homes is being used by the government to incite residents to move to other locations. The Caño CLT is watching this very closely to make sure that the residents may stay put safely on their land, relocating families only when needed and within the community, and with the support needed to overcome future extreme natural events.

A POLITICAL ECOLOGICAL APPROACH TO THE VULNERABILIZATION OF INFORMAL COMMUNITIES

Literature on political ecology can help us understand the vulnerabilization of informal communities and the ways in which the Caño CLT provides a counter mechanism to this vulnerabilization. Of specific use to this argument is literature on urban political ecology, which Swyngedouw and Heynen (2003, p. 914) describe as a combination of the concerns of ecology with those of political economy, and "provides an integrated and relational approach that helps untangle the interconnected economic, political, social and ecological processes that together go to form highly uneven and deeply unjust urban landscapes." In this regard, vulnerability is a thoroughly political ecological concept, as it is not an inherent property of social groups or individuals (Hilhorst & Bankoff, 2004, p. 5), but, according to Oliver Smith (2003: 10), deeply embedded in complex social relations and processes. Vulnerability, for him, "is the conceptual nexus that links the relationship that people have with their environment to social forces and institutions and the cultural values that sustain or contest them."

Rather than speaking about vulnerability as a fixed condition, we speak here about the vulnerabilization of informal settlements, because it better denotes how these communities are made and kept vulnerable.

When we speak about housing informality, we refer to those homes that have been self-built, without ownership over the land, without building permits or without following building codes, which is how the Government of Puerto Rico (2018, p. 52) defines informal housing. As to the term 'community', used repeatedly in this article and problematized in literature on the commons, we follow Oliver-Smith's thinking (2005, p. 54): a community is, in no way, a homogeneous group of people without differences, but rather "a group of interacting people who have something in common with one another, sharing similar understandings, values, life practices, histories, and identities within a certain framework of variation," or in the case of the Caño communities, people who share a highly politicized geographical living area.

In what follows, we will analyze how vulnerabilization happens in the housing sector. First, we will look at Puerto Rico's official discourse on housing informality, after which we will examine concepts of political ecology to draw lessons on how the Caño CLT counters this discourse. Hurricane María exposed the profound weaknesses of many of Puerto Rico's sectors, but especially its housing policies. At least one third of about 1.2 million occupied homes on the island were destroyed or suffered significant damage (Woellert, 2017). Additionally, roughly one third of homeowners risk foreclosures (Goldstein, 2017). More than anything, the hurricane brought to the fore the magnitude of the island's housing informality. A study commissioned by the Puerto Rico Builders Association estimated that 55 percent of residential and commercial construction was built informally (Government of Puerto Rico & Department of Housing, 2018). The exact number of informally built housing remains unclear, but even in conservative estimates it is widespread.

What is undebatable is that informality in Puerto Rico has been disregarded for decades. But now that, after María, residents are asked to prove property ownership to be eligible for repair grants from FEMA, the country is forced to face the situation of informality; 60 percent of FEMA applicants were initially found ineligible (Florido, 2018). Eventually, FEMA loosened its criteria and started –intermittently– helping owners, renters and occupants of informal homes who could prove residency.

Public Discourse on Housing Informality

The Government of Puerto Rico is determined to use Hurricane María as an 'opportunity' to tackle the issue of housing informality. We argue that this discourse of political and economic elites discredits informal settlements and reinforces –not reduces– the vulnerability of low-income people who live in these communities, and thus supports their vulnerabilization. In what follows, we discuss in what ways informality has been discussed in Puerto Rico and U.S. public discourse, following Hurricane María.

In the first place, informality is often portrayed as a choice. For example, the use of the word 'illegal' to describe informality (mostly referring to poor people and ignoring similar practices by other sectors of society), implies that people may have had a choice to build without permissions (and thus not officially building according to codes) or without the ownership of the land, as a way to 'illegally' avoid costs (see for example (Woellert, 2017)). It is often said that people take regulations lightly and build wherever they can, without looking much further. If they had looked further, this suggests, they would have been able to opt out of—to choose not to live in informality. This sentiment is to be found in popular discourse as well. Consider the words of a taxi driver we spoke to in April 2018 in San Juan, representative of many other similar conversations in the past few years: "People put their little houses wherever they want, and they don't think about it. And now nobody can help them." Even though there may be cases where building without ownership of the land was a choice, most informality results rather from necessity and a lack of 'formal' alternatives.

In the second place, we notice how the hurricane, the disaster relief funds, and the aftermath crises such as the foreclosures and mass migration are presented as an opportunity to eliminate informality and move residents out of their communities. When asked what solution he saw for those living in informality, the Governor of Puerto Rico said in an interview (O'Leary & Chiriguayo, 2018) that residents in informal housing will simply have to move out: "It's time to go, you know, it's not safe, it's not if, but when, another catastrophic event is going to happen, and it's just not worth it, and we do have the opportunity to use these funds effectively and transparently, why not take this opportunity to make this transition." And: "One of the opportunities I think we have is to start eradicating that informal housing component, [to] start pushing folks into safe, formal [home] ownership. […] We have had a significant decrease in population in the last couple of decades, and that has led itself to a lot of houses to be available or owned by the bank. [...] Make sure we are ready for another category 5 hurricane."

Even in the Caño communities, despite all the efforts of the Caño CLT, damage to homes and out-migration are being used as an excuse to pressure residents to move to other areas. This discourse and its corresponding policies remind us of the Puerto Rican government rhetoric in the 1950's, briefly discussed earlier in this article, when the Eradication of Slums Act aimed to rid the country of the slums. In the words of the president of the Puerto Rico Housing Authority in 1955, informal settlements are depicted as "almost an endemic abomination, like hookworm had been, which today has been eradicated by the iron will of men of science and government (Esterrich, 2013, p. 14)." Or in the 1956 newsreel *Puerto Rico Elimina El Arrabal*: "Each house that is moved or burnt down is another family taken away from the slums and turned into free citizens of peace and order, worthy of enjoying a true democratic life. And do not forget the slum is a pustule that threatens our entire social body" (Viguié Film Productions, 1950, *own translation*).

Here, in the third place, housing informality is presented not only as unsafe for residents themselves, but also as a threat to the social stability of the country. Today's discourse, again, blames informality for the vulnerability of the country. The coordinator of FEMA in Puerto Rico at the time of Hurricane María suggested that informal construction was to blame for the disaster that the hurricane caused, by saying that to reduce the risks: "We need to renew the building codes and eliminate informal construction. [...] We have to forget about the *¡ay bendito!* and reinforce building codes because we don't want to go through another María" (Sin Comillas, 2018).

Also, a Politico article (Woellert, 2017) mentions that "Squatters living on property without deeds are straining an already fragile infrastructure system throughout the island." 'Squatters'–the poorest people on the island– are blamed for the fragility of the country. Indeed, the damage caused to the housing stock was concentrated in those homes that were built informally: 98 percent of 'formal' housing suffered no or only slight damage (Sin Comillas, 2018). Informal housing is, as one would expect, built with less capital, and informal dwellers usually have no hazard or flood insurances against disaster damage. But putting all the blame on informal dwellers is simply too reductionist. Also, informality in Puerto Rico is so widespread that policies need to be adapted to that reality. The classic slum eradication policy of moving poverty from one place to another, as proposed once again by the government, will not work precisely because of this magnitude of informality.

Lastly, in the discourse today, housing informality is presented as unsustainable, and its residents are depicted as too vulnerable to resist new disasters (see for example the Governor's quotes on the previous page), and therefore need to be moved to other locations. Indeed, as we have discussed, informal communities are often located in a city's most vulnerable areas, while at the same time these areas are ecologically very important, and economically highly valuable. An example to draw comparisons is the situation in the favelas of Rio de Janeiro, some of which are located in the areas with the most spectacular views of the city's landscape, with plots being sold for ever higher prices. The Caño communities are also strategically located within the San Juan Bay Estuary and have a high potential for tourism development.

Politics of Unsustainability and Informal Settlements

In the context of more frequent climate change-induced disasters, it seems therefore urgent to ask fundamental questions on what is sustainable—or unsustainable—specifically in relation to urban informal settlements, and to examine the assumed links between informality and vulnerability. It is assumed, for example, when depicting housing informality as a choice, as a threat to the country, or as unsustainable, that it is this type of urbanization that makes people vulnerable, and that residents in informal housing are to blame themselves for their own vulnerability. But clearly, it is not this type of urbanization that most contaminates the environment, while informal dwellers must endure most of the impact of environmental degradation. It is also not only informal settlements that are vulnerable. In Puerto Rico, there are many middle- and higher-income neighborhoods that are located too close to the sea and other bodies of water, resulting often in erosion or regular flooding. Equally, it is assumed that informal dwellers, such as those who settled on the wetlands of the Martín Peña channel, have contaminated this ecologically valuable area, with the debris they used to fill the land and the wastewater that is discarded in the channel due to the lack of a sewage system. But putting the blame on residents who live in these conditions for their own vulnerability is vastly insufficient, because it does not address the broader causes of environmental degradation, nor those of the establishment of informal settlements.

The structural causes of climate change, and the structural causes of vulnerability, can be found instead in precisely those practices that also produce informality, pushing people to the city and, once in the city, pushing them into informal communities. Examples of those practices are the many ways that deregulation of environmental standards in favor of urban development purposes are promoted, especially now that the financial crisis and the crisis following the hurricane is used as an opportunity to further deregulate these standards. The sole aim of this deregulation is to attract investment, putting the economy before well-being of the people and the protection of the environment. Consider the many historical and contemporary examples of extractivism, mostly but not only in the Global South, contributing to climate change and the establishment of informal settlements by people who are pushed out of their valuable areas.

Ingelford Blühdorn (2013) calls this mode of governance 'politics of unsustainability'. This term can be useful when looking at the assumed link between vulnerability and informality. For Blühdorn, politics of unsustainability are those politics that merely manage the social and ecological consequences of unsustainability, rather than trying to tackle its causes. He says: "Rather than trying to suspend or even reverse the prevailing logic of unsustainability, its main preoccupation is to promote societal adaptation and resilience to sustained unsustainability" (Blühdorn, 2013, p. 21). Resilience, indeed, is a word that Caño residents associate with being ignored.

Hurricane María killed thousands of people, many of whom died because of the lack of power, clean water, and decent food. Rather than rebuilding the country so that it can withstand a future natural disaster, with democratically and locally managed renewable energy and food production systems, as well as increased environmental standards, the government has decided to sustain the unsustainable –"however self-destructive it is now widely acknowledged to be, ecologically, economically, socially, and also for democracy" (Wilson & Swyngedouw, 2014, quoted in Blühdorn, 2016, p. 260).

Puerto Rico's many informal settlements face infrahuman conditions. Its residents are told that they themselves are to blame for wanting to remain in their communities and that, therefore, they will have to show resilience and adaptability, while their conditions are kept the same.

Knowledges from the Caño Communities

The experience of the Caño communities allows us to understand the democratization of planning for sustainability measures, which help to mitigate vulnerabilization in a context of climate change-induced extreme natural events. As described above, the Caño CLT is the result of an extensive and ongoing process of grassroots planning, with the aim to democratize neighborhood development and achieve environmental justice and ecological sustainability. This process is led by the critical thinking of residents, who are encouraged and assisted by professionals to not accept their current living conditions and come up with alternatives. Along those lines, political ecology, as defined by Robbins (2012, p. 99), "seeks to expose flaws in dominant approaches to the environment favored by corporate, state, and international authorities, working to demonstrate the undesirable impacts of policies and market conditions, especially from the point of view of local people, marginal groups, and vulnerable populations."

Studying the resistance of the Caño communities from a political ecology lens helps us understand the role of critical thinking in social transformation. The Latin American political ecologist Arturo Escobar, studying that role, considers two key tendencies in critical thinking in Latin America: autonomous thinking—*autonomismo*—and *el pensamiento de la tierra*, the thinking of the land (2017: 58-64). In the *autonomismo* tendency, according to Escobar, the communal predominates over the individual, the connection with the land predominates over the separation between humans and nature, and *el buen vivir* (living well in harmony with nature) outweighs economic growth. *Autonomismo* in Puerto Rico is thinking in other directions than those imposed by the colonial capitalist state. This is essential in the Caño CLT and is strengthened every day through collective land management and stewardship. The other key tendency in critical thinking in Latin America, according to Escobar, requires listening to the land. In these processes, residents, and those accompanying and studying them, are required to learn to think and feel—*sentipensar*—with the land, while unlearning our fixation with the individual, private property, growth of the economy, science, and the market. Escobar argues that the knowledges connected with the struggles of those who think-feel with the land, are more appropriate in the study of social transformation than many of the forms of knowledge produced within the academy at present (Escobar, 2016, p. 24).

These struggles provide us with insight into the profound cultural and ecological transitions needed to tackle the environmental crises and reverse the politics of unsustainability. For Escobar (2016: 14), those who produce these knowledges "*sentipiensan con la tierra* (think-feel with the land) and orient themselves towards that moment when humans and the planet can finally come to co-exist in mutually enhancing manners. "Residents in the Caño communities think-feel with the land they have created, and with their body of water for whose protection they fight. Consider, for example, the words of Caño resident José Caraballo Pagán: "Waterways are living things. It doesn't talk, it doesn't walk, but it flows, it has a life. It grows. And when you've lived next to a thing that you saw as a young person, with a life of its own, to see it just die out, it affects your mind" (UNC, 2018).

Studying the knowledges produced by the struggles of the Caño communities to protect the land and restore the channel in an urban context can help us understand how social transformation in informal settlements can happen. The resistance of the Caño communities provides an antidote for informality by collectively regularizing land tenure and strengthening the existing affordable housing stock. This allows communities to remain on site, despite the government discourse focusing on the need to eliminate informal settlements by displacing people from their communities. As described above, the lack of land tenure documentation has been an impediment for many informal communities in Puerto Rico to access the help needed to get back on track after Hurricane María. Nevertheless, the residents of the Caño communities have found a foothold in their organization where they encounter guidance and a support system for their particular needs. No federal or local agency can legitimately say that the residents of the Caño communities lack land title. The collective ownership of the land has been proven to be a shield around the community residents, making them less vulnerable to displacements despite repeated government threats. The implementation of the District Plan will make them less vulnerable to floods and help them prepare to face the effects of climate change.

Collectivization of land ownership as a strategy to reduce the vulnerabilization of residents in unplanned settlements and the democratization of ecological sustainability are based on these processes of critical and autonomous thinking. Many community participation experiences in urban development processes are weakened by the antagonistic contexts in which they are taking place, despite their genuine commitment to social transformation (2017: 66). If the creation of instruments like community land trusts are not supported by processes of critical and autonomous thinking led by residents, efforts will turn into instrumentalism (where the instrument becomes the goal) and developmentalism. As full citizen control is not aimed for, these efforts will then in se be no different from other top-down interventions.

CONCLUSION

In what is described above, we have presented the Caño CLT as a mechanism which enables residents to hold, steward and manage their land with the aim to guide their own comprehensive neighborhood development. We have argued that through their CLT, the G-8, and the ENLACE Project, the residents have achieved a 'more inclusive mode of environmental production' (Swyngedouw & Heynen, 2003, p. 914), or the democratization of planning for social and ecological sustainability. This counters the vulnerabilization of their communities by strengthening them through participatory on-site rehabilitation, restoring the environmental qualities of the tidal channel and reducing the risk of flooding, while at the same time coming up with a solution to prevent gentrification and displacements that such an improvement of living conditions would cause. Community organizing and building strategic partnerships continue to be crucial to face these and other new challenges, such as ensuring CDBG-DR funds are used in support of their District Plan, rather than to displace those in need.

We have argued that studying the resistance of the Caño communities can help formulate political-ecological urban strategies and advance the search for examples of true democratic participation that counter the 'politics of unsustainability', which produce profound socio-environmental inequalities in Puerto Rico. Vulnerability in informal settlements, indeed, should not be studied without also looking at urban inequality, which deserves more attention than has been given in this article.

As one of the biggest landowners in San Juan, collective land ownership has given residents of the Caño CLT the political power to confront the state and control the development of their area and the protection of the channel, within a context of profound neoliberal globalization and colonialism. They are producing an urban environment that is in line with their worldviews and departs from market-led development while favoring socioecological preservation. In today's context of climate change and growing inequality, this is exemplary.

CHAPTER 4
COMMUNAL LAND AS SURVIVAL
Barbuda's Decolonial World View[25]

Authors: Line Algoed, Antonio Carmona Báez[26]

The Caribbean is at once the Earth's most geographic and ungeographic region. It is "the starting place," as Martinican scholar Malcom Ferdinand has said, "from which you conceptualize the Earth, the world, the people, the human, and non-human" (Ferdinand, 2021, p. 20). And yet it is still largely imagined as if it were not a real place. Globalization started here with the colonization of the Americas and the transatlantic "trade" in enslaved Africans. The region has long been seen as "a series of landscapes to be mined for their wealth or enjoyed for their beauty by outsiders" (Besson & Momsen, 1987, p. 39). Its global imaginary has been claimed by outsiders who have flocked to the region: the colonizers, the settlers, the real estate investors, the tourists, the shell companies, the remote workers. This imaginary belongs to everyone except its people.

---

25   This article is published in The Avery Review: Algoed, L. and A. Carmona Báez (2023) Communal Land as Survival: Barbuda's Counterhegemonic World View. The Avery Review. *https://averyreview.com/issues/61/communal-land-as-survival*.

26   Antonio Carmona Báez is President of the University of St. Martin.

The Caribbean is the region from where to consider the longevity of colonial notions of land use—which hinge on the supposed necessity of private property. Here we see the contemporary materializations of neocolonialism, the coloniality of power, and the decolonial resistance of its inhabitants. These three forces are particularly pronounced on the island of Barbuda, the smallest island of the independent Caribbean Commonwealth State of Antigua and Barbuda, located in the eastern part of the Leeward Islands. Although it is estimated that 65 percent of the earth's surface is communally held (Rights and Resources Initiative, 2015b). Barbuda is the only island in the world where all land is entirely held in common by Barbudans. The land is not property of the state, nor is there any private property; land cannot be sold. Communal land ownership has allowed Barbudans to keep the island out of the global land market, to limit the built environment, and to protect the delicate ecosystem of its coastal areas and lagoons. However, the island's centuries-old communal land is now threatened by the twin state's Central Government and its economic allies, who have used the devastating hurricanes of 2017 to capitalize on the island's unspoiled condition through land grabs, policy changes, and the advancement of luxury real estate projects—most notably Robert De Niro's "Paradise Found" and the Barbuda Ocean Club by John Paul DeJoria's "Peace, Love and Happiness "partnership. We see Barbuda's story of resistance against private property and these types of development as a fight for survival, not only of its people and environment, but also of the maintenance of its own sense of geography—of knowledge-practices that refuse to separate humans from nature.

BARBUDA DEFIES PRIVATE PROPERTY

Barbuda has a powerful history of resistance against Western forms of property and subjugation. When the Kalinago inhabited the island, they called it Wa'Omoni, Island of Herons. They fought to defend their land from European settlers (Sweeney, 2007, p. 2). In 1628, the island became the personal property of King Charles II, who in 1685 leased it for almost two centuries to the Codrington family for just "yearly one fat sheep if demanded" (Negga Melchior, 2018). A limestone island, Barbuda was too dry for large-scale sugarcane production, so the British enslavers used it to house their managers and overseers. A few hundred enslaved Africans worked under force to supply livestock and food staples to the Codrington's Antigua estates (Lawrence, 2015: 8-9). When Britain banned slavery in 1834, Barbudans were omitted from the Slavery Emancipation Act and had to fight to free themselves. The Codrington family left in 1870, and the Barbudans, who had lived and endured two hundred years of brutal enslavement on the island, refused to pay rent to the British Crown. The Crown eventually granted Barbudans legal status as its lawful tenants in communal possession in a 1904 colonial enactment (Negga Melchior, 2018). This communal possession was maintained throughout the twentieth century and was refined and ratified in the Barbuda Land Act of 2007. The Act, which states that the island is owned in common by the people of Barbuda, entitles each Barbudan to three plots of land: one for housing, another for agriculture (Figure 10), and a third for business.[27]

Figure 10: Arnel and Joanne at their agriculture plot. Source: Line Algoed

While the Crown remains the symbolic owner of the land, the Barbuda Council, composed of nine directly elected and two ex officio members serving four-year terms, is the legal land administrator. The Council has the power to allocate and lease plots of land. Some can be leased to international investors for a limited number of

---

27 The Act defines a Barbudan as "(a) a person born in Barbuda of whose grandparents at least one was born in Barbuda; or (b) the child, wherever born, of parents at least one of whom is a Barbudan." Many Barbudans live abroad, but when they come back, they are entitled to the three plots. All remaining land and other resources are held and managed in common (Antigua & Barbuda, 2007).

years, but major development[28] requires explicit approval by a majority of Barbudans of voting age (18+), who need to be fully informed of the complete plans during Village Meetings. With a population of about 1,500 people, the island's approval process includes three steps. First, Barbudans give their consent in principle to the proposal. The proposal is then considered in detail by the Cabinet of Antigua and Barbuda. Finally, the detailed proposal comes back to Barbuda for consideration and consent. Village Meetings are held regularly, whenever needed, and the entire community is invited.

This enduring legacy differentiates Barbuda from other Caribbean islands, including Antigua. In fact, Barbudans resisted independence from Britain in 1981 to avoid being forced to adapt their land system to Antigua's freehold system and its commitment to large-scale, coastal tourism. Unlike Antigua, Barbuda's coastline is preserved. Food is grown in small agroecological provision grounds or backyards, and people hunt and fish, selling food to the community. There are no fences. A typical plot for a private house is no larger than 0.5 acres. The built environment is limited to the roughly 600 homes in the island's only town, Codrington, and a few small-scale tourist resorts.

"PARADISE FOUND"

And yet, it is the island's immaculateness that has also attracted the rich and powerful to it. Princess Diana vacationed at (and made famous) the K-Club, which had a lease on the southern beach, Coco Point. In 2015, the American actor Robert De Niro announced his plans to redevelop the then abandoned resort into a 391-acre luxury, "Nobu-branded" residential community, which he and his billionaire partner James Packer have called "Paradise Found." The resort is anticipated to include a Nobu Hotel of fifty separate villas with private pools and Nobu residences for sale. The annual lease for the land is $62,000 USD (Frank, 2015), a small sum compared to the millions the proposed residences will cost.

There is, of course, nothing happenstance about the development of "Paradise Found." Prime Minister Gaston Browne—a former Antiguan banker and leader of the Antigua and Barbuda Labor Party—has explicitly sought out and legislated for this kind of development in Barbuda. His political attention has been devoted to attracting investors in tourism and real estate development, intended to turn the twin

---

28 Any development costing over $5,400,000 USD or having a significant impact on the economy, environment, or infrastructure of Barbuda (Antigua & Barbuda, 2007).

state into an "economic powerhouse" in the Caribbean (Caribbean Series, 2015). To authorize De Niro's project, Browne designed the Paradise Found Act in 2015 to override the community approval sections of the 2007 Barbuda Land Act—applicable to the 391 acres designated for the resort. Many Barbudans were resolutely opposed to the law. Community leader Mackenzie Frank called it a "direct undermining of the 2007 Barbuda Land Act," which provides for the "democratic participation of people in land alienation to foreign interests" (Frank, 2015). To garner legitimacy for the Act, the Central Government claimed that a (narrow) majority of Barbudans approved the Paradise Found project in a referendum, but according to the Barbuda People's Movement (BPM), the results were illegitimate as certain sections of the regulations governing the conduct of the Village Meeting were contravened (Johnson & Luscombe, 2015). For example, non-Barbudans were allowed to vote, and sufficient details of the proposed project were not provided prior to the meeting so that Barbudans could give their free and informed consent to the proposal. The Barbuda Channel filmed a widely attended Village Meeting in which the community unreservedly voiced its opposition to the prime minister's plan. Nevertheless, the Paradise Found Act was passed—and with it De Niro's project was approved—ultimately since Barbuda only represents less than 2 percent of the total population of Antigua and Barbuda. At the time this bill was passed, Barbuda's representative in the National Parliament was a member of Browne's Labor Party.

HURRICANE IRMA AS OPPORTUNITY FOR "PEACE, LOVE, AND HAPPINESS"

The encroachment did not end there. In September 2017, Hurricane Irma passed with unprecedented strength, devastating Barbuda. Flying in a helicopter over the island the day after the storm, Prime Minister Browne declared it "barely habitable" (BBC News, 2017). The army was deployed to evacuate Barbudans to shelters in Antigua, where they stayed for months. The official justification was that another storm, Hurricane José, was approaching. However, Barbudans resisted this evacuation, as they had wanted to start rebuilding their homes and participate in the international recovery efforts, especially after José passed without making landfall on the island. The official media worked to establish a different narrative, reporting: "95 percent of Barbuda's buildings were destroyed. Barbuda residents flee" (BBC News, 2017). The Wikipedia entry on Barbuda still states that after Hurricane Irma, Barbuda was left "empty for the first time in modern history." The US ambassador to Antigua and Barbuda declared in a 2017 Oxfam America forum, "There's not a single living person on the island of Barbuda—a civilization that has existed on that island for over 300 years has now been extinguished" (deGrandpre, 2017). The island was devastated, but not beyond repair, and its community certainly was not extinguished. Keeping the population off Barbuda for months[29] and exaggerating the island's uninhabitability served the political and economic interests of the prime minister and his allies, who saw the disaster as an opportunity to advance their goals for self-enrichment.

In the thirty days that Barbudans were not allowed to return, Barbuda became a textbook example of disaster capitalism (Klein & Brown, 2018). In that same month, Browne amended the Barbuda Land Act and called a snap election in March 2018 to cement his legitimacy. Despite Barbudans' extraordinary efforts to vote in large numbers, as a minority population, they could not stop Browne's reelection and thus the amendment.[30] The amended act effectively abolishes communal land ownership, stating that Barbudans have "the right to purchase the freehold interest in land situated in Barbuda" (Barbuda (Amendment) Act, 2018). Barbudans would be forced to apply for private land ownership and buy the plot of land on which their house is located for the symbolic price of 1 EC$. The other two plots in their name would be sold to them at market price. In opposition to this amendment, Barbudans have widely rejected this scheme. "I already own something, and you're telling me I have to pay a dollar for it—how insulting is that?" Barbudan Kendra Beazer asks in a New York Times video filmed a few months after the hurricane (Collier et al., 2017). "They want to put us in a reservation," Barbudan Tyreen Gift told us. "We own 62 square miles, but they want us to have only 2 square miles of that."

During the same period of evacuation, the government also began construction on an international airport, without approval of the Barbudan people or the Council, and without an environmental impact assessment. A ninety-nine-year land lease deal was also signed under the partnership "Peace, Love and Happiness" (PLH)—led by the self-proclaimed "self-made" billionaire John Paul DeJoria—for the development of the "Barbuda Ocean Club," an exclusive US $2B luxury residential community. Working with developers Discovery Land Company, DeJoria and partners intend to

---

29 Schools did not reopen until six months after Irma, making it impossible for families to return. The hospital was not fully restored until 2022.

30 As citizens were only allowed to vote in Antigua, campaigners chartered ferries to facilitate the Barbudan vote, which resulted in a record score for the Barbuda People's Movement (BPM) candidate Trevor Walker, who won a seat in the House of Representatives, where he is the only representative for Barbuda out of nineteen members.

construct 450 exclusive dwellings for ultrawealthy foreigners on the island's southern beaches of Coco Point and Palmetto Point. Promising "a spectacular private resort community" and an "unparalleled family-oriented, adventure lifestyle for discerning residents," the Ocean Club's website pictures mostly White people on a seemingly desolate island (BOC, n.d.).

Palmetto Point is protected by the Ramsar Convention on Wetlands (The Ramsar Convention Secretariat, n.d.). In a 2016 Village Meeting, only plans for the redevelopment of the existing hotel on Coco Point were presented. Plans for a golf course and more villas at Palmetto Point were not disclosed, which is a breach of the Barbuda Land Act. After a Village Meeting in early 2020, where Barbudans voiced their concerns, the Barbuda Council asked PLH to immediately halt construction, but this has not happened, and the Coco Point villas and the Palmetto Point golf course are now being built. The latter is already disturbed by heavy rains in early 2023—to be expected when building on wetlands. Feeling betrayed in their request to stop construction, deeply concerned about the ecological impact, and saddened by the loss of cultural practices like straw weaving—which depended on plants in the area— many Barbudans are vehemently against PLH (Handy, 2020).

RESISTING INDIVIDUAL LAND TITLES

From the moment the Codringtons left, Barbudans have collectively protected their land, natural resources, and common interests. There have been several previous attempts by the Central Government to privatize land in Barbuda, which Barbudans have constantly refused. In Barbuda Voice, a newspaper published in New York City in the 1970s, a Barbudan says: "The new Government is planning to give deeds to the people for their land… If… people accept deeds…, the Government will sell Barbuda piece by piece" (Potter, 2011). Now, individual land titles or deeds are seen as a technique to include Barbuda's land in the global real estate market, which will end up displacing the local population. According to the BPM representative, if "land were to be sold, the rich people will just come and buy it up. [Our] traditional way of life… will be extinct (Accheri et al., n.d.).

At present, Barbudans have filed four court cases against the Central Government: a challenge to the repeal of the Barbuda Land Act; a review of the construction of an international airport without Barbudans' consent; a challenge to the Paradise Found Act; and a challenge to the amendment of the Crown Act, which weakens the Barbuda Council's jurisdiction over land and resources. Despite this pattern of resistance, Barbudans' justice system is ultimately tied to the oversight of a settler court. In July 2022, Barbuda's case against the Paradise Found Act was also lost in the Privy Council in London, the highest court of appeal for Commonwealth countries and British Overseas Territories, after the case was previously heard and lost in Antigua and Barbuda's court. According to the Privy Council, the Applicants were not "deprived of any right or interest in land, which they enjoyed pursuant to the Barbuda Land Act 2007," as due to the Paradise Found Act "the Land Act does not apply to the leased land" (Judicial Committee of the Privy Council, 2022).

NEOCOLONIAL DEVELOPMENT AND "SUSTAINABILITY"

> *I will draw your memory back to the history of the region. When Columbus came, we had people living here, and he took over sovereignty. We have seen the effects of that, after 500 years, in how we suffered. One of our biggest challenges coming through the disaster in 2017 is that we were faced with that same principle going on, someone having different plans for the resources that we control.*
>
> —John Mussington, Barbudan marine biologist, and community activist (Stronger Caribbean Together for Food, 2020).

Contemporary "developers" settling in Barbuda, who use terms like "Paradise Found" and "Discovery Land Company," conjure colonialist notions of the "torrid zone," of "land left wholly to nature."[31] Colonial settlers, argues the Canadian legal scholar Brenna Bhandar, viewed the land they "discovered" as "lacking in civilized inhabitants, and therefore empty and ripe for appropriation" (Bhandar, 2018, p. 4). The inhabitants of those lands "were deemed to be in need of improvement as much as their waste lands were" (Bhandar, 2018, p. 8). This imaginary continues today, as Barbuda's "developers" see land as something to be discovered and "Paradise" to be found and appropriated on roaming expeditions. De Niro recalls how, while taking a boat trip from Antigua, he saw a beautiful island from afar (Volandes, 2020). In the project's commercial brochure, we read that "Barbuda glitters like a pristine yet understated diamond. The island is relatively untouched, rich in culture, natural wonders, and Indigenous wildlife." The island is "unspoiled, it's unique, you don't find

---

31   These notions can be traced back to the English philosopher John Locke, whose 1690 book The Second Treatise on Government introduced the hegemony of private property that currently organizes much of our world. A man obtains a right over land, Locke asserts, once he mixes his labor with it—thus he "improves" it. Locke writes: "Land that is left wholly to Nature, that hath no improvement of Pasturage, Tillage, or Planting, is called, as indeed it is, wast [sic]" (cited in Bhandar, 2018, p. 48).

places like this anymore" (Wattles & Harlow, 2017). Once De Niro found "Paradise," it could be claimed as his own, imposing particular forms of land use upon existing ones (Figure 11). Building a luxury resort for the mega-wealthy to replace the hotel where Princess Diana once vacationed reveals a commingled geology of colonial histories and present-day imaginaries.

The tactic of declaring the island's uninhabitability after Hurricane Irma also recalls the "torrid zone." In her writing on disaster capitalism, Naomi Klein talks of the "clean canvases" that only great ruptures—such as a hurricane—can create. She writes: "It is in these malleable moments, when we are psychologically unmoored and physically uprooted, that these artists… begin their work of remaking the world" (Klein, 2007, p. 21). We see this work as continuing neocolonial processes that render local practices of land use inferior and illegal.

Figure 11: The Paradise Found plot. Source: Line Algoed

Within this remaking, a large-scale environmental event provides yet another narrative "justification" for private developments. The Paradise Found marketing brochure communicates that the development is "an opportunity to create a greener, more sustainable Barbuda." PLH also states that the Barbuda Ocean Club will "advance sustainable infrastructure solutions, support environmental initiatives" (Business Wire, 2017). In an interview with the Barbuda Channel, Justin Wilshaw, the PLH project president, says they are in Barbuda "to assist, guide, train and educate" the local population and that they are "going to improve the environment by creating wetlands and building dune resistance" (Barbuda Channel, 2021).

But Barbudans are not in need of this kind of assistance. The island's coastline is mostly undeveloped and its wildlife unharmed because locals have applied their environmental knowledge-practices over hundreds of years. Against all odds, Barbudans have been able to protect the coastline from the large-scale built development that characterizes the rest of the Caribbean. Barbuda hosts the world's most important nesting sites for frigate birds (Figure 12) and other endangered species (Handy, 2020). The wetlands, which can serve as a flood zone if needed, have protected the population from worse outcomes after storms.

Figure 12: George at the Bird Sanctuary. Source: Line Algoed

Decades of sand mining promoted by previous administrations—despite community resistance—have already caused significant environmental damage, but Palmetto Point specifically was put under "special conservation concern" and identified as highly at risk for coastal erosion (OHCHR, 2021). The Central Government has pushed this extractive industry, which earned US $300 million over a 10-year period. Even when the Barbuda Council took over the sandmining industry, the players (international mining companies, government ministers) who were the major beneficiaries remained the same. PLH claims to be undoing the damage by restoring the dunes. However, the excavation of millions of tons of sand under the guise of creating artificial lagoons and the hundreds of luxury residences PLH is building will continue to alter the condition of the island beyond repair. The UN Special Rapporteurs reports that the Ocean Club poses a threat to safe drinking water, food security, biodiversity, and human rights (OHCHR, 2021). Leveling the dunes to erect buildings, removing mangrove wetlands, and replacing Indigenous flora, and introducing sewage and pollutants will destroy its fragile ecosystems.

In these campaigns, a Western imaginary of "sustainability" is mobilized to erase Barbudans' preservation practices and to justify neocolonial practices of land expropriation. Within these new highly contemporary narratives of sustainability, a centuries-old hierarchy is perpetuated. Natives are seen as "naïve savages" who need to be assisted, guided, trained, and educated, in short "improved" to adapt to modes of production—and environmental "protection"—that ultimately benefit others, not the local population. The purpose is to keep the working native population subordinate to investors and visitors from Europe and North America, reinforcing their dependency and vulnerability.[32]

By a similar token, these development projects offer a small number of mostly low-paid jobs to the community. De Niro's team asserts they are trying to help the island after Hurricane Irma, offering jobs to "every Barbudan that's willing to work" (Wattles & Harlow, 2017). DeJoria has also said that the hurricane encouraged him to "immediately advance development plans" of the Barbuda Ocean Club, calling themselves "community developers" (Business Wire, 2017). Mussington sees this as a standard practice of developers: "They approach small, resource rich communities they believe are poor and depressed. The jobs they hand out will never be owned by the people, and the wealth the communities hold in common is extracted. In the end the communities are left impoverished without the resources that sustain lives and livelihoods, and the 'developers' move on to the next place." The Discovery Land Company already demonstrated this conduct when they abandoned the Bahamas a

---

32   Quijano and Ennis (2000), Castro-Gómez and Grosfoguel (2007) and Maldonado-Torres (2007) see the legacy of colonialism as formerly colonized nations continue to struggle against the new structures, which keep their populations subordinate to the logic of Western modernity and transnational capital.

few days after Hurricane Dorian in 2019, leaving the Bahamas Ocean Club in pieces, its staff anguished and jobless (Sieff, 2019). Nevertheless, Wilshaw claims they are "pleased to be part of the Barbuda family and the Barbuda community" (Barbuda Channel, 2021). But the community they claim to be a part of is now divided, forced to compete for the jobs created by the Ocean Club. "Divide and conquer, the colonial program is known," the Guadeloupean novelist Maryse Condé writes (1999: 143).

De Niro, DeJoria, and their allies evoke the figure of the colonial White male possessive individual, to borrow from Brenna Bhandar. This figure was historically defined in contrast to the "Savage," the "Indian," who was painted as being unfit to be an owner (Bhandar, 2018, p. 183). Sylvia Wynter calls the possessive subject simply "Man," who "overrepresents itself as if it were the human itself" (2003, p. 260). Barbuda, like many places in the Global South that have struggled for self-determination, challenges this overrepresentation of "Man," who takes the shape now of a possessive individual interested only in the cash value of real estate, not in the non-monetized value of the natural environment. In Barbuda, resources are a part of the community. "We're not looking at natural resources turned into billions. They are the foundations of our existence," Mussington said. "I'm the richest man on earth! We own this whole island, together," a Barbudan fisherman told us when he took us around the island on his boat (D. Warner, personal conversation). The collective transcends the individual.

Figure 13: The Barbuda Ocean Club villa's being constructed on Coco Point in January 2023. Source: Gulliver Johnson

COLONIALITY OF DEVELOPMENT

Gaston Browne's economic model is well-known; it is the dominant model of the Caribbean region (and many others). It fits within the colonial matrix of power, in which former colonial subjects reproduce extractive strategies of development similar to those used by former European colonizers to fill their coffers, treating inhabitants of the land in question and as nothing more than potential workers or worse—obsolete in the project of creating wealth. The legacies, hierarchies, and knowledge-practices imposed by colonial institutions are reproduced in service to those in power (Quijano & Ennis, 2000). For the sake of "development, "resources—in this case, land—are extracted and monetized by these governments, until they run out (Figure 13). The current extractive model of the Caribbean region is mostly tourism and the related real estate sector.

In service of this mode of development, Browne has called Barbuda's collective property "a myth" (Accheri et al., n.d.) and Barbudans "deracinated imbeciles" (Human Rights Watch, 2018) for believing they are its lawful possessors. He thinks Barbudans occupy the land informally (Accheri et al., 2018). Like De Niro and DeJoria, by casting Barbuda's life in common as a fiction, Browne cultivates a colonial worldview, where systems of private property and development are deemed necessary and inevitable. This has significant material consequences. As Bhandar writes: "Rendering Indigenous and racialized populations as illegal or unlawful, often on the basis of their ways of living or relating to land, has been used as a primary means of dispossession. Owning land in common, without individual private ownership, reflected a "state of primeval simplicity." Without ownership, and the law that accompanies it, there could be no civilization" (Bhandar, 2018, p. 48).

"Do you [know of] any country in the world that has advanced without a well-developed property rights system? It is fundamental to growth and development in any country. What makes Barbuda so special?" Browne asked in an interview (Accheri et al., 2018). Liz Alden Wily, an international land tenure expert, disagrees. There is growing recognition, she says, that many of the world's communally held lands are not just lands that are occupied and used but are owned, that they are actual—well-developed—forms of property (CLT Center, 2020). The fact that Barbuda lost the court case in the Privy Council against the Paradise Found Act demonstrates that juridical techniques of appropriation and dispossession continue to inform ongoing processes of displacement as well as the struggles faced by Commonwealth nations in achieving self-determination through "legal" structures determined by settler states.

The context today is the global climate emergency. Locally entrenched lifestyles that have protected wetlands, biodiversity, and wildlife—and the ways of relating to the land that support these lifestyles—are invalidated and rendered "unsustainable." In this mentality, the threat of climate change and the population's vulnerability are used to dispossess people and clear the land for those who are deemed less vulnerable, which is attributable to their wealth. This is what happened in the months after Hurricane Irma when Browne forced Barbudans off the island while a ninety-nine-year lease was signed with PLH. Yarimar Bonilla writes in an article on the coloniality of disaster that "'Vulnerability' (both social and environmental) is not a natural state but the product of racio-colonial governance" (Bonilla, 2020: 1). We therefore prefer to speak of vulnerabilization, a political action making and keeping communities vulnerable so they can be easily moved around (Algoed & Hernández Torrales, 2019, p. 39) actively kept from rebuilding after a disaster,[33] and forced into the colonial framework of private property.

DECOLONIAL RESISTANCE FOR SURVIVAL

> "[Our land system] puts the wealth of our nation, the access to the resources, in the hands of the people first," Mussington says. "After the disaster, there was a concerted effort to change that. It was the repeat of things that took place during colonization. That's why we fight"
> (Stronger Caribbean Together, 2020).

Barbuda's ongoing struggle to maintain collective land rights has its roots in the struggle against slavery and historical colonialism in the Caribbean. Like other forms of collective lands in the region (family lands, maroon communities, customary tenure),[34] Barbuda's land system is a resistant response to colonial domination (Besson & Momsen, 1987, p. 39). The Haitian sociologist Jean Casimir calls this the "counter-plantation system." During the Haitian revolution and after independence, formerly enslaved Haitians turned their backs to paid forms of large-scale plantation labor and

---

33   Research has shown the importance of people affected by disasters in participation in rebuilding. (See, e.g., Oliver-Smith, 2005, p. 53). There is a need to expel stress hormones after the event, which can settle in the body if people are treated as passive victims (see, e.g. van der Kolk, 2015).

34   It is estimated that in the Caribbean region, 100,000 hectares of land is held by Afro-descendant communities under customary tenure (Rights and Resources Initiative, 2015a).

focused on small-scale subsistence permaculture on their own plots (Casimir, 2020, cited in Bogaert, 2023) which Casimir sees as sites of resistance.³⁵

We see Barbuda's world-making project as a decolonial struggle, as Barbudans stand up against the legacies of colonialism in their own country, transforming hegemonic ideas and established narratives and rejecting the Cartesian logic of divorcing humankind from nature, where the former dominates and exploits the latter (Maldonado-Torres, 2007). Through their ways of relating to the land, Barbudans challenge the global powers that continue to view nature as are source to be exploited in one particular way based on generating wealth, and the local population as expendable.

Figure 14: Barbuda Land Act Matters. Source: Line Algoed

Controlling their resources as a collective (Figure 14) has shielded Barbudans from worse outcomes after the storm. Unlike other islands that are increasingly dependent on food imports, Barbuda had local food security, even without electricity after

---

35   The differences between these ways of relating to the land are beautifully described by Anna Tsing in The Mushroom at the End of the World: On the Possibility of Life in Capitalist Ruins (2015, p. 24): "Since the time of the plantation, commercial agriculture has aimed to segregate a single crop and work toward its simultaneous ripening for a coordinated harvest. But other kinds of farming have multiple rhythms. In the shifting cultivation… farmers needed to attend to the varied schedules of maturation of [crops]. These rhythms were their relation to human harvests; if we add other relations, for example, to pollinators or other plants, rhythms multiply. The polyphonic assemblage is the gathering of these rhythms, as they result from world-making projects, human and not human."

the storm.[36] Every young person in Barbuda learns how to fish and hunt. The day after Irma, Barbudans went fishing, Mussington remembers: "We shared it among the community. A typical person in Antigua would not be able to do that, because they do not have the skills." The communal land system also prevented rising house prices, because the community still controls the land (Lulich, 2018). Importantly, the communal system shielded residents from displacement following Hurricane Irma. Despite the Central Government's attempts to fracture the community by forcing people off the island for months and by amending their Land Act, Barbuda's community returned and are still there. The Barbuda Land Act has been amended (and subsequently repealed); however, the government's offer of one dollar for purchase of their housing plot has been widely rejected by Barbudans. The Barbuda Council maintains its right to administer the lands of Barbuda and its resources under its communal ownership system based on the Local Government Act (1976). This law remains in force and cannot be changed unilaterally by the Central Government. Currently, the Barbuda Council Lands Department is upgrading its lands registration system by issuing certificates of allotment, which confirms ownership of the land under Collective Title. These triumphs give Barbudans we spoke to the confidence that they will also overcome the challenges presented by the new luxury developments.

The resistance of the people of Barbuda is destabilizing established narratives on property, progress, development, and sustainability. The dominant imaginary originates from colonial thought, which privileges Western practices of cultivation, exploitation, and domination of the land, leading to the land's destruction. The need for epistemologies that confront and substitute colonial thinking, and practice is urgent, and the example of Barbuda can help us think and act otherwise. From this small Caribbean Island emerges a decolonial worldview that sees land as "necessary for life" (Bhandar, 2018: 25) and as a basis for survival in times of climate crises. "Our land system is the reason we survive. As simple as that" Mussington affirmed.

---

36   The Caribbean imports 83 percent of food consumed (see Dorodnykh, 2017).

CHAPTER 5

NEITHER IRMA, NOR MARIA WILL TAKE WHAT'S OURS

Collective Land Tenure for Just Climate Change Adaptation in Puerto Rico and Barbuda[37]

Authors: Line Algoed, Ellen M. Bassett, Lyvia N. Rodríguez Del Valle [38]

Abstract

Following the devastation wrought by two hurricanes in the summer of 2017, the governments of Puerto Rico and Antigua and Barbuda announced reforms to address land tenure insecurity amongst their residents. While the two islands have different cultures, histories, and economies, their respective governments embraced one objective: promoting privatization and individual titling of land. Such actions, while not new, represent a policy prescription heavily promoted by the world's economic institutions, namely providing secure tenure as part of disaster preparedness. In contrast, on both islands residents have sought to defend and strengthen their collective land rights, asserting that it helps them face the realities of climate change.

---

34   This article has been submitted to Land Use Policy: Algoed, L., E. M. Bassett, and L. Rodríguez Del Valle, L. (forthcoming 2024) "Neither Irma, nor Maria will take what's ours": Collective land tenure in the fight against climate change in Puerto Rico and Barbuda. Land Use Policy.

35   Ellen M. Bassett is Dean of the College of Design at Georgia Tech, Atlanta, USA. 36   Lyvia N. Rodríguez Del Valle is co-founder of El Enjambre and former Executive Director of the Fideicomiso de la Tierra del Caño Martín Peña, Puerto Rico.

Drawing from ethnographic research, this paper presents two cases of communities who continue to embrace collective tenure and reject a state-sponsored push toward individual land titles because they see such tenure forms as rendering them more vulnerable to disasters and their aftermaths. In rural Barbuda, residents are fighting to protect a collective land ownership form established following the British abolition of slavery in 1834; in Puerto Rico, a Community Land Trust was created in the Caño Martín Peña, a historically self-built community, to fight gentrification and displacement threatened by a large-scale dredging project. Even though reducing vulnerability to climate change was not the driving force at the time of the creation of the Trust, it has proven to be a highly efficient land tenure method that has fostered just climate change adaptation. This paper explores the benefits and protections afforded by collective tenure in the fight against climate change. These cases contribute to a growing body of evidence challenging individual private property as the most superior form of ownership. Rather than eliminating communal land tenure, we argue that for the two studied communities collective land tenure means more secure tenure and that such tenures should be strengthened to assist communities seeking to adapt to climate change.

INTRODUCTION

In 2017, hurricanes in the Atlantic and Gulf of Mexico wreaked great damage to many islands in the Caribbean. Amongst the most powerful and destructive of the hurricanes were Irma and Maria. Maria, the strongest and most deadly storm of the season, made landfall in Puerto Rico in late September and was measured as a "high-end" Category 4 storm. Irma, the worst Category 5 to hit the Leeward Islands, caused catastrophic damage to Barbuda. While the death toll and the inept response to the damage wrought by Maria in Puerto Rico is well known, little attention has been paid to the aftermath of the storms and the processes of rebuilding and economic regeneration comparing different islands in the Caribbean. Most notably for this paper, in the aftermath of the hurricanes in these two Caribbean islands, the existing public debate over land tenure intensified. In Puerto Rico, after Hurricane Maria, federal policies required households to present property titles to receive assistance from the US Federal Emergency Management Agency (FEMA) and other disaster recovery programs. This rule disadvantaged the tens of thousands of Puerto Ricans living without recognized property titles—arguably those most in need of FEMA's assistance. All told, 60% of FEMA applicants were deemed ineligible, mostly due to a lack of proof of homeownership (García, 2022). In Barbuda, after Hurricane Irma, the Central Government of the twin State of Antigua amended the 2007 Barbuda Land Act to dismantle the communal land ownership system established after British abolition of slavery. The Prime Minister claimed it hindered economic progress and hurricane recovery. On both islands, the governments are using the hurricanes to promote individual land titles and private land ownership. These tenure policies have been met with skepticism and resistance by the communities. Undervalued is the importance of collective land tenure in withstanding extreme weather events and improving capacity to adapt to environmental disruptions (Shi et al., 2018).

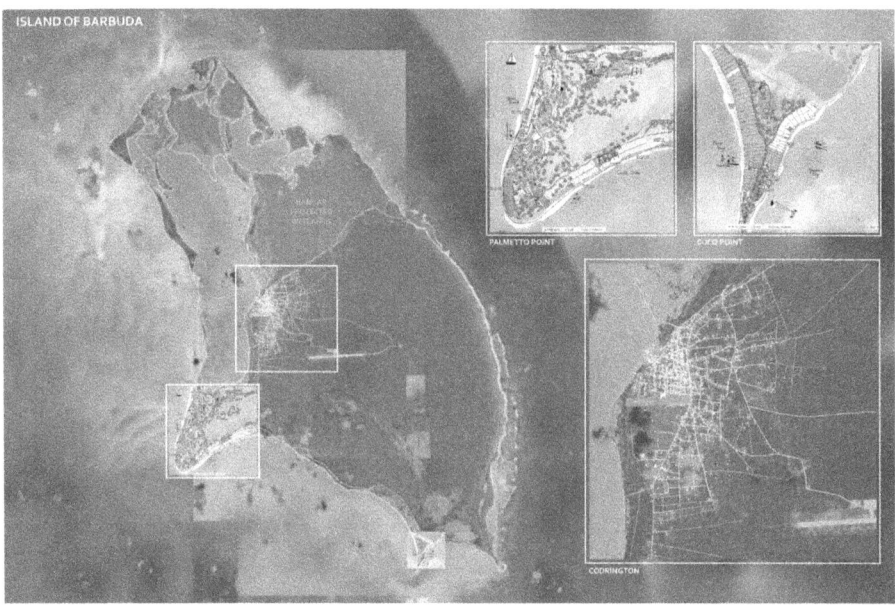

Figure 15: A map of Barbuda showing the low density of the island, the Ramsar Protected Wetlands, the excavation for the new airport, and the planned construction of 450 new luxury homes by the Peace, Love and Happiness Partnership at the Palmetto Point. Source: Line Algoed and Kyle Kalmar, using Google Maps and images of barbudaoceanclub.com, 2022

In Barbuda, the communal land tenure system was customary until two pieces of legislation formalized the communal ownership: the first, a colonial enactment in 1904; the second the Barbuda Land Act of 2007. Barbuda has a population of roughly 1600 people on an area of 40 000 acres. Figure 15 shows a map of the island of Barbuda. In Puerto Rico, a community land trust (CLT) established in 2004 in the self-built communities of Martín Peña is protecting residents against displacements following Hurricane Maria. A CLT is a nonprofit organization that holds land on behalf of a place-based community, while serving as the long-term steward for affordable housing, community gardens, civic buildings, commercial spaces, and other community assets on behalf of a community (CLT Center, n.d.-b). The Caño Martín Peña Special Planning District has a population of roughly 15 000 people and spans over 450 acres, with 280 acres being CLT lands. Figure 16 shows a map of the Caño Martín Peña Special Planning District.

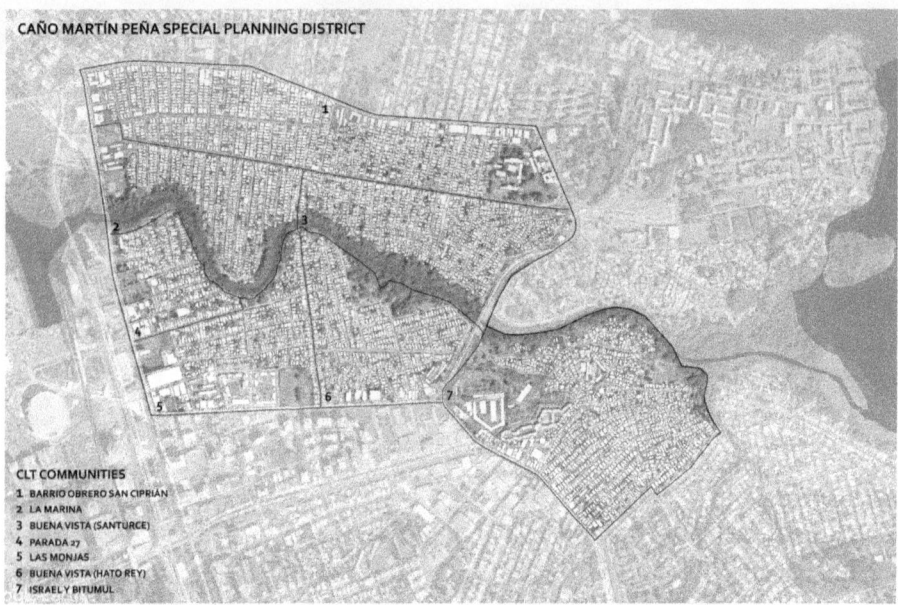

Figure 16: A map of the Caño Martín Peña Special Planning District showing the density of the seven barrios surrounding the Martín Peña waterway. Source: Line Algoed and Kyle Kalmar, using Google Maps, 2022.

This paper examines the importance of these two collective land tenure systems and in doing so contributes to a larger literature in economics and the social sciences on land tenure, economic development, and climate justice. We seek to understand why these communities, although very different in size, density, and biophysical features, continue to embrace collective land titles, when prevailing economic theory still argues that individual tenure is a superior form of land holding (Platteau, 1996). Drawing from ethnographic research, our findings demonstrate that residents see myriad benefits in their collective property regimes. To protect vulnerable communities in the face of climate change, we therefore argue that there is a need for tenure plurality–including the protection and strengthening of community-based tenure systems.

The paper is organized as follows. First, we present a brief overview of the theoretical debate over land tenure security and economic development. We then present the research design, namely a comparative case study approach, and outline the methods and data used. In the third section, we present case studies for the two islands examining why the Caño Martín Peña communities in San Juan, Puerto Rico, have opted for collective land tenure; and why Barbudans are resisting the push towards individual land titles led by Antigua and Barbuda's Central Government. Finally, we reflect on the cases and what they contribute to the literature on land tenure, as well as current policy perspectives for fostering climate justice in vulnerable communities.

LAND TENURE SECURITY AND JUST CLIMATE CHANGE ADAPTATION

Secure land tenure has long been recognized as an important factor for fostering economic development, enhancing agricultural productivity, and facilitating housing investment. Increasingly, secure land tenure is seen as a key element for community capacity to withstand the challenges arising from climate change and its accompanying severe weather events. In a 2019 report on land tenure and climate vulnerability, UN-Habitat contends that "given the evidence of strong linkages between tenure insecurity and climate vulnerability, improved tenure security should be considered to be an important enabler of climate-change adaptation" (UN-Habitat, 2019). Just what form of ownership facilitates land tenure security, however, has not been open to much debate. For decades, if not for centuries if one reflects on John Locke and his labor theory of property, individual land ownership or private property has been the dominant, almost unquestionable, way to hold land.

Theoretically the advantages of individual ownership are multifold. For economists, individual land ownership addresses the critical problem of negative externalities—by making the individual bear all the costs and capture all the benefits of land-based activities, private property is seen as "getting the incentives right" and fostering responsible land stewardship. In contrast, as is most famously argued by Garret Hardin (1968) community-based tenures have been cast as inherently flawed in relation to land management—suffering from negative externalities and free riding behavior. They are doomed to fail due to the "tragedy of the commons." The titling and registration systems established to prove ownership in the modern world are also lauded. Such systems enable landowners to harness the value of their land by using it as collateral in lending processes; this, in turn, enables entrepreneurial behavior and economic expansion. Hernando de Soto in his work, *The Mystery of Capital* (2000), argued that the lack of private ownership was a critical obstacle to economic development in the Global South, particularly Latin America. de Soto's policy prescription was simple: to kick start lagging economies all that needed to be done was to introduce well-documented private property and the "dead capital" tied up in unformalized land would be mobilized for economic investment. The previously identified advantages of private property are even more compelling for many economic theorists because private property has also been argued to be an inevitable end state. Land, as a finite resource, is confronted with an ever more hostile global land market, with the net result that local populations will ultimately face acute land scarcity.

In the face of scarcity, the most rational and secure form of tenure from an economic and environmental perspective is the one that centralizes control and fosters efficient economic behavior. This belief in the inevitability of private property has been given a rather Darwinian cast–evocatively dubbed "the evolutionary theory of land rights" by Pierre Platteau (1996).

In the face of such compelling arguments, it is not surprising that governments facing the threats of climate change would understand the importance of tenure security to facilitate investment in housing improvements and infrastructure to withstand severe weather. It is also understandable that they would view individual title as the best form of tenure to impart that security–particularly when their partners in development, namely prominent bi- and multilateral aid agencies, have been promoting individual titling for decades. Yet, the communities at the heart of this paper–those bearing the brunt of climate change–are forcefully resisting the push to individualize their land holdings and opting for innovative collective land tenure instruments. What advantages do they see in their common property regimes? What insights might they provide for economic theory in relation to land and tenure security? And what might we learn from their experiences to help prepare for the coming climate?

Much has been written about the inefficiencies of individual land titling programs (Varley, 2017; Rakodi et al., 2009; Pradilla Cobos, 1983) and even more about the contradictions in de Soto's theories (Clichevsky, 2003; Connolly, 2013). Yet, it remains understudied whether and how individual titles affect communities negatively when they confront (the aftermath of) extreme weather events. The ways in which land tenure insecurity connects to climate change-induced displacements also needs more scrutiny. Johnson, Jain, and Lavell (Johnson et al., 2021) start filling that gap with a book about risk and resettlement in the Global South, in which Yves Cabannes writes about climate-induced relocations in connection with other forms of land and housing evictions, arguing that climate change exacerbates evictions. He uses the Caño Martín Peña as a case study, saying that, although the community was affected badly by Hurricane Maria, it "demonstrated a remarkably higher level of resilience and recovery when compared to other communities" (Cabannes, 2021). Scott Leckie (2013) published a report with a series of possible land solutions to climate displacement, in which he argues "that many aspects of climate displacement can be resolved with land-based solutions and human rights-based improvements in domestic housing, land and property law and policy."

In this article we focus on collective land tenure and highlight its importance in withstanding and adapting to climate change. There are important academic contributions to the benefits of (mostly rural) collective land tenure systems (Alden Wily, 2018), less so in the Caribbean, with a few notable exceptions (e.g. Besson & Momsen, 2007). This paper builds on the work of scholars like Linda Shi et al (2018), who connect the benefits of collective land tenure specifically to current climate change debates, arguing that collective property increases the adaptive capacity of vulnerable communities confronted with climate change. Building on the work of Amorim-Maia et al., (2022), we understand this adaptive capacity to be intersectional, considering "the interconnected forms of social-environmental injustices that drive vulnerabilities." In the Caribbean those injustices are rooted in a historical lack of self-determination. As in the words of an art exhibition in which Caribbean artists explored the impact of the 2017 hurricanes: "A storm never comes alone. They're accompanied by political and economic storms, the origins of which can be traced to the colonial past" (Z33, 2021). Countering this, residents in the neighborhoods of this study see climate change adaptation as a community-led effort, where residents themselves are in control of all steps involved, from risk mitigation to disaster preparedness and recovery. The focus is on mitigating risk at the community level, and not at the level of the individual. This is what residents understand to be just climate change adaptation, which we have chosen to use in this article.

There are several collective, cooperative, or communal (CCC) forms of land tenure, categorized by Cabannes (2021) as "(i) collective or communal ownership, including co-operatives (ownership is vested in the co-operative or group of which residents are co-owners); (ii) community land trust (a non-profit organization develops and stewards affordable housing on behalf of a community) and (iii) customary ownership or use." This article zooms in on the latter two of these forms.

RESEARCH DESIGN AND METHODOLOGY

This research utilizes a comparative case study design. The two cases are: the Caño Martín Peña area in San Juan, Puerto Rico, a Caribbean Island that is an unincorporated territory of the United States; and the island of Barbuda, part of the sovereign Commonwealth nation of Antigua and Barbuda. The two cases were selected for comparison using two criteria: 1) the existence of common property tenure regimes, and 2) the devastating impact of the 2017 hurricane season and shared difficulties rebuilding. Despite these similarities, the islands are quite different, culturally, and economically. They are characterized by very different types of communal land ownership–a centuries-old system in Barbuda, and a more contemporary Community Land Trust (CLT), the Caño Martín Peña CLT (hereafter Caño CLT) in Puerto Rico. Despite the geographic closeness of the two islands, their similar colonial past and (neo-)colonial present, as well as present and future challenges brought about by the climate emergency, these communities do not often interact with one another–rather the islands share more direct connections with their metropoles (US and UK) than with other neighboring islands.

We have used triangulation to gather evidence to build the cases, relying on multiple methods and sources of data, including analysis of archives and government documents, participant observation at public meetings (in-person and online), participatory action research (PAR), and in-depth interviews with residents and community leaders. Table 3 gives a complete overview of the methods, sources, and types of analysis. Data for this research were collected by the first author over the course of six different field visits for a total of 5 months. The last author worked for almost two decades for the Caño communities in several capacities, was part of the process that led to the creation and operationalization of the *Corporación del Proyecto ENLACE del Caño Martín Peña* (hereafter ENLACE) and the Caño CLT and led the response to hurricane Maria. She is contributing to this article as a practitioner.

Table 3: Overview of research methodology and analytical approach

Method	Activity	Stakeholders	Material collected	Analysis
Ethnographic fieldwork	21 weeks of fieldwork between March 2018 and February 2023 divided over 3 research visits to Puerto Rico and 3 research visits to Barbuda.	Focus on residents, community leaders and accompanying professionals	Audio files of interviews and observations, field notes, artifacts, photos, video material	Triangulation using multiple sources of evidence
In-depth interviews	68 semi-structured in-depth interviews	Residents, community leaders, environmental activists, staff Caño organizations, members Barbuda Council, Member of Parliament for Barbuda in Antigua & Barbuda Parliament	Audio files of all interviews, video material of 13 interviews	Thematic narrative analysis of interview transcripts
Analysis of governance documents, archives, laws, government documents, leases, and environmental campaign documents	Puerto Rico: Caño governance documents: Comprehensive Development and Land Use Plan; CLT Regulations and Bylaws. Archives: Meeting notes from the Planning-Action-Reflection process meetings (2002-2004 and 2006-2008); Proceedings of the public hearings held by ENLACE regarding the regulations that govern the Caño CLT (2008); Letter from ENLACE to the Puerto Rico Secretary of the Department of Housing (2018); Fact Sheet ENLACE on Maximizing CDBG-DR funds; popular education materials; personal notes. Laws: Act 489-2004, as amended; Act 32-2009; Act 22-2012; Act 60-2019. PR Government documents: PR Disaster Recovery Action Plan for the Use of CDBG-DR Funds in Response to 2017 Hurricanes Irma and Maria (effective on July 29, 2018, and following 9 amendments).		Digital or hard copies of all documents	Qualitative content analysis

Source: Line Algoed

Table 3, continued

Method	Activity	Stakeholders	Material collected	Analysis
Analysis of governance documents, archives, laws, government documents, leases, and environmental campaign documents	Barbuda: Archives: Barbuda Channel footage of Village Meetings; archival research of deeds in Antigua & Barbuda national archives; commercial brochures of former and future real estate projects; Barbuda Council Press Releases. Laws: Barbuda Land Act 2007; Barbuda Amendment Act 2018; Crown Land Amendment Act 2018; Paradise Found Act 2015. Leases: Peace, Love, and Happiness (PLH) Lease 22 February 2017 version 1; PLH Lease 22 Feb 17 version 2. Environmental campaign documents: Environmental Impact Assessment prepared for PLH/Discovery Land Company by Deborah Brosnan & Associates; Antigua & Barbuda Department of Environment (DoE) Review on PLH development; Comments John Mussington on DoE review; Global Coral Reef Alliance comments on PLH development; Global Action Lawyers Network (GLAN) rebuttal to PLH.		Digital or hard copies of all documents	Qualitative content analysis
Participatory action research (PAR)	Organization of 3 peer-to-peer exchanges, in person and online: Aug 2018 In-person exchange in Rio de Janeiro; May 2019 In-person Peer Exchange in Puerto Rico with 49 people from 17 countries; online exchange: Reconectando: Entre la Pandemia y la Tenencia (17 June 2021).	Residents, community leaders, scholars, environmental and land rights activists, staff Caño organizations, Catalytic Communities, policymakers, lawyers	Notes of all meetings during these exchanges, audio files of several sessions, photos, videos	Thematic narrative analysis of transcripts and notes
Participant observation at public meetings	Puerto Rico: Caño Community Council meetings, ENLACE and Fideicomiso Staff meetings, Advisory Council meetings, Disaster Recovery meetings, Protests, Marches.	Residents and activists, staff Caño organizations, members Barbuda Council	Notes of all meetings, photos, short videos	Thematic narrative analysis of transcripts and notes

Table 3, continued

Method	Activity	Stakeholders	Material collected	Analysis
Participant observation at public meetings	Barbuda: Homecoming activities, Church services, Village meetings, Community walks, Bars.	Residents and activists, staff Caño organizations, members Barbuda Council	Notes of all meetings, photos, short videos	Thematic narrative analysis of transcripts and notes
Participation in research project 'Food, Land, and Climate Justice in the Caribbean' funded by the UK Global Challenges Research Fund (GCRF)	Monthly online meetings between 2019 – 2022, and organization of 3 webinars: Hunger, Covid-19, Resistance and farmer-based solutions (1 May 2020); Capitalism of Disaster in the Caribbean: Tourism, Development and Displacement of Local Communities (21 June 2021); Climate Change and Land Tenure in the Caribbean (24 March 2022).	Community activists and scholars from Barbuda, Belize, Jamaica, San Andrés (Colombia), Puerto Rico, Belgium, and UK, and invited people from Grenada, Vieques (Puerto Rico)	Video files of webinars, notes of all meetings, final report GCRF	Thematic narrative analysis of transcripts and notes

OPTING FOR COLLECTIVE LAND TITLES: THE CAÑO MARTÍN PEÑA CLT IN SAN JUAN, PUERTO RICO

Land is a topic of constant conversation in the Caño Martín Peña communities. Community leaders wear T-shirts that convey the central message: *¡La Tierra es Nuestra, Nadie Nos la Quitará!*—"the land is ours; no one will take it away from us." During one of the exchanges that were organized to help others get acquainted with the concept of the Community Land Trust, Evelyn Quiñones, a longtime Community Leader, talked about why she did not believe in the individual land titles offered by mayors, governors, or other politicians, looking for votes in the barrios, at several moments in the history of the US territory. She says: "They come and give us titles, and then the neighbors sell their titles one by one. That's displacement. The land belongs to all of us; we will stay."

Residents in seven communities of the Caño Martín Peña, *comunidades autogestionadas* (self-built and self-managed communities) 'informally' established in the 1930's without recognized ownership of the land, have found a way to address their lack of documentation and land tenure insecurity by creating the Fideicomiso de la Tierra del Caño Martín Peña (Caño CLT). The communities are located next to the financial district in San Juan and along the Martín Peña tidal channel, a body of water that became increasingly polluted due to the lack of a sewage system and was gradually obstructed with sediments, trash, and debris, so much so that it eventually stopped flowing. This causes recurring small-scale disasters in the form of constant flooding, which in turn creates a public health hazard for the communities. This method of collective ownership was chosen to regularize land tenure and increase tenure security, address poverty and marginalization, enable the implementation of a comprehensive plan that provides for proper infrastructure, but also with the express objective of preventing gentrification and involuntary displacements.

The initial impetus for the CLT formation was the proposed ecosystem restoration of the Martín Peña channel in the early 2000s. Due to the national significance of the channel, the US Environmental Protection Agency (EPA) chose the San Juan Bay Estuary, including the Martín Peña channel, to become part of its National Estuary Program. The San Juan Bay Estuary Comprehensive Conservation Management plan, adopted in the late 1990's, included the dredging of the environmentally degraded channel and addressing infrastructure challenges in the adjacent communities as the main actions required to uplift the ecosystem. In the early 2000's, the Government of Puerto Rico converted the dredging into a strategic project and assigned it to the Puerto Rico Highway and Transportation Authority (PRHTA), a public corporation under the Department of Transportation and Public Works. Employees of PRHTA took a rigorous approach to the involvement of the communities along the tidal channel (Algoed et al., 2018). The team, initially composed of planners and community social workers, assembled the community leadership, helped strengthen grassroots organizing, and started a planning-action-reflection process beyond the dredging of the channel, which included the comprehensive development of the communities along the channel and their stance within the city.

Community Displacements

Although supportive of the restoration in principle, residents were conscious of how such infrastructure projects have impacted low-income communities in the past. Their desirable location was of interest to a powerful and hostile real estate market. Market exposure, coupled with individual land ownership, might lead to the eventual displacement of community residents. Politicians spent decades promoting electoral interests by giving residents individual property titles. They were granted to very small lots, within blocks, without access to infrastructure or even water, without being accompanied by plans or concrete actions to address these precarious living situations. (idem). Speculators had already started buying some of those individually owned plots of land in the Martín Peña communities, particularly those closest to the main transportation corridors as they knew that the restoration of the channel would drastically increase the value of the area's land.

Martín Peña residents had also witnessed the displacement in two nearby barrios: Tokío and El Fanguito. The Puerto Rico Eradication of Slums Act of 1945, subsidized by the US federal government through Urban Renewal policies and the Model City program, wiped out a large part of the communities located along the western half of the channel. Approximately 30,000 inhabitants were displaced mainly to public housing projects conceived as temporary housing, but which turned out to be permanent. The former barrio El Fanguito now hosts a highway, parks, government buildings and housing blocks. Similarly, the government used eminent domain to evict the neighboring Tokío community, including those who had acquired individual titles, without providing relocation options to the families. Today, this area is home to middle- and high-income residents and urban facilities such as an arena (idem). With the establishment of San Juan's financial district on the border of the Martín Peña communities and the promotion of individual land-titling programs, gentrification had become a growing threat.

The threats became the impetus for community organizing by Martín Peña residents. The employees of the PRHTA facilitated a series of workshops, in which residents discussed the importance of the infrastructure project, while at the same time the need for mechanisms to regularize tenure and avoid displacements and community fragmentation. Participants were asked to explain why families wanted individual titles to the land, the tenure form most were familiar with. Common answers included: the desire of residents to bequeath the right to occupy a parcel of land to their heirs, access to public services, and access to mortgage credit. All participants agreed that avoiding the displacement of community members was a priority. After learning from experts (including an invited resident from a CLT in Boston) about the benefits and disadvantages of all tenure forms–individual land titles, land cooperatives, and community land trusts–participants were able to examine how each ownership instrument allowed them to reach their objectives. María Hernández Torrales (2020) synthesized the goals of the community in six critical rights indispensable for any instrument: the right to stay put; the right to secure land tenure; the right to adequate housing; the right to an individual property (house); the right to benefit from improvements to the area; and the right to participate in decision-making processes.

The Caño Martín Peña Community Land Trust

After examining priorities and land tenure options, residents decided that a form of collective land ownership was the only way to prevent displacements due to gentrification, speculation, or forced evictions. They chose a CLT as it would be supportive of the dredging of the Martín Peña channel, the construction of needed infrastructure, and the rehabilitation of their neighborhoods. A CLT separates individual homeownership from collective land ownership. The land is collectively owned in perpetuity, while each family who formerly lacked a land title obtains a legal document, a surface rights deed, to secure their right to use the land beneath their home, a right they would be able to bequeath to their legal heirs (see Figure 17). This deed would enable them to stay put and continue to pursue their livelihoods in the city, while securing their right to influence what happens in their own neighborhood (idem).

The planning-action-reflection process that took place between 2002 and 2004, facilitated by the employees of the PRHTA, included the discussion around land tenure and possible gentrification as an unintended result of the dredging. This process culminated in a Comprehensive Development and Land Use Plan ('the Plan') that was ultimately adopted by the PR Planning Board in 2008, and in the enactment of Law 489 in 2004. The Plan was designed by residents of the community with help of an interdisciplinary team that included urban planners, architects, engineers, economists, among others. Law 489-2004 created the CLT, and the *Corporación del Proyecto ENLACE del Caño Martín Peña*, a public corporation in charge of implementing the Development Plan. The Board of Directors of ENLACE was designed by the community, ensuring the continuity of the implementation of the Plan despite future changes in government. The Plan includes relocating families who live in the dredging area, if they so wish, within the Special Planning District of the Caño Martín Peña ('the District'). Before the establishment of the CLT, the leadership of the communities had set up the nonprofit organization, the Group of the Eight Communities Along the Caño Martín Peña, Inc. (G-8), which brought together all the grassroots initiatives in the District. It is this organizing and planning that led to the creation of the CLT.

The resultant CLT is a nonprofit organization governed by a majority of community residents, which manages the land collectively owned by 1500 households on 280 acres of non-contiguous urban land. Most of that land was previously owned by government agencies and was ultimately transferred to the CLT in 2009 through

ENLACE, as per the provisions of Law 489-2004. The Caño CLT regulations, which resulted from a participatory planning-action-reflection process led by ENLACE and the G-8 between 2006 and 2008, specify how the land is managed. As per the Caño CLT regulations, the relationship between the collective landowner and the individual homeowners is regularized through surface rights, evidenced by a notary deed, and recorded as a property separate from the land with the Puerto Rico Property and Real Estate Registry. Surface rights can be inherited, mortgaged, and sold with equity restrictions applicable to resales. The Caño CLT has the first right of refusal.

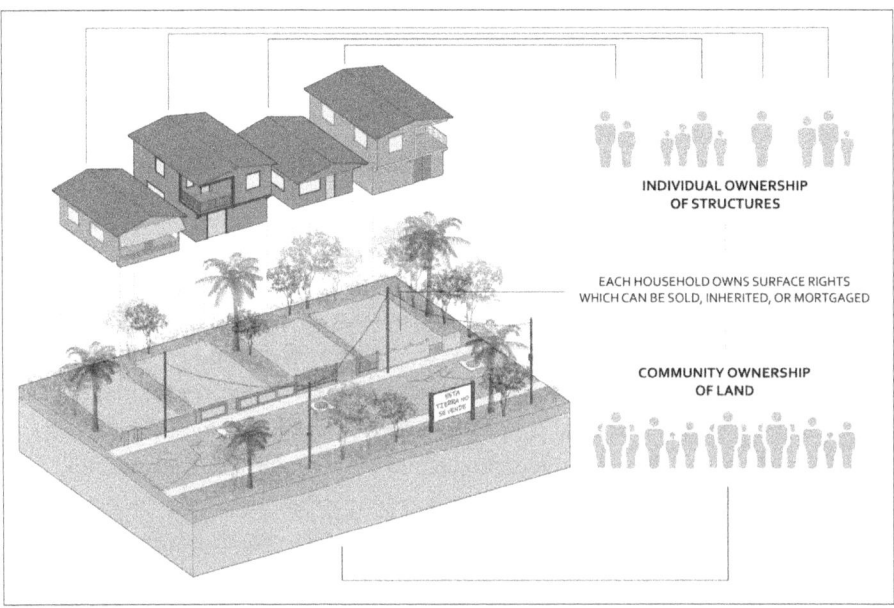

Figure 17: The Caño Martín Peña Community Land Trust. Source: Line Algoed and Kyle Kalmar based on a graph provided by ENLACE.

This arrangement was designed to balance the interests of individual families–to regularize tenure and have legal documentation of individual property rights–with the collective objectives discussed above, acknowledging the diversity of situations and interests within the communities. During the process to create the CLT and its regulations, concerns voiced by some residents included that individuals would relinquish decisions regarding their property rights to a board of trustees, that surface rights were short of full property rights, or that individuals that owned multiple structures other than that used as their primary home and acted as landlords would have to pay a fee to the Caño CLT for the surface rights (ENLACE, 2008). Governance concerns were addressed in the design of a multi-layered decision-making structure supported by technical assistance and community organizers, as well as provisions regarding transparency, and providing for checks and balances. The communities overwhelmingly prioritized the protections against gentrification and displacement above the right of individuals to accumulate properties and speculate with structures. Their decision was put to the test in 2009, when under the leadership of a former Mayor of San Juan, legislation was approved to return to the government agencies the land that ENLACE had transferred to the CLT, so that the municipality could issue individual land titles. During the four years under which the legislation was under judicial review, only 52 out of the 1500 families living in CLT land accepted individual land titles. The communities defended the CLT and were able to regain the lands in 2013 (Algoed et al., 2018).

Emphasis on Individual Land Titles and Individual Risk Mitigation after Hurricane Maria

Puerto Rico was badly hit by Hurricanes Irma and Maria in September 2017. Conservatively it is estimated that 2,975 people died in the aftermath of Hurricane Maria in Puerto Rico (AP News, 2021). Many of them died due to a lack of (clean) water, food, electricity, inadequate health care access, disrupted communications, or the disease leptospirosis caused by rats attracted by the hurricane debris (Sutter & Sosa Pascual, 2018). Around 1,000 Martín Peña houses lost at least part of their roofs. The hurricanes intensified the previously existing public discussion on the importance of secure land tenure. 'Informality' in impoverished areas was singled out as the underlying cause of significant damage to the housing stock, and dwellers of those areas were blamed for the fragility of the country (Algoed & Hernández Torrales, 2019). Federal and national policies required Puerto Rican households to present property titles to receive assistance from FEMA and other disaster recovery programs. As a result, thousands of families were denied FEMA individual assistance to pay for repairs, because they could not prove that they owned their homes (Florido, 2018). This disadvantaged those living in unrecognized settlements without formal tenure, even though they were the ones most in need of assistance.

Moreover, the Puerto Rican and federal government recovery programs that were intended to help the most deprived residents with reconstruction emphasized individual land titles and individual risk mitigation. The "Home Repair, Reconstruction, or Relocation Program" (R3), an element of the Community Development Block Grant funds for Disaster Recovery (CDBG-DR funds), is only available to those who can prove home ownership with an individual title deed. It does allow alternative methods to prove ownership, such an affidavit. Different from the norms applicable elsewhere in the US and its territories, until November 2021 homes located in areas designated a floodplain were not eligible for this program and would not be reconstructed even when mitigation was an alternative. It is estimated that roughly 10% of all the island's housing structures are in flood zones (Clancy et al., 2020).[39] Not surprisingly, construction permits are being approved within the floodplain in higher income areas near the beaches, such as Río Grande, Isabela, and Dorado. Another program, the Title Clearance Program, addresses the lack of documentation regarding property rights as is required for those seeking assistance under R3 or other CDBG-DR programs. It focuses on individual land titles and excludes other forms of property such as collective land ownership. Except for CDBG-DR applicants, this program also excludes properties located within the floodplains, again disadvantaging those residents most in need of assistance. It also prevents the community from using these funds to mitigate risk at community level, i.e., by strengthening infrastructure that may reduce flood risks. At no point in this policy response was there a recognition of the potential of community-based responses to the disaster and the potential of collective action for rebuilding.

BARBUDA'S HISTORIC RESISTANCE TO LAND PRIVATIZATION

In contrast to Puerto Rico, where collective land tenures are relatively new, Barbuda, the smaller island of the twin State of Antigua and Barbuda, has known collective land property for centuries. In the 17th and 18th centuries, Barbuda was a privately-owned sugar plantation of an enslaver family, the Codringtons. After Britain banned slavery in 1834 and the Codrington family left, Barbudans refused to pay rent for their homes on the island after having suffered 200 years of servitude. Based on that, in 1904, the British Crown granted Barbudans legal status as its lawful tenants in communal possession in a colonial enactment of 1904 (Negga Melchior, 2018).

---

39   Amendment #7 to the Action Plan, approved by the US Department of Housing and Urban Development on November 5, 2021, "incorporated elevation as an allowable construction activity under the Home Repair, Reconstruction, or Relocation Program (R3), when reasonable." According to the amendment, "[e]ligible applicants with homes located in the floodplain which qualify for substantial improvement rehabilitation will be offered elevated reconstruction when reasonable, or relocation when elevated reconstruction is not reasonable."

The Barbuda Land Act

Communal possession was maintained throughout the 20th century and subsequently refined and ratified in the 2007 Barbuda Land Act (BLA). While retaining the Crown as the symbolic owner of the land, the BLA entrusted exclusive possession of the land in common to the several thousand Barbudans living on the island (Alden Wily, n.d.). In this form of ownership, each Barbudan is entitled to three plots of land: one for housing, another for agriculture, and the third for business. (Frank, 2018) The Barbuda Council plays a de facto role as legal land administrator, with the power to allocate plots. It also leases land for several small hotels or other enterprises. Some of these plots are leased to international investors. Major development cannot happen unless there is consent of most of the people of Barbuda, who are informed during Village Meetings, pursuant to the Barbuda Land Act (Antigua and Barbuda, 2007). Thanks to this, Barbuda has been able to protect nature and biodiversity. It hosts the world's most important nesting sites for the frigate bird and other endangered species. The intact dunes and wetlands–protected by the Ramsar Convention on Wetlands– serve as a flood zone if needed. Barbuda's lifestyle distinguishes itself from other Caribbean islands. People can roam the island freely, as most if its land is not divided in plots. Residents hunt and fish for most of their food, there are not many shops, life is very quiet. "Do you hear that?" a resident asks during a research visit. "This is what silence sounds like."

Previous Attempts to Privatize Barbuda's Land

This communal land tenure form, and its related lifestyle, is not looked upon favorably by non-Barbudans. At various moments in history, the Central Government of Antigua and Barbuda has attempted to impose land privatization. But Barbuda has consistently refused to accept individual land titles for their plots of land. It even went as far as to resist independence from Britain in 1981 to avoid being forced to adapt their land system to Antigua's freehold system. Historian Amy Potter, who has studied the Barbuda Voice, a newspaper published for the Barbudan diaspora in New York City in the 1970's and 1980's, reviewed the outspoken opposition to these schemes (Potter, 2011). Barbudans anticipated it would lead to fragmentation and gradual displacement of the community: "The new Government is planning to give deeds to the people for their land. . . If [...] people accept deeds [...], the Government will sell Barbuda piece by piece" (Potter, 2011).

Land Tenure Reform in Barbuda after Hurricane Irma

Barbuda was devastated when Hurricane Irma hit early September 2017. Official sources alarmingly reported that 95% of buildings were destroyed (BBC News, 2017). Gaston Browne, Antigua and Barbuda's Prime Minister, called Barbuda "practically uninhabitable" (365 Antigua, 2017) and forced Barbudans to evacuate. Brought to shelters in Antigua, many felt disempowered and unable to participate in their community's rebuilding. Approximately one month later, some were allowed back onto their island, but schools remained closed for months after and the absence of other public services such as health, running water, banking and waste management made it impossible to restart community life (Algoed et al., 2021).

Barbudans resisted this forced evacuation for myriad reasons. Residents were suspicious that declaring the island uninhabitable and clearing out the population was not really about ensuring community safety. These suspicions were seemingly confirmed by a report issued in November 2017 by ACAPS (a group of independent specialists in humanitarian needs analysis and assessment), United Nations Office for the Coordination of Humanitarian Affairs, and the United Nations Development Program that stated that only 45% of buildings were destroyed as result of Irma (ACAPS et al., 2017)—not 95%. The island certainly was not uninhabitable. Residents interviewed asserted that declaring the island unsafe served the political and economic interests of the more powerful who embraced the disaster as an opportunity to advance capitalistic goals for self-enrichment, by pushing—once again—the privatization of the island's communal land tenure system.

In 2018, these fears seemed confirmed when the Central Government amended the Barbuda Land Act of 2007. In its place, the government sought to install a system through which Barbudans can apply for private land ownership of the plots on which their homes are located, for 1 EC$ (US$0.37 USD). In the amendment, communal land rights are taken away and land can now be sold to anyone, regardless of nationality or place of origin, a crucial difference from the Land Act that only gives the right to land ownership to Barbudans (Lightfoot, 2020). The justification was that title deeds would help Barbudans obtain bank loans to do repairs to homes, with the individual title deeds providing collateral. However, to date, no one in Barbuda has applied for private property under this scheme (Algoed et al., 2021).

On their return to their island, Barbudans found an international-length runway under construction to service tourist arrivals. A 99-year lease had also been signed on environmentally critical land to the Peace, Love and Happiness Partnership (PLH) for 450 exclusive dwellings for ultra-wealthy foreigners. This was done on top of the already existing lease for the American actor Robert De Niro's high-end tourist lodge, called Paradise Found (idem). In a protest in London challenging the decision to dismantle the BLA, Barbuda's Member of Parliament, Trevor Walker, says: "[If] land were to be sold, the rich people will just come and buy it up. […] [Our] traditional way of life, agriculture, fishing […] will be extinct […]. Land is power, land is wealth" (Accheri et al., 2018).

The residents we interviewed see private land titles as a capitalist mechanism to add land to the free market. They ask: In what ways would the commodification of land and the inclusion in global land markets benefit us? What would compensate us for the loss of control over common resources? Would we be able to continue to live on the island if property was owned not by us but by banks? Would there be enough well-paid employment to pay off loans, without banks repossessing the property? MP Walker stated in a personal conversation: "Banks won't lend any money unless you have a job, unless you have an income, to support or to service a loan. It's not because you have a title deed, the bank is going to give you money, you must pay it back."

The fear is that those who cannot get a job in the limited job market will need to leave the island, as the increasing loss of land will lead to a reduction in their self-subsistence. People leaving the island has always been a reality in Barbuda, as in many other Caribbean islands. Like Puerto Rico, more Barbudans live abroad than on the island, with the largest concentrations in Antigua, New York City, and Leicester (UK). However, in a crucial difference with Puerto Rico, those Barbudans who have migrated have an inalienable right to return and receive the same three plots of land as a Barbudan living on the island. Displacement due to economic reasons is, therefore, not permanent. Older residents often return after having worked abroad for years. Barbudans we spoke to agree there is a need for an economic development plan, one that helps Barbudans establish businesses that benefit the community and provide opportunities for younger people. But investment should happen on terms defined by the community, with the preservation of community control over common resources, not for the enrichment of foreign companies or their political allies.

THE BENEFITS OF COLLECTIVE TENURE FOR COMMUNITIES CONFRONTING CLIMATE CHANGE

The Importance of the Caño CLT in the Face of Climate Change

Protection Against Community Displacements

Children in a Martín Peña school painted a sign and hung it on the fence outside. It said: "Neither Irma, nor Maria, nor anyone will take what's ours: our Community Land Trust." It was a response against the closure of schools, one of the Puerto Rican government's actions of expedited privatization and austerity in the months after Hurricane Maria. It illustrates the security residents feel when it comes to their CLT, despite the challenges that have followed Maria. Community leader of the G-8, Evelyn Quiñones, puts it this way: "The CLT gives us security. It's a giant that takes care of us, watches over us, and protects us." Community leader Carmen Febrés: "It's because of the CLT that we are still here after the hurricane. We will stay, whatever happens."

Displacement and gentrification have significantly increased after hurricanes Irma and María and the COVID-19 pandemic, in part driven by local and federal policies (Torres Nieves & Todas, n.d.). Santiago-Bartolomei et al. (2022) argue that storm impacts are associated with increased socioeconomic segregation and higher real estate activities in certain areas of the San Juan Metropolitan Area. In the period of October 2017 to January 2018, there was a 17% increase in the number of Puerto Rican migrants moving to the U.S. (Alexander et al., 2019). Many have returned, but it is estimated that 130,000 people permanently left the island after Maria, (US Census Bureau, 2018) including people from the Martín Peña communities. The number of beneficiaries of the generous tax incentives offered by the government of Puerto Rico to foreign investors that buy real estate and become residents of the archipelago under Act 22-2012 increased.[40] Between 2015 and 2017, the government issued 676 decrees whereas in 2018 alone, the year after Maria, it issued 630 decrees, with a total of 4,645 issued by July, 2022 (Estudios Técnicos, 2019). Out of 301

---

40 Under Law 22-2012 (currently a chapter of Ley 60-2019), individuals that become Puerto Rico bona fine residents by living in the archipelago 183 days per year and comply with other minor requirements, can apply for a 15-year renewable decree that provides full tax exemption on US federal income taxes, Puerto Rico income taxes on all dividends, interests, capital gains accrued after becoming a resident, as well as 75% of real and personal property taxes for property used for export, promotion, and trade services. In 2019, the government reinstated as a requirement that decree beneficiaries must purchase a home in Puerto Rico.

real estate transactions made by Act 22-2012 beneficiaries examined by the Center for Investigative Journalism, 46.9% were homes in the price range accessible to workers and professionals (Sutter & Sosa Pascual, 2018). Some of these investors have hoarded properties, increased rents, and evicted residents in neighborhoods like Puerta de Tierra in San Juan (Santiago-Bartolomei et al., 2022). Additionally, the number of properties dedicated to short-term rentals has increased exponentially, driven by disaster activity (Idem). In contrast to the increased trends of displacement and gentrification in neighboring communities, the CLT's collective regularization of land tenure has made their property rights more secure within this context. The CLT's perpetual holding of the lands has made the communities less vulnerable to the pressure of global land markets exacerbated by government incentives to attract wealthy foreigners and the lack of regulation of the short-term rental market and of policies directed to protect the right to housing.

Disaster Preparedness and Recovery through Mutual Aid

The grassroots organizing that is at the core of the CLT facilitated the immediate disaster recovery and prevented Maria from becoming an even worse disaster for the community. Mere hours after the hurricane residents, community leaders, CLT and ENLACE staff, and volunteers were helping (Figure 18). Carmen Febrés recalls: "The aid we brought was the first aid our community received [...] We brought cash, water, tarps for the roofs, milk, Pampers [...] We fixed the homes of some elderly people." Quiñones is critical of the government's response: "We can't expect anything from anyone. That's what we learned with Maria. We, the residents, went to the streets to help each other. If we would have waited for the government, things would have been worse."

In the Caño, residents and volunteers cleaned entire streets in a few days, preventing further cases of leptospirosis. The ENLACE offices became a hub for aid and volunteers, where water and other supplies were stocked and given out to residents. Community leaders prepared and distributed food on squares. Blue tarps to cover the roofs of the most damaged homes were delivered days after Maria, the Caño being one of the first communities in Puerto Rico to receive them, through a personal connection with FEMA. Quiñones links the help they received to their level of organization: "We've always been organized, that's why we received help. We are recognized, people know that the help they give will reach each one of the residents of the community." The G-8 prepared residents for the arrival of the hurricane.

Febrés recalls: "We organized in brigades and distributed leaflets house to house, talked to people, explained that [this hurricane] was going to be much more disastrous [than Irma] and that they needed to prepare." Each hurricane season since 2017 the G-8 gives advice to residents, digitally via social media, or in the form of leaflets, or by loudspeaker in the streets, on how to prepare and stay safe in case of a hurricane.

Figure 18: Community leaders distributing food to residents in the Martín Peña communities after Hurricane Maria. Source: G-8

The same grassroots organizing helped residents successfully lobby government. Caño residents also faced challenges getting FEMA assistance for the reconstruction of their homes after Hurricane Maria. Unlike other communities, residents living on CLT lands with surface rights deeds were able to present documentation and receive assistance. This was the main direct benefit of the CLT after Hurricane Maria–it regularized the land ownership for hundreds of households. However, those households living on CLT lands who had not yet received such deeds (for they had not yet initiated or completed the lengthy registration process) were initially denied assistance. CLT staff provided documentation proving that the families were collective owners of the land, which after long negotiations, FEMA ultimately accepted. Families living outside of CLT lands, but within the Martín Peña communities, however, have struggled to get the necessary assistance. CLT staff organized legal assistance workshops funded by the Foundation for Access to Justice with volunteer notaries to help residents (both those living on and outside CLT lands) fill out FEMA forms to receive the necessary assistance and help them with the appeal when denied assistance. Many residents were successful.

Community-led Climate Adaptation Strategies

Another issue that the Caño community leaders were successful in lobbying for was the assignment of the CDBG-DR funds to the Martín Peña communities. These funds could not be assigned to communities located in the floodplain, and 89% of the area surrounding the Martín Peña waterway was mapped as floodplain. Informed by community leaders, ENLACE sent a letter with comments about the Action Plan on the use of the CDBG-DR funds to the Secretary of Housing of Puerto Rico. It stated that the Plan "should allow for construction of new homes and reconstruction within the floodplain, wherever mitigation is feasible, and flood prone conditions will change as those mitigation activities are implemented." The letter argued that by approaching recovery on the basis of individual households with disregard to the context and community, and therefore, not allowing for on-site rehabilitation and new infrastructure, the Action Plan promoted displacement, rather than community cohesion and on-site recovery. The Martín Peña communities made it clear that the CDBG-DR funds should be used to support just climate adaptation strategies at the community level to address the lack of adequate storm water management, the lack of wastewater sewer systems, and implement the plan to dredge the Martín Peña waterway. This would avoid the recurring small-scale disasters of constant flooding, as well as improve the neighborhood to better withstand a future extreme weather event. At the time of interviewing in early 2019, the Caño residents for this research, the funds had not yet been assigned. Quiñones interpreted this as a displacement mechanism, using tactics of exhaustion: "The government doesn't want to give us these funds. It's a way to displace us. [...] People are tired of so many floods. [...] Now the Secretary of Housing says you can't build here because of the floods. Puerto Rico gets flooded, not just here. [...] They tell us: I'll help you, but you must leave immediately. I'll buy another house for you in another area." After three years of intense lobbying, in 2020 the government of Puerto Rico finally assigned CDBG-DR funds to the Caño. They are used to repair people's homes to meet increased building standards.

The Importance of Barbuda's Communal Land Ownership in the Face of Climate Change

Protection Against Community Displacements

After they returned from the forced evacuation following Hurricane Irma, Barbudans were able to gradually restore their community. As in the Caño, the grassroots organizing at the basis of the communal land system helped them to act as a united front against the attempts of the Central Government to privatize the land. No one applied for the government scheme to buy the land for one dollar, making it fail. Also, community leaders returned to the island after 30 days despite the government's efforts to keep the community away–by, for example, keeping the schools and the hospital closed. These leaders were able to start restoring buildings, roofs and communication equipment, and were able to gradually convince others that it was safe to come back. Barbudans also initiated four lawsuits against the government, some of which were at the time of writing this article heard at the London Privy Council, (Williams & George, 2022) the Commonwealth's court of last resort. These united actions helped restore the community and prevent displacement after the hurricane. In the words of a popular Barbudan song: "United as one body / Surely we stand tall / Ready to defend the rights we possess / Knowing deep inside our hearts / We are blessed / I believe I must take a stand / For Barbuda / My precious native land."

Disaster Preparedness through Common Resources

Communal land tenure is regarded as an essential condition for survival by John Mussington, the principal of Barbuda's secondary school, marine biologist, environmentalist, and community advocate: "Our land system is the reason we have survived. As simple as that. Our resources are a part of us. The mindset of the Barbudan is different. We are not looking at resources turned into billions." This control over the resources made them stronger to withstand the hurricane than those in Puerto Rico. After Mussington visited Puerto Rico during one of the exchanges we organized as part of the research this article is based on, he remarked: "The people in Puerto Rico, when they were hit by that storm, suffered a lot […]. One of the reasons there was that difference […] was that our resources were pretty much still intact, the services provided by resources in good conditions helped protect us from that storm. After the storm and the disaster […], we came through stronger, because [we] have access to marine resources, like lobster and conchs, so we fish ourselves. We have access to land, where we can farm, and our biggest concern right now, is to ensure that we maintain that control."

Thanks to the preservation of these resources, Barbudans can provide for most of their own food consumption, cultivated in small-scale backyards and agroecology projects. To a lesser extent, council provision grounds yield fruit and vegetable produce that has fed the community, but these grounds have been disregarded in recent years due to a lack of Central Government investment. In more productive times, there was a rotation of the use of provision grounds, leaving some grounds to rest for a few seasons, considering the dry and harsh Caribbean weather conditions. Individual claims on land would not work in these conditions (Frank, 2018), as everyone would be left without arable land. A typical daily menu in Barbuda today consists of locally caught, hunted, or grown products such as lobster, conch, shark, deer, chicken, okra, zucchini, eggplant, and other seasonal vegetables (Figure 19). In contrast, other islands in the Caribbean region on average import 83% of food consumed (Dorodnykh, 2017). In the event of disruptions in international food distribution chains, as they have after hurricanes (or more recently during the COVID-19 pandemic), these communities become prone to hunger (ECLAC & FAO, 2020). As in Puerto Rico, electricity on Barbuda was unavailable for several months after Hurricane Irma (also after Hurricane Luis in 1995). Without refrigerators, storing food was a challenge on many other islands. In Barbuda, however, lack of refrigeration did not mean hunger, as they had options. Mussington explains: "We got on the boat and went fishing. [...] We shared it among the community. A typical person in Antigua would not be able to do that, because they do not have the resources, or the skills."

Community-led Climate Adaptation Strategies

Communal land ownership in Barbuda helped preserve other natural resources, such as marine life, mangroves, wetlands, and dunes, managed in common. One third of the island is wetland, and housing is concentrated in the inland settlement of Codrington. Locals have never built along the fragile coasts, knowing it would make them more vulnerable, and that the coastline needs to be protected. Mussington notes: "They say Barbuda is undeveloped. We are more developed than other countries [...]. Our coastlines are intact, there is no built development, so the sand and the beaches and the wetlands are there. Those systems are crucial for protections against storms and flooding." With most homes built in concrete, housing is also generally more solid in

Barbuda than it is among low-income communities on Antigua and other Caribbean islands, where that sector of society often lives in wooden homes. Without cost for the land, a larger share of disposable income can be spent on the building. In a key difference with Puerto Rico, where household debt is high with a default rate that has hardly gone down since the 2007 financial crisis (Brown et al., 2016) Barbuda's household debt is negligible, according to our informants.

Figure 19: Daily menu in Barbuda. Source: Line Algoed

DISCUSSION AND CONCLUSIONS

Despite declarations made in the New Urban Agenda, signed by all countries at the Habitat III conference in Quito in 2016, to include collective tenure and community land trusts among the "policies, tools, mechanisms, and financing models," individual tenure is still urged after natural disasters. The two cases described in this article demonstrate how and why to adhere to the commitments made in this international agenda.

For the two case study communities, collective land tenure means more secure tenure, since residents are less prone to forced permanent displacements that typically follow natural disasters induced by climate change. The communities hold land with a high potential for lucrative tourism-focused real estate development, making them more prone to displacement, as governments and their economic allies in both countries seek to monetize land in desperate attempts to allure wealthy investors by integrating into global land markets. Renewed attempts by both governments to debilitate or downright dismantle the communal land tenure systems have been met with resistance of the communities. The bankrupt government of Puerto Rico used the hurricane and its recovery policies to renew attempts to push residents out of informally established settlements. Despite having recognized tenure through the Caño CLT, community groups had to fight for funds to help repair homes and make it possible for residents to remain in the area. The Central Government of Antigua and Barbuda amended the Barbuda Land Act and offered Barbudans to buy their plots of land, but the latter saw this as a threat to control over their land and commonly managed resources on which their lives depend. The communal land tenure systems in both communities have so far withstood these threats thanks to the unfaltering struggle of residents, who recognize that their permanence and survival depends on their collective land tenure. Both communities are convinced that individual land titles would be used to sell off the land to investors. Thanks to their collective property, residents have been able to push government policies to benefit the community collectively. The participation processes at the core of the communal land systems created stronger community links, making it easier to act as a collective political voice. The common control of resources has put power in the hands of the residents, who have prioritized environmental protection above profit-making.

With an increased number of storms and other disasters, and the growing need for investment in durable architecture, housing and infrastructure, tenure security needs to be addressed. In discussions on the connections between tenure insecurity and climate vulnerability, insufficient appreciation is made for the different potential impacts of individual title and collective title. Individual land titles for the communities under review would clearly decrease tenure security, and therefore make communities more vulnerable to climate change, which is the reason why these communities have not opted for or strongly resisted individualization.

With this paper, we challenge land tenure theory orthodoxy that holds that private property is inevitable and superior. This ideology drives governments facing the threats of climate change to continue to push for individual land titles, as the one model for securing land rights for vulnerable communities. Rather than protecting these communities, individual titles threaten to bring more tenure insecurity after climate disasters. Communal land tenure, as practiced in these two communities, represents a highly developed, sophisticated, and flexible land tenure method that facilitates just and equitable climate change adaptation. The traditional form of communal land tenure in Barbuda and the newer Caño Martín Peña CLT in Puerto Rico have protected the land rights of these communities and have helped mitigate risks brought by the climate emergency at the community level. These cases help underline views that one size does not fit all—and that there is an urgent need to rethink land tenure theory in the context of the present climate emergency.

Collective land tenure is also challenging, particularly in a context that privileges individual property rights and promotes housing as a commodity. Such arrangements can face resistance from community members; they are vulnerable to being undermined by hostile governments and powerful private interests. The key to its long-term survival is maintaining relevance to its inhabitants and proving its centrality to community flourishing. Successful collective tenures require continual community organizing, popular education, transparency, and participatory practices that ensure intergenerational dialogue, inclusion of the youth, and the capacity to adapt to changing contexts. The solutions embraced in prevailing recovery policies—be it the land regularization policies to address FEMA's requirements for property titles, risk mitigation strategies for households following Hurricane Maria in Puerto Rico, or the claim of Antigua and Barbuda's Prime Minister that land titles will give households access to loans to rebuild–all cast the response to climate change as an individual act. These policies exclude alternatives that are addressing the risks associated with climate change from a collective perspective, which make the community, as a whole, less vulnerable. If we want to foster more adaptive capacity in our communities, we need a policy environment around land ownership at the local, national, and international level that supports more plural, innovative, and flexible land tenure options.

CHAPTER 6

COMMUNITIES AS GLOBAL ACTORS IN COUNTERHEGEMONIC POLICY MOBILITIES

Lessons from the Community Land Trust Movement[41]

Authors: Line Algoed, María E. Hernández Torrales

Abstract

This article argues that the connectedness among low-income urban communities is often undervalued by supporting organizations and in policy mobilities studies. These communities are considered local case studies, disregarding their global relational dynamics. To illustrate their role in the circulation of policy ideas, we explore the global Community Land Trust (CLT) movement as commons-based resistance which continues to expand through community-to-community collaborations. Emphasizing the contributions of these urban communities to counterhegemonic policy mobilities is crucial to develop more effective approaches that address the needs of the "urban poor." Describing the global trajectory of the Caño Martín Peña Community Land

---

[41]   This article is published in the International Journal of the Commons: Algoed, L., & Hernández Torrales, M. (2024). Communities as Global Actors in Counterhegemonic Policy Mobilities: Lessons from the Community Land Trust Movement. International Journal of the Commons, 18(1), 53-65. *https://doi.org/10.5334/ijc.1217*

Trust from Puerto Rico, we argue that long-lasting social change—and a true commoning of knowledge—can only occur when grassroots organizations are recognized as active stakeholders in the mobilities process, rather than being treated as mere subjects of study.

Keywords:
Policy mobilities; policy; circulation; community; exchanges; Community; Land Trust; South-South; counterhegemonic policy; mobilities

INTRODUCTION

We recall a formative moment, drinking expensive wine with scholars and professionals after a conference in Paris where we each presented our work on land issues in the Global South. Someone who works for a network of community-based organizations supporting the "urban poor" in the Global South talks about her work of bringing these organizations together. When we ask about the already existing links between these organizations, she answers: "They are not connected globally, that's where we come in." This is an urbane moment, and we consider ourselves cosmopolitan internationalists. After this conference, we will travel to other cities around the world. We assume the communities we work with do not travel; they remain in place, and only connected to the international stage because of people like us, and the global networks we work for.

This article argues that the connectedness between communities of low-income urban dwellers is often ignored or undervalued in the work of supporting organizations, as well as in policy mobilities studies. These communities are seen as mere local case studies, and their relationality remains disregarded and unsupported. A "community," for us, is simply a place-based group of people. Members of the community may be part of some type of organization, which we call a "community-based organization." We examine the role of "supporting organizations," defined as those organizations (NGO's, networks, institutes, foundations) that assist communities or community-based organizations in planning or development. The tensions that arise between professionals/scholars—often, but not always, from the Global North, or from wealthier neighborhoods—and residents in these communities in the Global South need to be analyzed. We use the global Community Land Trust (CLT) movement, which continues to grow because of ongoing community-to-community exchanges, as an example to highlight the importance of these exchanges of experiences and best practices in introducing new policies and planning instruments in cities. A more explicit focus on the contributions of low-income urban communities to policy mobilities can help the development of more effective approaches to address the needs of the "urban poor," who will soon represent two-thirds of the global population (Barthold, 2019, p. 149). According to one of our respondents, social change is only possible if grassroots organizations are treated as stakeholders in the process, thus not merely as case studies.

CLTs are nonprofit organizations that hold land on behalf of a place-based community, while serving as the long-term steward for affordable housing on behalf of that community (CLT Center, n.d.-b). We consider a CLT a policy—and therefore useful to study in a policy mobilities context—as it is created for the benefit of the (low-income) communities it serves. According to John E. Davis, "[t]he CLT is guided by—and accountable to—the people who call this place-based community their home. One-third of the CLT's board of directors is nominated and elected by members who live on the CLT's land. One third of the CLT's board is nominated and elected by members who reside within the CLT's targeted "community" but do not live on the CLT's land" (Davis et al., 2020, p. 4). The first CLT, in the form we currently know it, was established by members of the Civil Rights Movement in Georgia, USA, after its founders were inspired by other communities living with a variety of collective forms of land holding across the world, as we will describe below. CLTs have now become a widely used land instrument internationally fighting gentrification and ensuring permanently affordable housing.

A new push in the global movement has happened when a CLT in a self-built neighborhood in San Juan, Puerto Rico, the Fideicomiso de la Tierra del Caño Martín Peña (hereafter "Caño CLT"), won the 2015–16 World Habitat Award (WHA), a prestigious prize awarded by the British nonprofit organization World Habitat (WH)[42] in collaboration with UN-Habitat. The Caño CLT is one of the first CLTs in Latin America and the Caribbean. Planned and designed in 2004 by residents of seven neighborhoods surrounding the Martín Peña waterway ("caño" in Puerto Rican Spanish), a highly polluted tidal channel that is part of the San Juan Bay estuary, the Caño CLT regularizes land ownership and prevents displacements, which might have otherwise resulted from the planned dredging of the waterway. The WHA raised the Caño CLT's international profile and intensified their solidarity with and outreach to

---

42   WH is a non-profit organization supporting innovation in housing policy and practice: https://world-habitat.org.

similar communities in other countries, as we will describe. This article is based on historical data of the CLT movement and on data from participatory-action-research (PAR) during several international exchanges that occurred between 2017 and 2022, which the authors helped organize to facilitate the discussion on community-led mechanisms to tackle conditions of poverty and urban displacements.

We start with an overview of literature on policy mobilities discussing the lack of explicit focus in much of this literature on communities' lived experiences and mobilizations, followed by an explanation of our methodology. Next, we examine how the global CLT movement grew from community exchanges. We recount how the CLT was introduced in Puerto Rico, and how the Martín Peña communities reshaped the original instrument to fit their own realities. We explore how, doing so, the Caño CLT became an example for communities in other parts of Puerto Rico and the world, studying some key activities and institutions that have supported grassroots exchanges. We analyze exchanges that happened between the Caño CLT and the Brazilian NGO Catalytic Communities, leading to the latter spearheading the creation of a CLT in Rio de Janeiro. Finally, we make conclusions on the importance of community-to-community exchanges in policy mobilities.

WHOSE IDEAS TRAVEL?

There is a vast body of contemporary literature looking at urban policy mobilities (e.g. (Peck & Theodore, 2010; McCann & Ward, 2011; Roy & Ong, 2011); McCann, 2011; Oosterlynck et al., 2019). This literature looks at how new policies get introduced in cities, how ideas for policies travel globally, and who are the "agents of transfer." The traditional approach to "policy transfers"—i.e., models to be "replicated" or "adopted" by worldly decision makers from a global marketplace of policy solutions (Theodore, 2019)—has been replaced by a policy mobilities approach. This approach is geographically sensitive to the importance of sociospatial contexts in creating and validating effective policy solutions, and the interconnectedness of policymaking locations (idem). Policies "rarely travel as complete 'packages,' they move in bits and pieces—as selective discourses, inchoate ideas, and synthesized models—and they therefore 'arrive' not as replicas" (Peck & Theodore, 2010, p. 170).

Analyzing the role of elites in variegated neoliberalization, these authors describe the "agents of transfer" mostly as worldly experts and elite communities of practice. McCann, for example, in proposing an Urban Policy Mobilities research agenda, lists the communities of policy mobilizers as "local policy actors, the global policy consultocracy, and informational infrastructures" (2011, p. 114). Peck and Theodore write that traveling ideas are "constructing symbiotic networks and circulatory systems ... enabling cosmopolitan communities of practice and validating expert knowledges" (Peck & Theodore, 2010, p. 170). McCann and Ward define policy actors as "politicians, policy professionals, practitioners, activists, and consultants" (2011: xiv), and describe how they are "shuttling policies and knowledge about policies around the world through conferences, fact-finding study trips, consultancy work, and so on" (idem). None of these categories do, at least not explicitly, include the actual people whose lives are affected by those traveling policies, specifically low-income communities in urban settings.

These low-income urban communities, however, are making significant contributions to these policy mobilities. Their ideas travel too, and this demands a more direct analysis. In less than two decades two-thirds of the global population will be low-income urban dwellers (Barthold, 2019, p. 149). It is therefore urgent to be more explicit about the strategies, tactics, programs, and instruments the "urban poor" develop—and how these subsequently travel and get translated into policies elsewhere—as these are direct responses to their most pressing needs. A new focus on their contributions to policy mobilities can help the development of policies that are more effective to address the needs in these communities.

The Global CLT Movement as Commons-Based Resistance

This article centers the role of communities in the global CLT movement, using the circulation of ideas around CLTs as land-based commons to explore how policies grow from the ground-up, thanks to community-to-community exchanges. "Land-based commons" refers to the rights to access, use, and transfer of land that are shared among a community—or the community is claiming the right to do so (Simonneau, 2019). As Susanna Bunce (2016, p. 135) puts it in her article on East London CLT activism: CLTs are fascinating examples of commons-based resistance against land commodification as they challenge traditional land regulation and ownership, while resisting speculation and capital accumulation in urban contexts.

Following a policy mobilities approach, the growing international CLT movement recognizes that no two CLTs are the same. Too many local elements are at play for CLTs to function alike. A CLT is therefore hardly a model (Davis et al., 2020, p.

xxviii). This word—model—suggests it can be "brought" in a package from one place (by default, the USA) to another, underestimating the community organizing processes that require the establishment of each new CLT. Similarly, the CLT is not an American model. The first CLT as we know it today was inspired by preceding forms of collective land tenure worldwide, as we will discuss. A growing number of communities around the world use key elements of the CLT: community-led development on communally owned land.

In tracing Liverpool's urban CLT movement, Thompson (2020) uses a policy mobilities perspective to analyze the assemblage of elements, components, discourses, practices, materials, and actors, sourced from both local and global contexts that make the movement. The intricate integration of globally mobile ideas with historical "place effects" generates, he says, novel compositions of policy models and social movements (2020, p. 85). Thompson highlights the importance of conferences and study tours in the dissemination of the CLT idea, which he refers to as "convergence spaces" borrowing the term of Temenos (2015).

There is a large body of literature that explores the importance of South-South learning in the circulation of best practices in urban policy. Of interest is the study by Claire Simonneau (2019) on the global circulation of CLTs between the USA, Belgium, and Kenya. Contributing to literature on South-South policy mobilities, she argues for fully reintegrating the South into the analysis of the circulation of ideas for urban policies, and for highlighting "non-dominant", nonconformist, anti-neoliberal ideas. Foregrounding the South into the analysis of the circulation of urban models allows us, she writes, to focus on drivers of change other than finance, such as human rights approaches, and anti-poverty strategies (Simonneau, 2019, p. 6). Françoise Vergès, (2021, p. 16) writing about the people who resisted against Western colonization, says: "Ignorance of the circulation of people, ideas, and emancipatory practices within the Global South preserves the hegemony of the North–South axis; and yet, South–South exchanges have been crucial for the spread of dreams of liberation."

Similarly, postcolonial theorists increasingly acknowledge that cities in the Global South do not adhere to Western-centric policy trajectories. Instead, these cities are recognized as fertile grounds for experiments that redefine the notion of "global" urban practices (Ong, 2011, p. 2). Jennifer Robinson argues against the academic division that centers theoretical approaches solely on the West, whereas the once-called 'third-world' is seen from a passive, receiving, development lens (Robinson,

2002, p. 531). In much of this literature, however, policymaking "from below" refers to the political agency of the city; the analysis fails to go further "down," i.e. to the level of the residents. The role of urban dweller communities—those most affected by traveling policies, and how they influence city policy—is, at best, implicit. When their role does get acknowledged, the analysis remains on the local—not the global—scale.

New International Solidarities

Many scholars have studied international solidarity and transnational activism as a vector for traveling ideas and policies. This literature indeed recognizes that ideas of social justice travel globally and are not just driven by local and national contexts. Temenos (2015, p. 15) argues that looking at who is able to be mobile, who is excluded from mobility, is a key question for the geographies of social movements. Almeida and Chase-Dunn (2018. pp. 1-3) discuss the influence of worldwide economic and cultural developments on social movements. But even in some of this literature on transnational social movements which recognizes the role that non-state actors play, the focus is mostly on NGO's or other types of supporting organizations (see for example Sikkink, 2005). The role members of urban communities play in the growth of these movements—or how these supporting organizations collaborate with the communities—is not made explicit.

Other authors do call for the inclusion of local people's experiences and mobilizations in policymaking. A "peopling" of urban policy mobilities research is needed to enrich urban policy mobilities research, Temenos and Baker write (2015, p. 842). Mehta et al. (2014), who studied the right to water in the Global South, observed the role of elite biases in policy making in the failure to achieve certain rights to environmental justice. "It is the poor who largely bear the brunt of environmental degradation and pollution," she writes, but "their interests are both ignored and by-passed due to elite biases." Baker et al. (2020) argue to advance our understanding of the role of "nonelite" actors in mobilizing policy knowledge and advocate for an analytical expansion "into the ordinary" involving often ignored actors who influence policymaking from the "front-line" or "street-level."

Crucial to our argument is Doreen Massey's (2011) term "counterhegemonic policy mobility," which denotes how this "ordinary" knowledge can challenge hegemonic thought and can alter power relations. She writes about the relationship between "relationality" and "territoriality" in policy circulation. According to her there is a contrast between a focus on connections (and lack of connections—"relationality"—on the one hand, and a focus on places, on the other"—"territoriality" (Massey, 2011, p. 3). Indeed, we see that the "relationality" between community-based organizations and communities—among themselves—is often underestimated (for example as described in the opening sentences of this article), undervalued, and understudied. Instead, their "territoriality" is exaggerated, seeing communities as mere local case studies. When communities are mentioned in literature, they are often described in the phrase "local communities", as if communities only act locally. Almeida and Chase-Dunn (2018, p. 1.3) in their study of the globalization of social movements agree that there indeed is a greater synchrony and connectedness among groups than currently described in literature.

Epistemic Justice and Traveling Knowledges

In earlier studies of international policy transfer, an "epistemic community" was understood as "a network of professionals with recognized expertise and competence in a particular domain and an authoritative claim to policy-relevant knowledge" (Haas, 1992, p. 3). In this view, knowledge can only be produced in institutions, universities, laboratories, companies, not in the everyday context of streets or communities. The ways in which such institutional knowledge or urban policies are actually based on the work of communities are ignored. Perhaps, this perspective is still partly in existence today. Contrasting to these earlier studies, in more recent literature on for example environmental justice, we read that "conflicts over the environment are epistemic struggles wherein other forms of the political, other economies, other knowledges are produced and theorized, and hegemonic worldviews are questioned and reformulated" (2016, p. 42). This applies equally to conflicts over the tenure, use, and development of land. To question the hegemonic worldview that individual forms of land ownership are the only path of development (e.g. De Soto, 2000) is to resist the whole epistemology of the political, economic, and cultural world system and its perceived absolute institutions. The radically different knowledge practices that emerge from these conflicts also travel; these ideas are mobile and influence other communities. The communities who resist injustices collectively construct another, counterhegemonic worldview. In these types of policy mobilities a global "counterhegemonic solidarity" (Massey, 2011, p. 5) emerges. Similarly, Arturo Escobar sees land struggles as fundamentally epistemic struggles: "The knowledge connected with these struggles is actually more sophisticated and appropriate for thinking about social transformation than most knowledge produced within the academy" (Escobar, 2016: 14). Without this knowledge actual social change becomes impossible.

Hess and Ostrom (2007, p. 5) describe knowledge as a commons: it is a resource that is jointly produced, used and managed by groups of varying sizes and interests. But the question we address in this article is: Who gets to participate in these groups that produce, use, and manage knowledge? Or better said: whose participation is acknowledged at the different levels at which knowledge construction happens—not just the local level? Participation in policy construction is emphasized as a crucial factor for successful commons management, by scholars such as Hayes and Murtinho (2023). However, granting decision-making rights to communities, they say, does not automatically guarantee inclusive or equitable decision-making processes. For a true commoning of knowledge all voices need to be heard, acknowledged, and made explicit.

Our article calls for the explicit inclusion of those voices in policy mobilities studies. It tracks the global CLT movement which results from community-to-community learning on collective land tenure and zooms in on the role of the Caño CLT in the circulation of ideas around CLTs in the Global South. Community-to-community exchanges of knowledge and ideas need to be included as a critical, highly effective component in the analysis of policy mobilities.

COMMUNITY-ENGAGED RESEARCH

Both authors of this article have directly supported the Caño communities during a period of eight and 20 years respectively. The first author got involved with the Caño communities since they won the WHA for which she was an evaluator. The data used for this article were collected during her doctoral research. The second author was on the Board of Trustees of the Caño CLT and instrumental in its establishment. Both authors are on the Executive Committee of the Center for CLT Innovation (hereafter "the CLT Center"), an organization we helped establish with the aim to encourage the international CLT movement and support community land trusts and similar strategies of community-led development on community-owned land in countries throughout the world.

The data we used for this article are retrieved from the historical archives of the CLT movement compiled by the two founders of the CLT Center, John E. Davis, and Greg

Rosenberg, and from interviews with people directly involved in the described events. We retrieved data from PAR with the Caño communities during 10+ international community exchanges that we helped organize. Our conclusions are also based on data retrieved from helping other communities establish CLTs, in the frame of a study conducted on the potential for CLTs in Rio de Janeiro for the Lincoln Institute of Land Policy (LILP) in 2018. We kept notes during these meetings and conducted in-depth interviews with participants and community leaders. The research was multi-sited, conducted in different locations where the community exchanges took place, in Puerto Rico, Brazil and online. We actively helped create these transnational networks and policy circuits that are used as the sites for this research, and these continue to develop and be active.

We do not claim to be "objective" observers of communities, as we are very much a participant in this research ourselves, with our own feelings, contradictions, and political stances. We employ the research method of autoethnography, inserting personal experiences in the analysis. Several events and partnerships in which we have been closely involved were critically analyzed, using emails, WhatsApp exchanges and personal fieldnotes as data. This method helps us address the paradox of being a researcher writing on behalf of the communities whereas we argue for their participation in all matters that affect them. Many of the ideas presented in this article are generated by members of these communities and the supporting staff, but we had the time and the university funding to do the largest portion of the work of writing it down. These divisions of responsibilities were discussed among all participants.

In her essay on "Situated Knowledges" Donna Haraway (1988: 581) writes: "I would like a doctrine of embodied objectivity that accommodates paradoxical and critical feminist science projects." Traditional ideas of "objectivity" are illusory, she says, all knowledge is constructed through social, political, and historical processes. But, as Sherry Ortner (2019) says, taking such an engaged feminist stance does not stand in the way of a commitment to the "principles of accuracy, evidentiary support, and truth," the basis of all scientific work. "The only difference," Ortner writes, "is that the biases of work that does not define itself as engaged tend to be hidden, while the biases of engaged [research] are declared up front."

THE COMMUNITY-DRIVEN HISTORY OF THE CLT MOVEMENT

The global CLT movement grew because of community-to-community exchanges. The first CLT, New Communities Inc., was founded in the 1960's by members of the civil rights movement. A community of tenant farmers in Georgia, USA, on land owned by white landowners was evicted because of their participation in the movement, after which they sought true economic emancipation through ownership of the land they had been cultivating for decades. Pooling money they bought 6,000 hectares, combining communal land ownership with individual home ownership and cooperative organization of agriculture.

Charles and Shirley Sherrod, among the founders of New Communities Inc. were inspired by other similar forms of landholding around the world, such as communal lands of different Indigenous peoples who live on indivisible collective land property with common use of the natural resources on which all depend. They were also inspired by the "land gift movement" in India, whereby wealthy people would donate land to groups of impoverished people. The donated land was to be held in "trust" by a village council and leased to local farmers (Sholder & Hasan, 2020). Another precedent is the moshav ovdim founded by Jewish settlers in the early 20th century on land in what was then Palestine and now Israel. The Moshavim are "workers' cooperative agricultural settlements," where the land was cultivated collectively, but households were managed independently by their members. The Sherrods, among others, went on a study trip in 1968 where they met residents of the moshav ovdim, after which they founded New Communities Inc. (CLT Center, n.d.-a).

Currently, there are around 545 CLTs around the world. No two of these CLTs are the same, never traveling as "complete packages," to use Peck and Theodore's phrase. This demonstrates the integration of a global idea—the combination of collectively stewarded land ownership with individual home ownership—with historical "place effects," which is what makes the CLT movement so diverse. Several CLTs were founded after community activists and professionals visited other CLTs or learned about them at conferences, demonstrating the importance of Temenos' "convergence spaces," and the role of supporting organizations.[43]

---

43   Three activists founded the Brussels CLT after visiting Champlain Housing Trust in Burlington during a peer exchange organized by WH (De Pauw & de Santos, 2020).

The Caño CLT: Born from Community-Driven Mobilities

The Caño CLT also demonstrates the importance of community-to-community exchange in policy mobilities. Learning about core elements of the CLT from residents living in one, Martín Peña residents created a new organization that serves their specific needs, living in an "informal" settlement, i.e. a neighborhood built without recognized ownership of the land. The Martín Peña communities are home to approximately 21,000 residents, and strategically located adjacent to the financial district. In the 1930's, impoverished landless farmers constructed precarious crowded towns on mangroves swamps along the Martín Peña waterway, looking for jobs in the city. By 1975, the government adopted on-site rehabilitation public policies and provided paved streets with sidewalks, potable water, and electric power. A law was enacted for families to acquire a formal individual land title for the symbolic price of $1 US, but in the Martín Peña communities, by 2002, almost half of the households lacked those titles. By that time, the waterway was completely degraded and contaminated, and life was harsh.

In 2002, the residents were informed of the government's plan for dredging the Caño. Represented by their elected community leaders, they demanded participation from the very beginning of the planning process. From experience, they knew that dredging would lead to gentrification, as it would make the area significantly more attractive. After two years of intensive participatory planning-action-reflection with 700 community activities assisted by professional urban planners and social workers, the communities were designated as a special planning district (the District).

They drafted a Comprehensive Development and Land Use Plan that contemplated community control of the 200 acres of the District. Residents without land titles expressed a need for secure and inheritable land tenure. After thorough analyses of the type of land tenure that would fulfill the expressed necessities, residents opted to explore the CLT, hardly known in Puerto Rico at that time. Needing to hear from someone skillful in CLTs, they invited Julio Henríquez, the then President of the Board of Directors and resident of the Dudley Neighborhood, Inc., a CLT in Boston, Massachusetts. This meeting reaffirmed that a CLT could address their needs, although it had to be transformed to their context with valid recordable perpetual surface right titles to the approximately 1,500 families that lacked security of tenure.

The Caño CLT was born because of this community mobilization. This CLT allows the restoration of the ecosystem, while avoiding the involuntary displacement of residents that such an infrastructure project would entail. The government transferred the 200 acres of public land within the District to the CLT. The CLT's Board of Trustees comprises a majority of members of the communities, who have control of the land within the District and made it available for the projects related to the dredging of the Caño and the construction of new infrastructure.

The Caño CLT as a Driver for Circulation of CLTs in the Global South

The nonconformist approach to addressing tenure insecurity and the community planning practices of the Caño CLT were recognized with the 2015–2016 World Habitat Award. Since then, the CLT became an inspiration for communities living in insecurity of tenure around the world. Residents actively engage in global solidarity work, driving circulation of ideas. This demonstrates they are not just a local case study (Massey's "territoriality"), but an actor of policy mobilities ("relationality"). First, this solidarity work led to the creation of two other CLTs in Puerto Rico, with a third one being considered. The Fideicomiso para el Desarrollo de Río Piedras is intended to revitalize the distressed economy of Río Piedras in San Juan and provide affordable housing for low- and moderate-income residents. The other CLT, the Fideicomiso de Tierras Comunitarias para la Agricultura Sostenible was created to acquire farmland and make it affordable for landless farmers. Another CLT is being considered in an African Puertorrican community in the municipality of Loiza. The community hopes a CLT will halt displacements, because investors, attracted by the astonishing ocean views, started grabbing land for short-term rentals after the 2017 hurricanes.

Secondly, the Caño CLT organized several international exchanges that drove the mobility of ideas around collective land tenure in the Global South, especially in "informal" settlements. The Caño CLT organized 10+ international exchanges with organized communities and accompanying professionals eager to learn new ways to alleviate the globalized housing crisis and strengthen ties of solidarity. In 2017 an international peer exchange was organized in collaboration with World Habitat hosting 14 professionals who traveled to Puerto Rico to learn about this new application of the CLT instrument. One of the participants was Greg Rosenberg from the USA who, inspired from what he learned during the visit, later co-founded the CLT Center to help support this innovation in CLTs, an initiative the authors of this article quickly joined, alongside Caño CLT staff. The CLT Center now promotes and supports CLTs and similar strategies in countries throughout the world. The Center also publishes under its imprint Terra Nostra.

In May 2019, 49 people from 17 different countries from Latin America and the Caribbean, Africa, Asia, Europe, and the USA traveled to the Martín Peña communities, sponsored by the Ford Foundation, to share strategies on fundamental rights and the strengths of collective land ownership in response to the major political economic, social, and environmental challenges. The methodology of these workshops facilitated critical thinking among community leaders, who were accompanied by one person from a supporting organization. Attention was given to community residents being a majority in the room, not the employees of the supporting organizations, which significantly influenced the dynamics of the sessions. People felt safe to share experiences and think of ways to overcome challenges, without professionals guiding the discussions based on what, according to them, is possible or not. It was a safe space to reflect on different forms of communal land tenure, not to be "trained" about the CLT instrument.

Figure 20: Community-to-community exchange hosted by the Caño CLT in May 2019. Source: Line Algoed.

In the evaluation of this exchange, participants said that by sharing experiences, they realized how global the fight for social justice and equity is. "This fight is everyone's, and collectively we are stronger," Caño community activist José Caraballo Pagán remarked. These experiences must be shared among those who face injustice, not (only) among professionals or scholars of these issues. It sounds like a truism to say that there should be no discussions about "the community" without members of that community participating; yet this still happens very often. "Nothing for us, without us," the T-shirt of a participant read (see Figure 20). In these exchanges the emergence of Massey's "counterhegemonic solidarity" becomes noticeable, by way of questioning ingrained institutions such as private property. "We are fighting ancestral battles against the displacement of our people," a participant said. These "convergence spaces" facilitate the discussion on epistemologies that may lead to social transformation. It is in these discussions that commoning of knowledge happens, acknowledging all voices and all levels at which knowledge construction happens—a global, not just local level.

The global connectedness/relationality generated by these peer exchanges materialized after Hurricane Maria hit Puerto Rico in 2017. The Martín Peña communities were severely affected: 75 families were left without homes, approximately 800 roofs were lost or severely damaged, and 70 percent of the community's land was flooded with contaminated water (Algoed & Hernández Torrales, 2019). The international work of the Caño CLT was the foothold for an immediate response from the Puerto Rican diaspora and people from around the world. "We've always been organized, that's why we received help. We are recognized, people know that the help they give will reach each one of the residents of the community," a Caño community leader remarked in an interview, demonstrating the importance of the CLT's global connectedness (including with diasporic networks) in the community-driven hurricane response. Resources for swift relief were provided, facilitating recovery, and ensuring the safety of residents (Vincens, 2017).

The Relation between Communities and Supporting Organizations

One of the most salient contributions of the Caño CLT internationally has been the exchanges with Brazilian nonprofit organization Catalytic Communities (CatComm)[44] and favela residents in Rio de Janeiro (see Figure 21). With funding from the Lincoln Institute of Land Policy (LILP), a think tank based in Cambridge, Massachusetts

---

44   CatComm is an American/Brazilian NGO supporting Rio's favelas since 2000 through empowerment, research, and advocacy at the intersection of community development, human rights, communications, and urban planning (Catcomm.org).

(USA), the Caño CLT and CatComm conducted a research project to study the feasibility of establishing similar CLTs in other informal settlements in the Global South, specifically in favelas in Rio de Janeiro. LILP has been a crucial actor in the global circulation of land policies for decades. Their publications in the early 2010's have facilitated the dissemination of knowledge on CLTs, leading to new CLTs emerging across the Global North (see e.g. Davis, 2010). Thanks to the importance of the Caño CLT for other informal settlements in the Global South, the LILP took a renewed interest in CLTs.

In organizing the research project on the feasibility of CLTs in Brazil, it needed to be stressed that the Caño CLT residents had to be directly involved, and that it should not just be carried out only by appointed researchers, who were not favela or Martín Peña residents. In an article published by a fellow of the LILP, it appeared that the Caño CLT initially was seen as a local initiative and a powerful case study, but not as an active participant in the internationalization of CLTs in informal settlements. The article described that the Caño CLT was "one of the first attempts to create a CLT in an informal area," and that "the Lincoln Institute is supporting [Catalytic Communities'] efforts to ascertain the legal and political feasibility of CLTs in Brazil" (Flint, 2018). The Caño's leading role was set aside. The Caño CLT and CatComm pushed back, insisting that an exchange between the communities should be central in these efforts. Later, the LILP recognized how important it had been to actively involve the community in this and other projects (CLT Center, 2021).

Figure 21: Exchange between Caño CLT and a Favela community in Rio de Janeiro, August 2018. Source: Line Algoed.

This suggested that there was a different understanding about the role of professionals. One of the reasons of success in the Caño is that from the onset the community leads in the discussions on why CLTs may be a potential way of addressing tenure insecurity. Professionals take a step back and collaborate by providing sound information that would help residents in the decision-making process when needed. The role of professionals is to accompany the community's own thought process, not to suggest to them a certain "model" or instrument. The residents of the community must be a majority in the room, and the conditions should be conducive to ensure they do not feel intimidated when participating with professionals. In the Caño, community social workers were involved from the beginning to facilitate—not to lead—the planning-action-reflection process. Lawyers, urban planners, architects, and engineers only stepped in after the community had defined its goals; professionals would then help to implement that vision. If professionals lead, they may guide the discussions towards what is possible and what is not possible, according to them, possibly stifling ambitions. Organizing an exchange on the potential of CLTs in favelas in Rio without community leaders present would have given a completely different outcome. Eventually, a community-to-community exchange took place in Rio in August 2018 with a strong presence of community leaders, which successfully led to the creation of the organization "Favela CLT," who are supporting pilot CLT projects in three favelas, with increasing interest across Brazil. In December of 2021, thanks to the efforts of this organization and numerous community leaders, a first Brazilian law acknowledging the CLT was approved, effectively making the CLT instrument a reality (Termo Territorial Coletivo, n.d.). The exchanges between Favela CLT and the Caño CLT continue with regular virtual meetings and other visits of the Caño CLT staff and community leaders to Brazil. In this example, we clearly see the connectedness among low-income urban communities, which brings about transnational commons-based resistance to land commodification.

CONCLUSION

Policy mobilities scholars and organizations supporting low-income urban communities often underestimate the relationality of these communities, instead focusing on their territoriality. The history and current development of the CLT movement—and specifically the role of the Caño CLT—demonstrates that policy ideas do travel among communities which leads to noteworthy counterhegemonic solidarity movements. We have argued that these communities need to be recognized as key actors in policy mobilities if we want to truly understand how effective policy solutions are created and validated, and how social transformation happens.

We described how the idea of a CLT found fertile ground in the Martín Peña communities through a visit from a community leader living in the Dudley Neighbors CLT in Boston, USA, at that time also the President of the Board of Trustees of this CLT. Martín Peña community leaders found convenient the idea of this form of collectively stewarded land ownership to put a halt to speculation and community fragmentation that had been happening in the decades prior. Yet, they did not "adopt the model;" it was not "transferred" to their community. Instead, during a two-year in-depth community-led "planning-action-reflection" process, Martín Peña leaders designed a whole new application of the CLT, using key elements from existing CLTs and devising others to serve the specific needs of their communities. Subsequently, these ideas traveled around the world, creating a movement of communities sharing lifeworld concerns. The example of the Caño Communities does not represent a "transfer process" of any "model" intended to "solve" problems. In narrating this success story, our aim is rather to prompt scholars, professionals, and consultants to recognize the pivotal role that communities play in generating ideas that evolve into public policies capable of addressing situations and problems. Although quite different from the elite networks described by policy mobilities scholars mentioned in this article, in this grassroots movement we also clearly see that ideas mutate in the circulation process, and that global mobile ideas conglomerate with historical place effects.

Massey's term of counterhegemonic policy mobilities has been useful to understand how these South-South circuits are challenging power relations. Communities are learning from each other to question the hegemonic worldview that prescribes individual forms of land ownership as the only viable path of development. We see this questioning and the ensuing creation of new applications (or the continuous protection) of collective forms of land tenure as "commons-based resistance" against the political, economic, and cultural world system and its perceived absolute institutions.

We have argued that, if we are to consider knowledge as true commons, all those who produce, use, and manage knowledge need to be included in the analysis. These communities are sharing ideas and influencing policy, and an explicit focus on their contributions to policy mobilities—at local and global levels—can help the development of more effective approaches to address the needs of the "urban poor" who will soon represent most of the world population.

This work is far from completed. The transnational networks and policy circuits described continue to develop. Recently, for example, a new initiative was launched inside the CLT Center to support the circulation of knowledge and best practice on collective land tenure in Latin America and the Caribbean, which will be led by the Caño CLT and CatComm. To be continued.

CHAPTER 7
CONCLUSION

This study has looked at the critical role of communal land ownership amidst the climate emergency, spotlighting two historically marginalized Caribbean communities: the Martín Peña communities in Puerto Rico, and Barbuda, part of the twin state of Antigua and Barbuda. Both communities reside in environmentally fragile yet resource-rich areas and embrace communal land systems. Concentrating on the aftermath of the 2017 hurricane season, this research investigated external influences contributing to the production of vulnerability (vulnerabilization) within these communities and examined their resistance strategies and resultant knowledges.

The study frames the 2017 hurricane season as a turning point for a heightened awareness of vulnerabilization in the Caribbean region. Both communities witnessed the prioritization of international capital interests over local needs, particularly evident in a focus of foreign elites on coastal land. Following the hurricanes, a surge in land grabbing by political and economic elites occurred in both countries, aided by policies favoring individual land titles. Under the pretext of safety concerns, authorities mobilized vulnerability discourse to justify deregulation, displacement, and attempts to replace the population. Community strategies leveraging communal land to counteract these vulnerabilization processes involved mobilizing the community organization processes inherent to communal land structures to prepare for, aid during, and recover from storms while establishing mechanisms for sustained long-term support. They coordinated collective responses to government policies perpetuating vulnerability and used collective regularization and communal resource stewardship for recovery. Legal avenues were taken to defend community rights and resist oppressive measures, exercising control over development initiatives to align with community interests in climate change adaptation. Both communities gave priority to preservation of natural environments.

Despite hegemony of private land ownership, communal lands still encompass most of the Earth's surface. By centering tenure plurality, this study offers a different perspective on property, contending that forms of communal land are not just an alternative to the norm of private ownership. By exploring the Caribbean's intersection of colonialism and climate change, this study seeks to uncover connections between land tenure systems and global crises. It argues that these Caribbean communities are decolonizing property notions and redefining human-earth relations, rooted in struggles against colonial legacies accelerating environmental degradation. Communal land ownership emerges as a vital strategy in confronting the climate emergency and challenging the narrative that private land ownership is the only path for development.

Rather than framing these communities as passive disaster victims, the study portrays them as active agents crafting crucial counterhegemonic knowledges "from below," transcending local boundaries to inform global responses. Countervailing Caribbean perspectives on land ownership and ecological thought provide a pathway away from land as mere property. This approach acknowledges the intricate relationship between communities and the land, challenging Western sustainability narratives used to justify land and resource expropriation. Ultimately, the study advocates for a reevaluation of land ownership paradigms, stressing the need to amplify local voices and strengthen countervailing knowledges to navigate the challenges posed by the climate emergency.

SUMMARY OF THE FINDINGS OF THE CHAPTERS

The overarching research question of this study was formulated as: "In what ways do communities use communal land tenure as a shield against the impacts of climate change and resist vulnerabilization processes produced by political and economic elites?" This question was addressed in four empirical chapters: detailing vulnerabilization and resistance processes in the Caño Martín Peña area in Puerto Rico (Chapter Three), examining similar processes in Barbuda (Chapter Four), analyzing in what ways these communities use communal land as a shield against vulnerabilization (Chapter Five), and exploring the epistemological mobilities of the Caño CLT in a final chapter (Chapter Six).

Chapter Three looked at the Caño CLT, highlighting how political and economic elites produce and perpetuate residents' vulnerability in self-built communities while championing the Caño CLT's effectiveness in countering this process. It stressed that self-built communities, such as those in the Martín Peña area, are located in environmentally fragile zones, often making them the most in need of post-disaster assistance. However, due to their geographically strategic locations, they become targets for land grabs. The chapter dissected the assumed connections between informality and vulnerability, illustrating how these notions fuel public support for displacements. By documenting the resistance of Martín Peña communities, the chapter underscores the importance of real democratic participation in disaster recovery. Instead of reconstructing the country to withstand future natural disasters through democratically and locally managed renewable energy and food systems, along with heightened environmental standards, the Puerto Rican government persisted in "sustaining the unsustainable," exacerbating socio-environmental inequalities by deregulating environmental standards in favor of real estate development, leveraging the financial crisis and aftermath of Hurricane Maria to further this agenda.

The Caño CLT, along with the community organizing underpinning this collective land tenure system and the strategic partnerships built around it, exemplifies a more democratic approach to planning for social and ecological sustainability while resisting displacement. Empowered by collective land ownership, which made them one of San Juan's largest landowners, Martín Peña residents exert political influence to challenge government authority and control urban development. Against the backdrop of profound neoliberal globalization and colonialism, they crafted an urban landscape aligned with their values, departing from market-driven development in favor of socioecological preservation and co-existence with landscape.

Chapter Four examined similar processes of vulnerabilization and resistance on the island of Barbuda. It argued that Barbuda serves as a crucial locus for understanding the persistence of colonial land use ideologies rooted in the concept of private property.

Following Hurricane Irma, the interplay of neocolonialism, the coloniality of power, and decolonial resistance became starkly evident on this island. My co-author and I frame Barbuda's struggle against private property and related development paradigms as a battle for survival, not only of the well-being of its people and environment but also of the preservation of its unique geographical and knowledge-based practices that reject the separation of humans from nature. Despite narratives of sustainability employed to justify land expropriation, Barbudans' preservation methods were sidelined, perpetuating a centuries-old hierarchy wherein locals are viewed as needing guidance and improvement to align with external interests, reinforcing dependency and producing vulnerability. Development projects, purportedly aimed at post-hurricane recovery, offered limited employment opportunities while ultimately dispossessing residents of communal resources and leaving them impoverished. Barbuda's resistance emerged as a decolonial struggle, challenging hegemonic ideas and narratives while advocating for an alternative worldview that sees land as essential for survival, particularly in the face of climate crises. The island's example calls for the urgent study of epistemologies that counter colonial thinking and practice, offering a path forward for reimagining relationships with land and challenging dominant paradigms of property, progress, development, and sustainability.

Chapter Five explored the interplay of the two case studies, examining how urgent it is to understand the nature of secure land tenure in the context of climate change. My co-authors and I explored the resistance of the communities in Puerto Rico and Barbuda against pressures for individual land titling, a narrative often pushed by governments and aid agencies, even more so after disasters strike. Residents advocated for preserving and enhancing collective land rights to address climate realities, challenging the prevailing notion of individual private property as inevitable and superior. Instead, they endorsed tenure plurality to strengthen adaptive capacity in the face of the climate emergency. Drawing from ethnographic data, my co-authors and I illustrated how collective land tenure provides vital benefits for communities confronting the consequences of climate change-induced threats. It shields against forced displacements, facilitates disaster preparedness and recovery through mutual aid, and empowers community-led adaptation strategies. Despite the pressures of lucrative tourism-driven real estate development, residents in both Puerto Rico and Antigua and Barbuda resisted individual land titling, recognizing its threat to their collective control over essential resources. Through community solidarity and collective action, they protected communal land systems, advocating for policies prioritizing community well-being over profit-making. Real participation processes inherent in communal land tenure fostered stronger community ties and enable collective political action, with a shared focus on environmental protection. In contrast, individual land titling policies promoted by governments—be it the land regularization policies to address FEMA's requirements for property titles, risk mitigation strategies for households following Hurricane Maria in Puerto Rico, or the claim of Antigua and Barbuda's Prime Minister that land titles will give households access to loans to rebuild—overlooked the collective dimension of climate change adaptation, further vulnerabilizing communities.

Finally, Chapter Six emphasized that low-income urban communities' interconnectedness is frequently overlooked by supporting organizations and in studies on policy mobilities, which tend to treat them as local case studies, disregarding their broader global dynamics. To illustrate their role in disseminating policy ideas, my co-author and I explored the global CLT movement as a form of commons-based resistance, expanding through community-to-community collaborations. We highlight the contributions of these urban communities to counterhegemonic policy mobilities, crucial for addressing the needs of the "urban poor" effectively. The Caño CLT's recognition with the World Habitat Award in 2015–2016 served as a turning point, inspiring communities worldwide grappling with tenure insecurity. Through international solidarity work, the Caño CLT helped to drive the circulation of ideas, challenging perceptions of being merely a local case study and becoming an active participant in policy mobilities. By fostering "counterhegemonic solidarity" through international exchanges, the CLT questions entrenched institutions like private property and encourages discussions on transformative epistemologies.

This global connectedness proved invaluable during Hurricane Maria, with the CLT's international networks enabling a swift community-driven response. Furthermore, the CLT's exchanges with organizations like Catalytic Communities in Rio de Janeiro underscore its significant role in the internationalization of CLTs, also in non-Western contexts, highlighting the power of counterhegemonic solidarity movements spurred by shared struggles and the exchange of ideas among communities worldwide. We argued that enduring social change and genuine knowledge sharing require grassroots organizations to be recognized as active stakeholders in the mobility process, rather than passive subjects of study. Central to our argument is Doreen Massey's concept of "counterhegemonic policy mobility," emphasizing how ordinary knowledge can challenge dominant ideologies and change power dynamics. We asserted that while the relationality between community-based organizations and communities themselves is often underestimated, undervalued, and understudied, their territoriality is exaggerated, portraying communities as mere local entities, thereby limiting our understanding of their broader impact and interconnectedness.

The next segment of this concluding chapter is structured into different sections, initially addressing the research sub questions before answering the main research question. The initial two subquestions give an account of the dynamics of vulnerabilization and resistance within the two Caribbean communities ("What happened?"), also describing the differences between them, while the final subquestion examines the implications of these dynamics and their intersection with decolonial epistemologies ("What does this mean?"). The response to the main research question then synthesizes these insights.

VULNERABILIZATION AND RESISTANCE THROUGH COMMUNAL LAND IN PUERTO RICO AND BARBUDA

Research sub question 1: In what ways are these communities being vulnerabilized through land encroachment?

I studied the intricate nexus of political and economic forces that culminate in the production of vulnerability, particularly evident in historically marginalized communities grappling with the aftermath of natural disasters and the consequences of climate change. Throughout the preceding chapters, my co-authors and I examined how the devastating 2017 hurricane season served as a catalyst for political and economic elites to vulnerabilize these communities, pushing forward a free-market agenda through persistent land encroachment and prioritization of land titling programs.

The post-disaster vulnerabilization process in both locations can be summarized as follows, elaborated for each community below:

- In the wake of the disaster, recovery efforts in both communities disproportionately favored foreign capital (real estate interests) over addressing local needs.
- A surge in land grabbing activities by political and economic elites ensued in both communities following the hurricanes, aided by policies that prioritized individual land titles.

- Utilizing the pretext of "uninhabitability," "unsustainability," and safety concerns, authorities in both islands mobilized the discourse around vulnerability to justify deregulation, displacement and attempted population replacement.

Vulnerabilization in Puerto Rico

Disaster Recovery Focusing on Foreign Capital. The preceding chapters described the pivotal role land played in the unfolding of disaster capitalism in Puerto Rico. Following Hurricane Maria, a surge of external investors flocked to the island, aggressively acquiring land, particularly in desirable coastal regions. This rush drove property prices upward and catalyzed the process of gentrification (Marcos & Mazzei, 2022). The Puerto Rican government's tax incentives fast tracked this phenomenon, their significance magnified in the wake of the hurricane's devastation. During my fieldwork, I had a meeting with Lyvia Rodriguez Del Valle, the former Executive Director of the Caño CLT, a central person in my work and a co-author in Chapter Four. Our meeting took place in a lively open-air bar nestled along the trendy Calle Loiza in the Ocean Park coastal district of San Juan. As she animatedly shared her insights on the island's experience of disaster capitalism, while I observed the clientele, predominantly Americans in fashionable surfer attire, Lyvia remarked, "After Maria, Americans came to realize that Puerto Rico belonged to them."

In Chapter Five, we described one of these tax incentives, the controversial Law 22-2012 (now a component of Law 60-2019), which grants full tax exemption on US federal income taxes, Puerto Rico income taxes on dividends, interests, capital gains, and 75% exemption on real and personal property taxes for properties used in export, promotion, and trade services. Importantly, these incentives required beneficiaries to purchase property in Puerto Rico, facilitating land rushes. Almost half of these real estate transactions fell within a price range accessible to local workers (Suárez et al, 2022). In a manifestation of David Harvey's accumulation by dispossession (2004), investors, such as cryptomillionaires or tech workers, are thus leveraging these tax incentives to buy up affordable housing, hoarding extensive property holdings and building real estate empires. This was disaster-driven, with an increase of up to 31% in average daily Airbnb listings after Maria. Many of these properties are turned into short-term rentals, escalating rents, and displacing residents in neighborhoods across the island (Santiago-Bartolomei et al., 2022). Grappling with these escalating costs of living, unprecedented numbers of Puerto Ricans left the island.

Emphasis on Individual Land Titles Targeted at Displacement. In Chapter Three, we described how Hurricane Maria spotlighted the extent of "informality" in Puerto Rico's housing stock. Many households live in "informal" neighborhoods, characterized by a lack of formal ownership of the land, or in housing that was built without building permits or without following building codes. This type of building had been disregarded, tolerated and even supported for decades due to the government's failure to provide affordable housing for low-income households. Governor Rosselló's response post-Maria was to forcibly "clear" informal areas and encourage residents to transition to "safe, formal ownership" (O'Leary & Chiriguayo, 2018), targeting displacement.

We described how the Puerto Rico Disaster Recovery Action Plan in Response to 2017 Hurricanes Irma and Maria ("the Action Plan") presented for the use of the first $8.3B CDBG-DR funds promoted the displacement of vulnerable communities, even where on-site risk mitigation was feasible. The housing strategy focused on providing individual families options to relocate outside the floodplain and prohibits reconstruction and rehabilitation within the floodplain. We argued that flood reduction was feasible in the Martin Peña area, and that denying the possibility to build in the current floodplain above the flood level can have the effect of displacing families in need.

In Chapter Five, we described how federal and national policies placed a heavy emphasis on individual land titles and required Puerto Rican households to present property titles to receive assistance from FEMA and other disaster recovery programs. As a result, thousands of families, or 60% of all applicants, were initially denied FEMA individual assistance to pay for repairs, because they could not prove that they owned their homes. This also disadvantaged those living in self-built settlements without formalized tenure, even though they were the ones most in need of that assistance.

Similarly, in this chapter we detailed how the Action Plan presented the "Home Repair, Reconstruction, or Relocation Program" (R3) which only served households with documented home ownership. The "Title Clearance Program" addressed that lack of documentation, but only by providing individual land titles to households. Both programs excluded properties located in floodplains, despite those areas hosting 10% of the island's housing structures, often low-income areas most in need of assistance who could have used these funds to significantly mitigate risk at a collective level.

Conversely, construction permits are being approved within floodplains in wealthier coastal areas, demonstrating the double standards in these recovery practices.

One of my research collaborators, Evelyn Quiñones, a G-8 community leader, interpreted the allocation of funds as a mechanism of displacement driven by what we have termed "tactics of exhaustion." Remarking that the government's reluctance to disburse funds is a way to displace their communities, Quiñones observed how their weariness of incessant flooding is exploited. Despite floods being a common issue across Puerto Rico (and many other areas suffering from other risks such as landslides or earthquakes), the then Secretary of Housing insisted on immediate relocation from flood-prone areas, offering to purchase alternate housing elsewhere.

Discourse of Unsafety and "Unsustainability." Former Governor Rosselló's assertion that self-built neighborhoods must transition to "safe, formal ownership" implicitly labeled these communities as inherently vulnerable. In Chapter Three, we dissected these presumed connections between informality and vulnerability, revealing how such notions are mobilized to garner public support for displacements. Housing informality is painted as "unsustainable," portraying residents as too susceptible to withstand future disasters, thus justifying their relocation. We noted that many of these informal settlements occupy the island's most environmentally fragile yet ecologically and geographically valuable areas. Recovery strategies prioritizing private property rights facilitated the acquisition of land by foreign investors, perpetuating the vulnerability of residents in these settlements. This occured even as the use of funds in these neighborhoods could mitigate risks. The absence of private land titles considered tenure ambiguous and presupposed vulnerability among residents, disregarding alternative forms of land tenure and their potential in collectively addressing risks. Our examination looked into the "politics of unsustainability," (Blühdorn, 2013) revealing how the post-hurricane Puerto Rican government promoted the deregulation of environmental standards to prioritize real estate development. This deregulation, solely aimed at attracting investment, prioritizes economic interests over the well-being of the population and the safeguarding of the environment.

Vulnerabilization in Barbuda

Disaster Recovery Focusing on Foreign Capital. In Chapters Four and Five we detailed the aftermath of Hurricane Irma in Barbuda, describing how the Central Government of Antigua and Barbuda favored foreign capital over addressing urgent local needs. Exploiting the hurricane's chaos by evacuating the community, the Central Government initiated the construction of a new international airport during the period of enforced evacuation of the local population. This move lacked approval from the Barbudan people or the Council, and an environmental impact assessment was not presented. The construction was a fulfillment of promises made to luxury real estate developers, most notably Robert De Niro's "Paradise Found" and the Barbuda Ocean Club by John Paul DeJoria's "Peace, Love and Happiness" (PLH) partnership, whose target clients are global financial elites[45] in another clear manifestation of accumulation by dispossession. Not restoring the schools, the hospital, and other essential services such as the ATM, was also an example of the tactics of exhaustion, making the restoration of community life difficult.

In the same post-disaster period, the Central Government greenlit the development of a lavish $2 billion residential community under a ninety-nine-year land lease deal with PLH. Teaming up with Discovery Land Company, DeJoria and partners started construction of 450 exclusive residences and a golf course for the ultrawealthy on the island's pristine beaches of Coco Point and Palmetto Point—the latter being protected by the Ramsar Convention on Wetlands. When the journalist with whom I produced the documentary and I flew to Barbuda in a tiny propellor plane from Antigua, we saw how the newly constructed golf course on Palmetto Point area was completely flooded. When we asked Barbuda activist Gulliver Johnson about this, he remarked,

> "Of course! The water comes not only from the sea, but from below. These are wetlands, that's how it works. No matter how much digging you do there, how many pumps you put there, how much money you put in, you can't just recreate what has taken nature millions of years. Look, we know that, but they obviously didn't think that through at PLH."

Emphasis on Individual Land Titles Targeted at Displacement. In the same month as the coerced evacuation, Browne made significant amendments to the

---

45 A friend in Barbuda calls these projects places "for the billionaires to get away from the millionaires" (Imran Thomas, personal conversation, 2020).

Barbuda Land Act. Like in Puerto Rico, this deregulation was also an example of the "politics of unsustainability" as it was solely aimed at accommodating investment and prioritized economic interests over the well-being of the population and the safeguarding of the environment. The revised act effectively dismantled communal land ownership, removing the clause guaranteeing collective land ownership to the people of Barbuda and stating that Barbudans now possess "the right to purchase the freehold interest in land situated in Barbuda" (Barbuda (Amendment) Act, 2018). The development approval procedure was also seriously curtailed, no longer required permission or consultation of the people. To secure private land ownership, Barbudans were required to apply and purchase the deed to the land on which their residence stands for the nominal price of 1 EC$. The other two allotted plots would be obtainable at market price. Browne called the communal ownership a "myth," falsely stating that no developed country has communal ownership, and underlining the supposed necessity of private property for national progress.

We described how, in stark opposition to this amendment, Barbudans vehemently rejected the proposed scheme, contending that it aimed to fragment and displace the community, to pave the way for the integration of Barbuda's land into the global real estate market, as speculators acquire deeds and the privatization of communal areas, notably the coastal regions. These coastal areas, pivotal for protecting the population during hurricanes, serve as natural defenses. Mangrove areas and other wetlands act as flood zones, while the presence of natural dunes impedes water flow. The plan to level these dunes for construction, eliminate mangrove wetlands, replace Indigenous flora, and introduce sewage and pollutants poses an imminent threat to the fragile ecosystems, undermining local climate change mitigation strategies. The establishment of a coastal real estate market, ostensibly designed to aid Barbuda's economic development and post-hurricane recovery, is causing environmental harm and vulnerabilizing Barbudans.

During my interview with John Mussington for the documentary on Barbuda's struggle, he passionately expressed his frustration as we waded through mangrove wetlands. Rather than helping the community in adapting to climate change, he argued, they are being further vulnerabilized:

> "For years, we have had the solution and actually practicing it, and when you are now hearing of a development policy and you're going to be taking out things like this (pointing at the mangroves) […]. How can you justify

that when you're taking out the insurance policies that you have and the things that allow us to withstand climate change. This is what protects us, and the world. That's why it's so important to us" (Bulckens & Algoed, 2023).

Discourse of Unsafety and "Unsustainability." Much like the Maldives government's post-tsunami actions, as described by Naomi Klein, Gaston Browne of Barbuda labeled the island as "unsafe" and "barely habitable" to rationalize the evacuation of its population. Much like in Puerto Rico, residents were portrayed as too vulnerable to withstand future disasters, thus justifying their relocation. Similarly, like in the Martín Peña area, Barbuda is an environmentally fragile yet ecologically and geographically highly valuable area. Chapter Four explored how this discourse of "uninhabitability" and safety concerns conveniently aligned with the political and economic interests of the prime minister and his allies. They perceived the disaster and the subsequent emptying of the island as an opportunity for self-enrichment.

Furthermore, we described how the discourse of "unsustainability" has been actively propagated also by PLH. In an interview with the Barbuda Channel, Justin Wilshaw, the project president, articulated their mission to "assist, guide, train, and educate" the local population, with promises of environmental improvements such as creating wetlands and bolstering dune resistance. Their website echoes this, declaring efforts to restore Barbuda's pristine environment, highlighting the global wetlands destruction and how "until recently, the island of Barbuda followed this same tragic trend" (BOC, n.d.). However, Barbudans do not need such interventions, as they have historically safeguarded their coastline and wildlife through environmental knowledge-practices recognizing the interconnected web of life over centuries. Despite daunting challenges, Barbudans have successfully shielded their coastlines from the rampant development prevalent in other Caribbean islands.[46]

Both communities illustrate the themes explored in this book's literature review and theoretical approach, demonstrating that disasters do not necessarily result in a flight of capital. Rather, reconstruction endeavors tend to prioritize the concerns of foreign investors over local necessities. Residents face an onslaught of hypercapitalism and

---

46   These discourses of unsustainability are a standard technique of dispossession of land and resources. In the novel "Crooked Plow" geographer Vieira Junior describes a scene where in a context of modern slavery, people organize to fight for their land rights. "They even forbid us from fishing, with the excuse of protecting the rivers— but we are the protectors. We're a part of this" (2023)

fresh enclosures reminiscent of colonial frontiers, facilitating capitalism's global spread into once-overlooked areas like the Martín Peña communities or pristine islands such as Barbuda. This underscores the perpetuation of what Harjo (1991) termed "a half millennium of land grabs and one-cent treaties." In line with decolonial thought, I conclude that inhabitants are positioned as "naive savages" requiring rescue, education, and development, appropriating land to conform to production methods benefiting only a small group of people.

Research Sub Question 2: How are these communities resisting this vulnerabilization, mobilizing their communal land tenure systems to halt the encroachment?

Framing the 2017 hurricane season in the Caribbean as a turning point—referred to as "the Hurricane Moment" by Sir Hillary Beckles (Popke & Rhiney, 2019)—marking a heightened awareness of the links between disasters and colonialism, as well as of the use of disasters for vulnerabilization in the region, this book examined the strategies employed by these communities in leveraging their communal land to counteract the processes of vulnerabilization delineated in the preceding section. Both the Martín Peña communities and Barbuda residents have employed their land structures as a shield against practices that render and keep them vulnerable, concurrently engaging in diverse forms of resistance against exploitative actions.

The resistance efforts within these communities can be synthesized as follows, elaborated for each community below:

- Harnessing the foundation of community organization inherent in communal land structures to prepare for the storm, offer mutual aid during the storm, orchestrate immediate recovery efforts after the storm, and establish mechanisms for sustained long-term mutual support.
- Coordinating collective responses to governmental policies and practices that produce and perpetuate vulnerability.
- Deploying collective regularization and communal stewardship of resources to foster recovery.
- Engaging in legal avenues to defend community rights and resist oppressive measures.

- Exercising control over development initiatives to align with community interests in context of climate change adaptation.
- Prioritizing the preservation of natural environments within communal territories.

Resistance against Vulnerabilization in Puerto Rico

The Martín Peña community strategically utilized their land system as a shield against exploitative actions aimed at capitalizing on their vulnerabilities. In the words of community leader Quiñones: "The CLT gives us security. It's a giant that takes care of us, watches over us, and protects us." Throughout the entire hurricane ordeal, from initial severe weather warnings to the aftermath, the Caño organizations—namely, the CLT, Proyecto ENLACE, and G-8—exhibited advanced levels of organization. They mobilized effectively, disseminating crucial information and distributing essential provisions to support residents. Chapters Three and Five elaborated on how the G-8 prepared residents for the hurricane's arrival and how communities promptly responded to the crisis, recognizing that waiting for government assistance would be too slow. Besides facilitating vital material aid, this response empowered residents to retain agency post-disaster, rather than being relegated to the status of victims—an aspect essential for community recovery following catastrophes as articulated by Oliver-Smith (2005).

In Chapters Three and Five, we illustrate how these organizations, by leveraging their communal land system, orchestrated a coordinated response to challenge government practices perpetuating vulnerability. This involved addressing issues like the misallocation of CDBG-DR funds, which failed to reach the most disadvantaged communities, and the imposition of reconstruction and rehabilitation restrictions within flood zones. By underscoring the feasibility and importance of neighborhood-level risk mitigation and genuine participation in disaster recovery, they asserted their presence in national post-disaster discussions. Warning against the potential displacement of families in need, the communities successfully advocated for the redirection of CDBG-DR funds towards equitable climate adaptation strategies at the community level. Through their advocacy for equitable climate adaptation, the Martín Peña communities aimed to make a lasting impact on residents' overall well-being and fortify defenses against future weather extremes.

In a similar concerted effort, community leaders addressed FEMA's decision to exclusively assist households with ownership documents. This highlighted the CLT's significant impact post-Hurricane Maria: by regularizing land ownership for numerous households, residents on CLT lands with surface rights deeds could furnish documentation and receive aid, unlike those in other self-built communities. Initially, households on CLT lands lacking such deeds faced assistance denials. However, CLT staff furnished legal documentation proving collective land ownership, which FEMA eventually accepted after prolonged negotiations.

This illustrates how, unlike the rising trends of displacement and gentrification in adjacent San Juan communities, the CLT's collective regularization of land tenure has bolstered property rights amidst climate change. Legalized through Law 489-2004, the CLT's perpetual land holding has mitigated vulnerability to global land market pressures, exacerbated by government incentives to attract affluent foreigners to invest in Puerto Rican property.

We elucidated how the communal land effectively empowered the community with governmental tools and resources, democratizing planning for social and ecological sustainability. Their endeavors to safeguard the natural mangrove waterway environment while asserting their right to remain in the area illustrate the possibility of "coexistence between humans and the planet" (Escobar, 2016, p. 14) and their anti-Cartesian approach to the land.

Resistance against Vulnerabilization in Barbuda

Barbudans similarly leveraged their land system as a protective barrier against exploitative actions increasing their vulnerabilities. Like the Martín Peña communities, they demonstrated remarkable levels of community organization throughout the entire hurricane ordeal, from the first weather warnings through the aftermath.

Chapter Five delineated how the community collectively rallied in response to the disaster: fortifying homes before the hurricane, providing refuge to neighbors during the storm, and collaboratively orchestrating recovery efforts such as communication restoration and food distribution. Their shared access to food rendered them less vulnerable compared to other islands, as Barbudans predominantly rely on locally sourced food from small-scale backyard cultivation, agroecology projects, fishing, and hunting—traditional practices that sustain them.

This collective control over resources helped them withstand the hurricane better compared to counterparts in Puerto Rico. Chapter Five further examined how this collective control was mobilized against the escalating threats of displacement and gentrification observed in Puerto Rico and other Caribbean islands. Despite government efforts to deter their return post-disaster—such as by keeping schools and hospitals closed—Barbudans who returned 30 days after the hurricane initiated building restoration, roof repairs, and communication equipment reinstatement. Gradually, they reassured others of the safety in returning, countering attempts to keep the community away.

In Chapters Four and Five, we look into how Barbudans orchestrated a unified response to challenge governmental practices perpetuating vulnerability. Following Hurricane Irma, when the Central Government amended the Barbuda Land Act allowing Barbudans to apply for private land titles of their home plots for a nominal fee of 1 EC\$ (US\$0.37 USD), very few Barbudans did so, effectively stalling land privatization sought by the real estate developers flocking to the island post-disaster. Subsequently, the Barbuda Council worked towards establishing a Collective Title covering the entire island to counteract the amendments to the Barbuda Land Act.

Moreover, over recent years, Barbudans have initiated four legal cases against the Central Government. These legal battles encompass contesting the repeal of the Barbuda Land Act, scrutinizing the construction of an international airport without Barbudans' consent, challenging the controversial Paradise Found Act, and contesting the amendment of the Crown Act, which diminishes the Barbuda Council's authority over land and resources. In November 2023, the Privy Council heard a case brought forth by two Barbudans against the Central Government, contesting the Eastern Caribbean Court's decision to deprive them of the right to challenge the commencement of the new international airport's construction. In February 2024, at the time of writing this conclusion, the Privy Council ruled in favor of the two Barbudans, granting them the right to challenge the construction, emphasizing its violation of local consultation laws and threat to fragile ecosystems (GLAN, 2024).

Throughout the preceding chapters, we showcased how communal land in Barbuda has preserved community control over development allowing the protection of natural resources such as marine life, mangroves, wetlands, and dunes—essential ecosystems for climate change adaptation. With one-third of the island comprising wetlands and housing concentrated in the inland settlement of Codrington, locals have refrained from coastal construction, recognizing the need to safeguard the coastline to protect the community.

Both communities embody the ontological struggles described earlier. These struggles advocate for a world "where many worlds fit" (Escobar, 2023) challenging the colonial and patriarchal legacies of the "world-as-resource," (Ghosh, 2021, p. 76) privileging separation, appropriation and exploitation. This endeavor epitomizes the decolonization of the concept of property, particularly in urban and tourism-centric areas.

Differences Between Communities in Vulnerabilization and Resistance

In the preceding discussion, my emphasis was primarily on explaining the shared experiences of vulnerabilization and resistance within the two communities. Yet, there are also significant disparities that exist between them. Firstly, a fundamental contrast lies in their respective communal land systems. The Martín Peña communities have used a relatively new form of collective land tenure through the establishment of a CLT, while Barbuda has a deeply ingrained and refined communal land structure cultivated over centuries. Both were safeguarded by legal frameworks. Although the Barbuda Land Act has been significantly amended, effectively dismantling communal land ownership, the longevity of Barbuda's communal land imbues it with a sense of stability that leads to a broader segment of the island population defending it compared to the relatively new CLT in Puerto Rico, where even in the Martín Peña communities some residents are against it, citing fear of tax increases or a perceived sense of tenure security even without official documentation.

Secondly, disparities in sovereignty status distinguish the two islands. Puerto Rico is a non-sovereign present-day colony, whereas Barbuda is part of a sovereign twin state. Nevertheless, Barbuda's reliance on the more dominant Antigua underscores the enduring coloniality of power.

Thirdly, while in Puerto Rico residents strive for restoration of the natural environment through the dredging and cleaning of the mangrove waterway, in Barbuda the battle is for preservation of natural resources. In the fourth place, the notion of community diverges substantially between the two locations. The Martín Peña district is a highly diverse arrival neighborhood, characterized by a dynamic influx and efflux of residents coming from various Caribbean nations (such as the Dominican Republic, Haiti, Colombia and Venezuela), while Barbuda has a close-knit, longstanding population with intricate familial ties spanning generations.

Finally, engagement with global networks manifests differently across the communities. The World Habitat Award given to the Caño CLT launched them into the sphere of global housing advocacy and Right to the City movements, also fortifying their ties with the global CLT movement. Conversely, Barbuda's diaspora assumes a more important role, facilitated by the right to return, with many individuals returning to the island after extended periods of overseas employment while maintaining close contact with the island. Additionally, Barbuda's integration into global legal frameworks reinforces their capacity for resistance through legal avenues.

Research Sub-question 3: How do these Caribbean land struggles shape emerging decolonial epistemologies on land property, fueling a counterhegemonic worldview?

In this section I analyze the importance of the knowledges produced by the struggles of these communities. I discuss how these struggles unveil enduring colonial legacies and generate lessons for sustainability. The importance of these knowledges is summarized as follows:

- A radically different imaginary of relating to land emerges from these struggles.
- These knowledges unveil the enduring legacies of colonialism in property (the coloniality of property).
- The struggles to defend collective land rights is characterized as decolonial resistance.
- These knowledges travel to construct a counterhegemonic worldview that is crucial as we move towards a more sustainable future.

A Radically Different Imaginary of Relating to Land. In my study, I responded to urgent calls by scholars to understand other ways of relating to the land (e.g. Bhandar, 2018, p. 193). I contended that these communities play a pivotal role in shaping a radically different imaginary of land relations, unveiling the colonial roots embedded within the concept of private property. Through their determined resistance against encroachments and affirmation of communal ownership, these communities directly confront the prevailing narrative that privileges individual ownership and exploitation of land.

Furthermore, they illuminate the persistence of plurality of land tenure regimes. In the Martín Peña communities, the workshops held prior to the establishment of the CLT fostered discussions on various tenure forms, emphasizing that private titles are not the exclusive avenue for securing rights like permanence and improved living conditions, or for coexisting with a restored mangrove waterway. Similarly, in Barbuda, the insistence on alternative tenure models underscores their validity, rejecting the notion that they must conform to Western frameworks, a supposed condition for progress. Instead, they assert the full development and efficacy of their property system, aligning closely with their needs and aspirations. Collectively, these examples disrupt the dominance of private property and advocate for a more varied approach to land ownership and governance. They lay the groundwork for a significant shift in how we perceive and engage with land.

Enduring Legacies of Colonialism. The persistent emphasis on private property as the sole "developed" mode of land relations is a deeply entrenched colonial notion. I illustrated how this belief continues to dictate which ownership forms are deemed legitimate. Authorities in both islands have long abided by land titles, even prior to the hurricanes, as a means of assimilation of land into the global market, perpetuating colonial land policies. These titles are also mean to turn its inhabitants into proper "citizens" who do not endanger the safety and progress of the nations. I described how the hurricanes further intensified these policies.

Another enduring colonial concept is *Terra Nullius*, which still influences land tenure, enabling the appropriation of land for the benefit of a select few at the expense of many. Wherever tenure diverges from private property, it is often labeled as confusing, "empty," or "wasted," terms which serve as justifications for its seizure. These ideologies manifest in the communities central to this study. In Puerto Rico, the existence of numerous "informal" self-built communities represents such confusing tenure systems, leading to policies that prioritize land titles, often resulting in displacement under the guise of safety concerns and the hindering of national development or national safety (informality as a threat to the social stability of Puerto Rico). Similarly, in Barbuda, Prime Minister Browne dismissed communal land ownership as a "myth" and as an impediment to national progress, stating that Barbudans occupy the land "informally." This discourse had to justify the displacement of Barbudans or the pushing through of private land titles and major development projects not wanted by Barbudans and reflects Western values that dictate land improvement and ownership, marginalizing those who do not conform to these standards.

Communities practicing communal land ownership are frequently depicted as "uncivilized" or underdeveloped due to their land relations, another enduring colonial legacy. Browne's derogatory remarks towards Barbudans, labeling them as "deracinated imbeciles" for defending their communal land system, exemplify the coloniality in his attitude toward land. Such attitudes suggest that those who adhere to different land-holding practices require "civilizing," echoing the stereotypes that underpinned the colonization of the Americas as well as the land allotment programs (Harris, 1993). This perpetuates the notion that epistemological, ontological, and cosmological relationships with land are inherently "savage," as articulated by Tuck and Yang (2012, p. 5). Moreover, the billionaires flocking to Barbuda enticed by PLH's "spectacular private resort community" (BOC, n.d.) and tech millionaires gravitating towards Puerto Rico to purchase coastal property evokes the concept of Bhandar's "Self-possessive individual" (2018) or Wynter's "Man, which overrepresents itself as if it were the human itself" (2003). These individuals now hide behind a discourse of "development" through tourism, disregarding the demands of the local population to have a say.

This book delineated the intricate links between land, colonialism, capitalism, and climate change, as evidenced in the struggles of these Caribbean communities. Barbudans are embroiled in a relentless battle against the destruction not only of the web of life sustaining them but also of the enduring thought systems that have sustained their existence for centuries. Similarly, residents of the Martín Peña area are fighting to preserve alternative land relations that serve their needs, advocating for formalizing their ties to the land and asserting their right to live alongside an ecologically restored mangrove waterway, which protects not only their communities but the entire island.

The post-hurricane land encroachments my co-authors and I chronicled in both islands resonate with Malcom Ferdinand's notion of "Colonial inhabitation," (2022) wherein land is seized for the benefit of a privileged few, enforcing a singular mode of inhabiting the world that subjugates both lands and peoples to the desires of colonizers. Furthermore, the experiences of both islands during and after the 2017 hurricanes echo Bonilla's concept of the "Coloniality of disaster," (2020) wherein disasters unveil and exacerbate existing inequalities rooted in entrenched racial and colonial histories. These land encroachments also evoke Patel and Moore's notion of "Colonial frontiers," (2018) characterized by continual expansion into so-called "unconquered" territories, where always more places are created to serve market interests, a crucial factor in enabling the global land rush. These connections highlight the lasting imprint of colonialism on land struggles, ecological degradation, and conceptions of ownership, prompting us to critically assess and challenge these legacies as we strive for a more sustainable future.

Decolonial Resistance. In these settings, I perceive the resistance of these communities as inherently "decolonial," actively defending their non-extractive relationships with the land. Their resistance challenges fundamental tenets of post-Enlightenment thought which have contributed to the ongoing environmental crisis by delineating a separation between humans and nature. Land for them is not measured for its exchange value, nor is it an investment product; rather, it is a crucial community need. It is not a resource "turned into billions" as Mussington put it. This stance opposes the global land grab jeopardizing both people and environments while upholding knowledge-practices that prioritize land as vital for community and for life. These struggles highlight the persistence of common land, with half of the world's surface being commonly held, countering the notion of private property as a natural state or universality.

In the Martín Peña area, land equals community; in Barbuda, land is synonymous with life. Ultimately, this book foregrounds these representations of property. This resistance embodies Casimir's concept of the "counter plantation system," (2020) emerging from parallel knowledge systems. Additionally, it resonates with Wynter's idea of the "plot system," (1971) a cultural guerilla resistance to the plantation system wherein the "land remained the Earth." The provision grounds and backyard gardens in Barbuda, along with the small community gardens in the Martín Peña area, exemplify these resistant responses to the widespread lack of food sovereignty across the Caribbean region.

This resistance gives rise to 'epistemologies of the land' that transcend physical boundaries, encompassing the universe, including water bodies, beaches, and mangroves. This sharply contrasts with colonial perceptions of land as devoid of meaning. Martín Peña resident Caraballo Pagán eloquently expressed this thinking: "Waterways are living things. They don't talk, they don't walk, but they flow, they have a life. They grow. And when you've lived next to something that you saw as a young person, with a life of its own, to see it just die out, it affects your mind" (UNC, 2018).

Studying the struggle of these communities, we can conclude that mainstream interpretations of "sustainability" are steeped in Western paradigms, often serving to perpetuate existing power structures and practices. In Chapter Four, we examined how the rhetoric of sustainability is manipulated to uphold the status quo, exemplified by PLH's Barbuda Ocean Club. This project purportedly aims to restore vital dunes and wetlands crucial for the entire island's protection, yet paradoxically, it destroys these ecosystems to erect a golf course catering to a select elite. Ironically, the very colonial practices that have contributed to our current environmental crisis, persist under the guise of sustainability, reducing land to a mere commodity for exploitation.

In contrast, this study centers Caribbean perspectives on "sustainability," foregrounding communities disproportionately affected by climate change. Rather than being passive victims, they produce invaluable insights into climate adaptability, embracing methods that transcend land's utilitarian value. By foregrounding these perspectives, I seek to broaden the discourse on sustainability and amplify the voices and experiences of historically marginalized communities in shaping more equitable and effective approaches to environmentalism.

Counterhegemonic Mobilities. As Angela Davis put it when saying, "local issues have global ramifications" (2016, p. 95) this study asserts that the experiences of these communities transcend mere case studies. Instead, they offer profound insights that challenge conventional notions of local communities' "territoriality" and underscore their "relationality," in line with Massey's terminology (2011). By acknowledging the interconnectedness between communities combatting poverty, colonial oppression, and climate change, the knowledges emerging from struggles to defend collective rights hold transformative potential. This matters not only for communities grappling with similar challenges but also for a broader counterhegemonic worldview, essential for a more sustainable future.

I illustrated how these insights travel beyond their immediate contexts. Initiatives like the "Stronger Caribbean Together" project, involving the Martín Peña communities, Barbuda, and various other Caribbean regions confronting similar challenges related to climate change and ensuing disaster capitalism, exemplify the dissemination of transformative ideas. Furthermore, exchanges facilitated by the Martín Peña communities have spurred the establishment of Favela CLTs in Brazil, demonstrating how these insights transcend geographical boundaries and inspire similar movements globally. Ultimately, this interconnectedness of social struggles holds the promise of "collective liberation," (Davis, 2016) emphasizing the significance of international solidarity and shared knowledge in confronting systemic oppression and fostering a more equitable and sustainable world.

Building on what is written above, I now formulate a general answer to the main Research Question.

Main Research Question: In what ways do these communities use communal land tenure to resist against the consequences of climate change and the vulnerabilization imposed by political and economic elites?

In the preceding sections, I outlined the processes of vulnerabilization within these communities and highlighted the emergence of counterhegemonic knowledges and strategies providing a platform for resisting these processes. Expanding upon these discussions, I now present a comprehensive response to the main research question. The ways in which communal land protects these communities against the consequences of climate change and vulnerabilization can be summarized as follows:

- Communal land protects communities against post-disaster displacements caused by encroachment from foreign capital, ensuring the permanence of communities.
- Communal land helps nurture a stronger sense of community.
- This stronger sense of community serves as a foundation for mutual aid initiatives, amplifies political influence, and fosters international solidarity.
- Communal land embodies an understanding of the interconnectedness between humans and nature, nurturing the formation of counterhegemonic 'epistemologies of the land.'

This study has illuminated how the communal land systems in the Martín Peña area and Barbuda, serve as protectors against the widespread displacements often triggered by severe hurricanes, such as those witnessed in 2017. These displacements are not random occurrences; rather, they result from policies that systematically dispossess communities, especially in areas where land tenure is ambiguous, as seen in the case of "informality" in Puerto Rico or the contested land system in Barbuda, which lacks recognition from the majority government of Antigua.

Through my research, it has become evident that the post-disaster emphasis on private land titles is aimed at integrating these territories into the global property market, thereby subjecting them to the pressures of the global land rush. This trend is observable through the proliferation of short-term rentals in Puerto Rico, driven by policies emphasizing the "visitor economy," as well as the rush on "pristine" beachfront real estate in Barbuda. However, the pursuit of such titles poses a direct threat to the sovereignty, self-determination, and benefits derived from these lands, often falling prey to foreign capital interests. In Barbuda, these benefits manifest in the form of common resources, including wildlife, fish, and the island's serenity, while in the Martín Peña area, they encompass strategically located urban lands near public transport hubs and the advantages of residing alongside an ecologically restored waterway.

The communities have used communal land as a shield against the encroachment of external forces, safeguarding their sovereignty and self-determination against major odds. Despite concerted efforts by governments and their economic allies, these communities have resolutely retained control over their land and its resources, fortifying their sovereignty. The main direct benefit of the Martín Peña CLT after Hurricane Maria is that it regularized the land ownership for hundreds of households which facilitated receiving FEMA assistance, which in turn allowed residents to reconstruct their homes *in-situ*. Even those households living on CLT lands who had not yet received surface right deeds and who were initially denied assistance, were aided by CLT staff and the G-8 with documentation proving that the families were collective owners of the land, which after long negotiations, FEMA ultimately accepted. In Barbuda a direct benefit of living with communal land for centuries is that it has allowed residents to spend larger amounts of their household income to build concrete homes that are relatively more extreme weather-proof than the wooden homes observed in similar communities in other islands. Thanks to the preservation of common resources, Barbudans can also provide for most of their own food consumption, cultivated in small-scale backyards and agroecology projects. After the hurricane freshly caught fish and hunted meat was readily available to share among the whole community.

Another benefit of communal land is that it helped nurture a stronger sense of community. This stronger sense of community is captured by Martín Peña community leader Juanita Otero, who reflects,

"The greatest achievement is for the eight communities to speak the same language. We were close physically and, despite having so many things in common, we were not working together. Now we can support each other" (Hernández Torrales, 2007: 794).

Similarly, during my interview with Martín Peña youth leader Zorimar Rodríguez, she echoed this sentiment, stating, "The CLT created a sense of belonging. Before we were divided, and that made us more vulnerable. Now, together, we have control over our own future." This collective empowerment is also depicted on one of the murals in the Martín Peña area. A parallel sentiment is expressed in a popular song I first heard at an ecumenical church service during Barbuda's Homecoming event, ten months after Hurricane Irma. Hundreds of Barbudans gathered under a tent erected for the occasion, sang together:

"United as one body / Surely we stand tall / Ready to defend the rights we possess / Knowing deep inside our hearts / We are blessed / I believe I must take a stand / For Barbuda / My precious native land."

This sense of community has been leveraged in impactful ways facing the hurricanes. Firstly, it facilitated mutual aid efforts throughout various stages of the hurricanes: residents collaborated before the storms hit, assisting each other in preparations such as boarding up windows and safeguarding documents. Amid the hurricanes, mutual support continued as residents provided shelter and maintained contact for as long as possible. People told me agonizing stories of rushing out during the deceitful calm of the eye of the storm to check on neighbors. Immediate recovery efforts were also driven by the community itself, without reliance on government assistance. As articulated by Martín Peña community leader Quiñones, "We, the residents, went to the streets to help each other. If we would have waited for the government, things would have been worse."

Secondly, this stronger sense of community bolstered political influence, countering government actions that threatened further vulnerabilization. The Martín Peña communities successfully advocated for the allocation of CDBG-DR funds to their area. In Barbuda, few residents participated in the government's land purchase scheme, leading to its failure. Despite forced evacuations, community leaders initiated restoration efforts and gradually persuaded others to return, despite governmental delays in restoring essential services. Strengthened by this restored community, led Barbudans to pursue legal action against the government through four lawsuits.

Lastly, the sense of community and grassroots organizing facilitated the establishment of international solidarity networks crucial to the recovery process. Quiñones remarked, "We've always been organized, that's why we received help. We are recognized, people know that the help they give will reach each one of the residents of the community." Similarly, in Barbuda, Mussington noted, "We have the eyes of the world following what's going on here." Their organizing efforts have garnered significant media coverage in major international news outlets.

Communal land embodies a profound awareness of the vital interconnectedness of humans with land and nature, emphasizing co-existence in mutually enhancing ways, as articulated by Escobar (2016, p. 14). This perspective views land not merely as a resource but as a nurturing force essential for life and the reproduction of a common shared by all, resonating with decolonial feminist ideologies (Escobar, 2023). In this context, communal land helps to mitigate the consequences of climate change. Land becomes necessary for survival, echoing the ethos of Indigenous communities worldwide. The stewardship of communal land serves to preserve nature and its indispensable ecosystems, including vital natural barriers such as mangroves, wetlands, dunes, and beaches, crucial in mitigating climate change impacts. It is this acute consciousness of nature's functions that drives community leaders in their determined advocacy for its protection.

This consciousness represents a significant form of knowledge that transcends individual communities facing similar challenges. It contributes to the formation of vital counterhegemonic 'epistemologies of the land,' which challenge the dominant discourses of "sustainability" wielded by the "colonial inhabitation" of those who exploit communities for the benefit of a privileged few. In essence, this consciousness not only serves as a guiding principle for communal land management but also as a catalyst for collective liberation of systems of oppression, fostering solidarity and empowering communities to reclaim agency over their land and futures.

IMPLICATIONS

In its contribution to disaster studies, this research underscores the pivotal role of communal land in understanding the intricate interplay between land tenure security and climate vulnerability. By centering the perspectives of affected residents, this study sheds light on the experiences of communities grappling with the impacts of climate change. It highlights that these communities are not passive victims of natural disasters but active producers of invaluable knowledges regarding disaster preparedness, collective risk mitigation strategies, and post-disaster recovery efforts. Furthermore, this book advocates for the integration of decolonial perspectives in disaster recovery frameworks, acknowledging the colonial legacies embedded within disaster narratives and policies. It emphasizes the importance of recognizing and preserving existing community-led risk mitigation practices, rooted in local knowledge, which are often overlooked in disaster management approaches. It also calls for a critical stance towards narratives of "sustainability", employed to justify land and resources expropriation.

This research contributes to decolonial feminist research by emphasizing the imperative for feminist methodologies that is not just about centering the experience of women but as much about closely collaborating with historically marginalized communities, who are further vulnerabilized by climate change. In line with these methodologies, it underscores the importance of taking an engaged stance in research, rather than merely indulging in academic critique, as well as being upfront about political and emotional biases. This decolonial feminist perspective also emphasizes the enduring colonial ontology of patriarchy on the way land is used, thus on the way space is organized, perpetuating appropriation, conquest, domination, and subjugation. I argued, thinking with the work of authors such as Sylvia Wynter, Brenna Bhandar, Arturo Escobar, Malcom Ferdinand, Amitav Ghosh, and Robert Connell that this ontological framework, epitomized by Cartesian dualism between humans and nature, lies at the heart of the planetary crisis we face.

Integrating critical environmentalism into decolonial thought is therefore crucial, acknowledging that Global South communities bear the disproportionate burden of climate change, and that its roots are embedded in colonial legacies. Furthermore, this research underscores the inherently political and cultural nature of all fields within geography. It highlights how landscapes, whether beaches, mangroves, dunes, or glaciers and volcanoes, are inherently connected to humans and produce meaning. Through this study, the significance of land as a bearer of meaning is underlined, revealing the interplay between space, culture, and history. This specifically matters to those fields studying these landscapes, i.e. (Physical) Geography, Biology, Environmental Studies, etc.

In the realm of land policy, this research untangles the colonial origins of land titling programs and their implications for the ongoing expansion of capitalism dating back to colonialism. It emphasizes that land policy initiatives such as land regularization programs, necessitate the active involvement of communities at all stages. Specifically, in the context of CLTs as tools to combat gentrification, evictions, and dispossession, this research underscores the importance of recognizing CLTs as resistant responses to oppression, rather than mere instruments that can be implemented from above without real participation from communities. By contextualizing CLTs within broader struggles against systemic injustice, this research highlights their potential to liberate communities and challenge hegemonic structures of oppression.

Limitations and Research Outlook

During presentations at conferences, seminars, or guest lectures, I was often asked questions regarding potential shortcomings within these communities. It seemed as though I was portraying communal lands through rose-tinted glasses, depicting idyllic scenes where people, untouched by capitalistic individualism, coexist harmoniously amidst picturesque landscapes. Obviously, this is not the case. These communities are diverse and multifaceted, experiencing conflicts like in any other collaborative setting. Consciously, this research refrained from poking into these conflicts, a methodological decision I made early in the process. Upon observing both communities, it became evident that the collective pursuit of common objectives outweighed internal divisions, leading me to focus on these collective drivers.

In a more comprehensive ethnographic study, involving at least a year's immersion in each community, deeper insights into community dynamics, conflict resolution processes, and the delineation of conflicts along gender, class, or racial lines could have been possible. In the Martín Peña communities, where I spent more time than in Barbuda, I have seen how conflicts are a part of daily community organizing. "*Chica*, these things happen," remarked my colleague Mariolga Juliá Pachecho at the Caño CLT, acknowledging tensions that I found visibly affecting. "The important thing is to address it." This experience underscored the importance of confronting tensions rather than disregarding them, a fundamental aspect of effective community organization (or any type of organization for that matter).

In Barbuda, land is a contentious issue, overshadowed by the omnipresence of party politics. A small group, aligned with the Central Government, advocates for the use of land to "develop" Barbuda, and there are rumors of political clientelism. While I did not explore these assertions, most people I met advocated for the preservation of communal land, albeit differing on strategies for its maintenance, including support for the construction of an international airport and luxury tourism.

Early on, I aligned myself unequivocally with the "Barbuda resistance," those who are defending communal land rights and natural resource preservation. I did so, not only because I knew it would give me more intimate access to that struggle, which is at the center of this research, but also because it resonated with my personal convictions. I was unable (and did not want) to hide these convictions. As explained throughout the preceding chapters, I deeply respect this struggle, which I believe is of global importance. These divisions may also echo historical "divide and conquer" tactics that have always been integral to the colonial project. Further research could unravel the manifestation of these tactics in neocolonial contexts.

Such research would also ask for a deeper engagement with the "vulnerabilizers", not solely focusing on the communities undergoing vulnerabilization as this study did. At the start of my research, I intended to talk to Robert De Niro, John Paul De Joria, PLH customers, Prime Minister Gaston Browne, Puerto Rican Governor Ricardo Rosselló, and beneficiaries of the then Act 22 tax incentives, among others. But I quickly abandoned that idea as they were unresponsive to interview requests. Even for the documentary we filmed in 2023 or the article I wrote for a Belgian newspaper about the struggle in Barbuda, neither the Prime Minister nor PLH management replied to the numerous attempts via calls, Facebook messages, WhatsApp, and other communication channels, even when prompted by media outlets seeking their perspective, adhering to journalistic due diligence. Consequently, as discussed, in this study, I conducted a thorough discourse analysis of statements made by these figures in interviews conducted by other journalists. While I do not anticipate significant divergence from their potential responses in interviews, a longer ethnographic study, still in close collaboration with those doing the resistance, encompassing the perspectives of these "vulnerabilizers" could provide deeper insights into their motivations and tactics—and how to counter them.

Although this study touches upon aspects of post-disaster financialization, it does not examine sufficiently the existing literature or contribute substantially to it. The phenomenon of global land grabs is intrinsically tied to financialization, requiring further exploration in future research. In the Caribbean context, financialization manifests through proliferating real estate development, particularly in coastal regions, exerting mounting pressure on local populations, especially in the context of climate change. State-sponsored initiatives such as tax exemptions for wealthy foreigners and Citizenship by Investment programs (which exploded during the COVID-19 pandemic, something I witnessed firsthand in St Martin), coupled with a surge in short-term rentals, are displacing Caribbean inhabitants. Despite the burgeoning discourse on housing and land financialization, the implications for Caribbean populations, particularly the most marginalized, remain inadequately addressed, presenting a critical avenue for future research.

Another potential avenue for future research involves conducting broader comparative analyses between the processes of vulnerabilization and resistance occurring in these communities and those in other regions of the global south. The communities I studied represent small places, who are affected by large global issues. John Mussington, upon learning about similar narratives from other islands participating in the Stronger Caribbean Together project, noted a "textbook" response to post-disaster situations worldwide. "We can predict it. Every time a disaster happens anywhere, people come and make use of it to take the land," he observed. This hypothesis presents an intriguing avenue for further exploration. As land tenure expert Liz Alden Wily, whose work primarily focuses on Africa, stated, "It's not an event, it's ongoing, it's a global land grab" (CLT Center, 2020). Understanding how these dynamics unfold in Africa, Asia, Latin America, and other parts of the Caribbean is crucial. Other communities living on unacknowledged communally held land are protecting themselves from this land grab by formalizing their relationship with the land in a myriad of ways, representing a tenure plurality that requires urgent scientific attention as it can help us address the climate emergency. Equally important is exploring how communities worldwide are interconnected in addressing these challenges and identifying key actors within international solidarity networks.

Furthermore, exploring the activities of important community-based organizations advocating for the return of communal lands to Indigenous Peoples, such as the Landback movement in the USA, could be fascinating. Does decolonization, as envisioned by scholars like Tuck and Yang (2012), who advocate for a complete return to communal lands, offer a viable pathway forward as we confront the increasing urgency of climate collapse? This question deserves thorough investigation.

OUR LAND, OUR SURVIVAL

As demonstrated in this book, communal land plays a vital role in protecting communities against the adverse impacts of climate change and ensuing vulnerabilization processes. Firstly, it shields them from post-disaster displacements spurred by foreign capital encroachment, ensuring community continuity. Secondly, communal land fosters a deeper sense of community cohesion, serving as the foundation for mutual aid endeavors, bolstering political influence, and fostering international solidarity. Thirdly, by embodying an ethos of interconnectedness between humans and nature, communal land cultivates the development of counterhegemonic 'epistemologies of the land,' challenging dominant narratives and promoting sustainable land stewardship practices.

The title of this book conveys the idea that land signifies survival not only for the communities examined but for humanity at large. With more than half of the world's land still held, used, or managed communally (Rights and Resources Initiative, 2015b), this study has underscored the central role of communal land in addressing the climate emergency. Communal land is not an aberration, nor something of the past. A plurality of land tenure systems exists demanding attention in disaster research, land policy, and recovery endeavors. The communities acting as the custodians of such lands present a path forward for reimagining relationships with the land. These communities are therefore not only essential in their role as protectors but also as generators of invaluable knowledge and innovative strategies integral to critical environmentalism. As we navigate towards a more equitable and sustainable future, their contributions will be indispensable. It's time to listen.

APPENDIX 1: LIST OF INTERVIEWS, OBSERVATIONS AND EXCHANGES

	Puerto Rico	Barbuda
Interviews	Staff Fideicomiso de la Tierra del Caño Martín Peña Staff Corporación Proyecto ENLACE del Caño Martín Peña Staff Centre for New Economy Staff Ayuda Legal Puerto Rico Staff Hispanic Federation / Association of Planners Housing Expert Scholars University of Puerto Rico Staff Foundation for Puerto Rico Staff Foundation Access to Justice Residents Barrio Obrero La Marina Resident Las Monjas Community Leaders Barrio Obrero La Marina Community Leaders Las Monjas Community Leaders Líderes Jóvenes Acción (LIJAC) Fideicomiso de Tierras Comunitarias para la Agricultura Sostenible Community Leaders Loíza	Barbudan diaspora Members Barbuda Council Staff Peace Love & Happiness Pastor Former Director National Archives Antigua and Barbuda (in Antigua) Staff UNDP (in Antigua) Member of Parliament Antigua and Barbuda for Barbuda (in Antigua) Farmer Fisherman Restaurant owner Writer Shop owner
Observations	Post-Hurricane Community Meeting Prevention of Violence Community Meeting Street Meeting Caño CLT Advisory Committee Community Assembly Las Monjas Community Assembly La Marina Session LIJAC Universidad del Barrio Assembly G-8 Evaluation Exchange May 2019 Proyecto Matria on Feminism in Puerto Rico Ayuda Legal Puerto Rico Social Justice and Right to Housing Post Maria Architecture Colegio de Arquitectos Post Maria meeting Foundation for Puerto Rico on Resiliency Protest March for Independence Protest March for Public Education Public presentation UPR Planning Public presentation UPR Women and Colonialism Public presentation UPR De-urbanizing the City David Harvey Lecture UPR	Homecoming events Ecumenical church service Community walk Village Meeting Community clean up Daily Community hangouts Church Barbuda People's Movement celebration Barbuda People's Movement community celebration
Community-to-Community Exchanges	Exchange Caño CLT and Favela CLT Rio De Janeiro - August 2018; International Exchange "Community Development and Collective Land Tenure" - May 2019; Online Exchanges Caño CLT 2020/2021; Online Exchanges Stronger Caribbean Together 2021/2022	

REFERENCES

365 Antigua. (2017, September 7). "We may have to evacuate all of Barbuda." PM Gaston Browne, when discussing another storm (Jose) possibly arriving in a couple days. *365 Antigua.* https://www.facebook.com/365antigua/posts/10155014833708727

ACAPS, OCHA, & UNDP. (2017). *Regional Overview: Impact of Hurricanes Irma and Maria.* https://reliefweb.int/sites/reliefweb.int/files/resources/UNDP%20%20Regional%20Overview%20Impact%20of%20Hurricanes%20Irma%20and%20Maria.pdf

Accheri, C., Baring, M., & Suliman, A. (n.d.). Communal land ownership in Barbuda a myth, says prime minister. *Thomson Reuters Foundation.* Retrieved May 9, 2022, from https://news.trust.org/item/20180425114248-rgfzn/

Ahmed, S. (2017). *Living a Feminist Life.* Duke University Press. https://doi.org/10.1215/9780822373377

Alden Wily, L. (n.d.). *A land rights storm brewing in Barbuda?* Land Portal. Retrieved May 9, 2022, from https://landportal.org/blog-post/2017/10/land-rights-storm-brewing-barbuda

Alden Wily, L. (2012). *The Global Land Grab: The New Enclosures.* The Wealth of The Commons: A World Beyond Market & State. https://wealthofthecommons.org/essay/global-land-grab-new-enclosures

Alden Wily, L. (2018). Collective land ownership in the 21st century: Overview of global trends. Land, 7(2). https://doi.org/10.3390/land7020068

Alexander, M., Polimis, K., & Zagheni, E. (2019). The impact of Hurricane Maria on out-migration from Puerto Rico: Evidence from Facebook data. *Population and Development Review,* 45(3).

Algoed, L., Alden Wily, L., & Mussington, J. (2021, December 14). *The disaster for Barbudans and their fragile homeland continues.* Land Portal. https://landportal.org/fr/node/94513

Algoed, L., & Hernández Torrales, M. E. (2019). The Land is Ours. Vulnerabilization and resistance in informal settlements in Puerto Rico: Lessons from the Caño Martín Peña Community Land Trust. *Radical Housing Journal,* 1(1), 29–47.

Algoed, L., Hernández Torrales, M. E., & Rodríguez Del Valle, L. N. (2018). *El Fideicomiso de la Tierra del Caño Martín Peña: Instrumento Notable de Regularización de Suelo en Asentamientos Informales.* Lincoln Institute of Land Policy.

Almeida, P., & Chase-Dunn, C. (2018). Globalization and Social Movements. *Annual Review of Sociology,* 44, 1.1-1.23. https://doi.org/10.1146/annurev-soc-073117

Amorim-Maia, A. T., Anguelovski, I., Chu, E., & Connolly, J. (2022). Intersectional climate justice: A conceptual pathway for bridging adaptation planning, transformative action, and social equity. *Urban Climate,* 41, 1–18. https://doi.org/10.1016/j.uclim.2021.101053

Antigua and Barbuda. (2007). *The Barbuda Land Act, 2007, nr 23 of 2007.*

Bahr, S. (2023, October 20). What to Know About 'Killers of the Flower Moon': A Guide to the Osage Murders. *The New York Times.* https://www.nytimes.com/2023/10/20/movies/killers-of-the-flower-moon-osage-murders-explained.html#:~:text=There%20was%20a%20legal%20wrinkle,of%20one%20or%20more%20shares.

Baker, T., McCann, E., & Temenos, C. (2020). Into the ordinary: non-elite actors and the mobility of harm reduction policies. *Policy and Society,* 39(1), 129–145. https://doi.org/10.1080/14494035.2019.1626079

Baptiste, A. K., & Devonish, H. (2019). The Manifestation of Climate Injustices: The Post-Hurricane Irma Conflicts Surrounding Barbuda's Communal Land Tenure. *Journal of Extreme Events, 6*(1).

Barbican. (2023). *RE/SISTERS: A Lens on Gender and Ecology*. Barbican.

Barbuda (Amendment) Act, 2018 (2018).

Barbuda Channel. (2021, January 20). *Special Interview with Team from PLH* [Video recording]. Facebook. https://www.facebook.com/profile/100004071112259/search/?q=PLH

Barbuda Ocean Club (BOC). (n.d.). *About*. Barbuda Ocean Club. Retrieved April 12, 2024, from https://barbudaoceanclub.com/about

Barthold, S. (2019). Greening the global city. The role of C40 cities as actors in global environmental governance. In S. Oosterlynck, L. Beeckmans, D. Bassens, B. Derudder, B. Segaert, & L. Braeckmans (Eds.), *The City as Global Political Actor* (pp. 147–167). Routledge.

BBC News. (2017, September 8). Hurricane Jose: "Barely habitable" Barbuda residents flee. *BBC*.

Bernard, R. (2011). *Research Methods in Anthropology: Qualitative and Quantitative Approaches (Fifth Edition)*. AltaMira Press.

Besson, J. (2015). *Transformations of Freedom in the Land of the Maroons: Creolization in the Cockpits Jamaica*. Ian Randle Publishers.

Besson, J., & Momsen, J. (1987). *Land and Development in the Caribbean*. Macmillan.

Besson, J., & Momsen, J. (2007). *Caribbean Land and Development Revisited*. Palgrave Macmillan.

Bhandar, B. (2018). *Colonial Lives of Property: Law, Land, and Racial Regimes of Ownership*. Duke University Press.

Blühdorn, I. (2013). The governance of unsustainability: ecology and democracy after the postdemocratic turn. *Environmental Politics, 22*(1), 16-36.

Blühdorn, I. (2016). Sustainability–Post-sustainability–Unsustainability. In *The Oxford Handbook of Environmental Political Theory*. Oxford University Press.

Bogaert, K. (2023). *In het Spoor van Fanon: Orde, Wanorde, Dekolonisering*. EPO.

Bonilla, Y. (2020). The coloniality of disaster: Race, empire, and the temporal logics of emergency in Puerto Rico, USA. *Political Geography*. https://doi.org/10.1016/j.polgeo.2020.102181

Brown, M., Haughwout, A. F., Lee, D., Scally, J., Solimano, M., & van der Klaauw, W. (2016, August 12). *Puerto Rico's Evolving Household Debts*. Liberty Street Economics. https://libertystreeteconomics.newyorkfed.org/2016/08/puerto-ricos-evolving-household-debts/

Bruyneel, K. (2021). Reconstructing Political Memory: The Reconstruction Era and the Faint Trace of Settler Colonialism. In *Settler Memory: The Disavowal of Indigeneity and the Politics of Race in the United States* (pp. 45–75). https://doi.org/10.5149/9781469665252_bruyneel.8

Bulckens, L., & Algoed, L. (2023, November 4). *"Paradijs Niet te Koop"* [Broadcast]. Vranckx & De Nomaden. https://www.vrt.be/vrtmax/a-z/vranckx---de-nomaden/2023/vranckx---de-nomaden-s2023-paradijs-niet-te-koop/?ndl=true.

Bunce, S. (2016). Pursuing Urban Commons: Politics and Alliances in Community Land Trust Activism in East London. *Antipode, 48*(1), 134–150. https://doi.org/10.1111/anti.12168

Business Wire. (2017, September 13). Community Developers Committed to Barbuda Recovery after Hurricane Irma. *Business Wire*. https://www.businesswire.com/news/home/20170913006278/en/Community-Developers-Committed-Barbuda-Recovery-Hurricane-Irma

Cabannes, Y. (2021). Climate change, land and housing-induced evictions: another round of accumulation through dispossession? In C. Johnson, G. Jain, & A. Lavell (Eds.), *Rethinking Urban Risk and Resettlement in the Global South*. UCL Press.

Calle 13. (2010, November 22). *Latinoamérica*. Genius. https://genius.com/Calle-13-latinoamerica-lyrics
Caribbean Series. (2015, December 4). Honourable Gaston Browne. *Caribbean Series*. http://www.peninsula-press.com/caribbean_series/antigua-and-barbuda/interviews/gaston-browne/
Casimir, J. (2020). *The Haitians: A Decolonial History*. The University of North Carolina Press.
Castro-Gómez, S., & Grosfoguel, R. (2007). *El giro decolonial: reflexiones para una diversidad epistémica más allá del capitalismo global*. Siglo del Hombre Editores.
Center for CLT Innovation. (2020). *Line Algoed (of the Center for CLT Innovation) Interview with Liz Alden Wily*. Center for CLT Innovation. https://cltweb.org/wp-content/uploads/2020/11/Liz-Alden-Wily-Transcript-Final.pdf
Center for CLT Innovation. (2021). *The Experience of Community Land Trusts in Latin America* [Video recording]. https://vimeo.com/637867077
Chaillou, A., Roblin, L., & Ferdinand, M. (2020, June 4). *Why We Need a Decolonial Ecology*. Green European Journal. https://www.greeneuropeanjournal.eu/why-we-need-a-decolonial-ecology/
Clancy, N., Dixon, L., Elinoff, D., Kuznitsky, K., & Mckenna, S. (2020). *Modernizing Puerto Rico's Housing Sector Following Hurricanes Irma and Maria Post-Storm Challenges and Potential Courses of Action*.
Clichevsky, N. (2003). *Pobreza y acceso al suelo urbano: algunas interrogantes sobre las políticas de regularización en América Latina*. Naciones Unidas, CEPAL, División de Medio Ambiente y Asentamientos Humanos.
CLT Center. (n.d.-a). *History of the Community Land Trust Movement*. Center for CLT Innovation. Retrieved June 5, 2023, from https://cltweb.org/timeline/
CLT Center. (n.d.-b). *What Is a Community Land Trust?* Retrieved September 6, 2022, from https://cltweb.org/what-is-a-community-land-trust/
Collier, N., DeKornfeld, O., & Laffin, B. (2017, November 26). *No Man's Land: Barbuda after Irma* [Video recording]. The New York Times. https://www.nytimes.com/video/world/americas/100000005425833/barbuda-after-hurricane-irma.html
Condé, M. (1999). *Le Coeur à Rire et à Pleurer*. Pocket.
Connell, R. J. (2017). *The Political Ecology of Maroon Autonomy: Land, Resource Extraction and Political Change in 21st Century Jamaica and Suriname*. https://escholarship.org/uc/item/5n1665b6
Connolly, P. (2013). La ciudad y el habitat popular: paradigma latinoamericano. In *Teorías sobre la ciudad en América Latina (Vol. II)* (pp. 505–562). Universidad Autónoma Metropolitana.
Cornish, F., Breton, N., Moreno-Tabarez, U., Delgado, J., Rua, M., de-Graft Aikins, A., & Hodgetts, D. (2023). Participatory action research. *Nature Reviews Methods Primers*, *3*(1). https://doi.org/10.1038/s43586-023-00214-1
Crichlow, M., Ferreira da Silva, D., & Cavuto, M. (n.d.). *Climate Change, Decolonization and Global Blackness Lab*. Duke. Retrieved April 12, 2024, from https://fhi.duke.edu/research/entanglement-project/climate-change-decolonization-and-global-blackness-lab/
Cruz-Martínez, G., Fernández Arrigoitia, M., Ortiz Camacho, J., & Román-Velazquez, P. (2018). The Making of Caribbean Not-so-Natural Disasters. *Alternautas*, *5*(2), 4–12. "http://www.alternautas.net/blog/2018/9/7/introduction-to-the-special-issue-themaking-of-caribbean-not-so-natural-disasters"

Davis, A. Y. (2016). *Freedom Is a Constant Struggle Ferguson, Palestine, and the Foundations of a Movement*. Haymarket Books.

Davis, J. E. (2010). *The Community Land Trust Reader* (J. E. Davis, Ed.). Lincoln Institute of Land Policy.

Davis, J. E., Algoed, L., & Hernández-Torrales, M. E. (2020). *On Common Ground: International Perspectives on the Community Land Trust* (J. E. Davis, L. Algoed, & M. E. Hernández-Torrales, Eds.). Terra Nostra Press.

De Pauw, G., & de Santos, J. (2020). Beyond England: Origins and Evolution of the Community Land Trust Movement in Europe. In J. E. Davis, L. Algoed, & M. E. Hernández Torrales (Eds.), *On Common Ground: International Perspectives on the Community Land Trust*. Terra Nostra Press.

De Soto, H. (2000). *The Mystery of Capital: Why Capitalism Triumphs in the West and Fails Everywhere Else*. Basic Books.

deGrandpre, A. (2017, September 15). On tiny Barbuda, a 300-year-old civilization has been 'extinguished.' *The Washington Post*. https://www.washingtonpost.com/news/capital-weather-gang/wp/2017/09/15/on-tiny-barbuda-a-300-year-old-civilization-has-been-extinguished/

Dorodnykh, E. (2017). *Economic and Social Impacts of Food Self-Reliance in the Caribbean*. Palgrave Macmillan.

Dyal-Chand, R. (2010). Leaving the Body of Property Law? Meltdowns, Land Rushes, and Failed Economic Development. In D. B. Barros (Ed.), *Hernando de Soto and Property in a Market Economy* (pp. 83–96). Ashgate.

Echenique, M., & Melgar, L. (2018, May 11). Mapping Puerto Rico's Hurricane Migration with Mobile Phone Data. *City Lab*. "https://www.citylab.com/environment/2018/05/watch-puerto-ricos-hurricanemigration- via-mobile-phone-data/559889/."

ECLAC, & FAO. (2020). *COVID-19 Report ECLAC-FAO Preventing the COVID-19 crisis from becoming a food crisis. Urgent measures against hunger in Latin America and the Caribbean*.

Encylopedia.com. (n.d.). *Private Property and Property Rights: What It Means*. Encyclopedia.Com. Retrieved April 12, 2024, from https://www.encyclopedia.com/finance/encyclopedias-almanacs-transcripts-and-maps/private-property-and-property-rights

Engels, F. (1884). *Origins of the Family, Private Property, and the State*. Marxists. https://www.marxists.org/archive/marx/works/1884/origin-family/ch02c.htm

Escobar, A. (2016). Thinking-feeling with the earth: Territorial struggles and the ontological dimension of the epistemologies of the south. *AIBR Revista de Antropologia Iberoamericana, 11*(1), 11–32. https://doi.org/10.11156/aibr.110102e

Escobar, A. (2017). "Desde abajo, por la izquierda, y con la tierra: la diferencia de Abya Yala / Afro / Latino / América." In H. Alimona, C. Toro Pérez, & F. Martín (Eds.), *Ecología Política Latinoamericana. Pensamiento Crítico, Diferencia Latinoamericana y Rearticulación Epistémica* (pp. 51-68.). CLACSO.

Escobar, A. (2023, June 21). *Against Terricide: Envisioning Paths Towards Pluriversal Transitions with Arturo Escobar* [Video recording]. John Hope Franklin Humanities Institute at Duke University. https://www.youtube.com/watch?v=8UKXg_Agw3c

Esterrich, C. (2013). "Singing the City, Documenting Modernization: Cortijo y su Combo and the Insertion of the Urban in 1950s Puerto Rican Culture." In L. Shaw (Ed.), *Song and Social Change in Latin America* " (pp. 9–26). Lexington.

Estudios Técnicos. (2019). *Update: Economic Assessment Act 20/22*. http://www.estudiostecnicos.com/projects/act2022update2019/2019-Summary-results.pdf

Fanon, F. (1963). *The Wretched of the Earth*. Grove Press.

Ferdinand, M. (2021). A Future Named "Ayiti": Thinking Decolonial Ecologies from The Caribbean World. A Conversation with Malcom Ferdinand. *THE FUNAMBULIST*, 20–23.

Ferdinand, M. (2022). *Decolonial Ecology: Thinking from the Caribbean World*. Polity Press.

Ferrars, M. (2024, February 25). *"Birth of the Dream: Friedrich Engels' the Origin of the Family, Private Property and the State" (1884)*. Ferrars & Fields Magazine 02/24. https://ferrarsundfields.de/2024/02/25/birth-of-the-dream-friedrich-engels-the-origin-of-the-family-private-property-and-the-state-1884/

Fidalgo Ribeiro, T., Algoed, L., Hernández-Torrales, M. E., Rodríguez Del Valle, L., Cotté Morales, A., & Williamson, T. (2020). *Community Land Trusts in Informal Settlements: Adapting Features of Puerto Rico's Caño Martín Peña CLT to Address Land Insecurity in the Favelas of Rio de Janeiro, Brazil* (J. E. Davis, L. Algoed, & M. E. Hernández-Torrales, Eds.; On Common Ground).

Flint, A. (2018, February 23). *Letting Slum Residents Control Their Own Destiny*. Bloomberg. https://www.bloomberg.com/news/articles/2018-02-23/a-just-model-for-integrating-slums-into-the-formal-city

Flint, C., & Taylor, P. J. (2018). *Political Geography: World-Economy, Nation-State and Locality (Seventh edition)*. Routledge.

Florido, A. (2018, March 20). Unable To Prove They Own Their Homes, Puerto Ricans Denied FEMA Help. *NPR*. https://www.npr.org/2018/03/20/595240841/unable-to-prove-they-own-their-homespuerto- ricans-denied-femahelp? utm_campaign=storyshare&utm_source=facebook.com&utm_medium=social

Fontánez Torres, É. (2008). "The contingency of property policies: A review of the assumptions related to the political theory of property in the contexts of social and environmental justice in Puerto Rico." *Derecho y Propiedad: Seminario En Latinoamérica En Teoría Constitucional y Política*.

Foundation for Puerto Rico. (n.d.). *Visitor Economy 101*. Retrieved August 21, 2024, from https://foundationforpuertorico.org/en/visitor-economy-101/

Frank, A. (2018). *Dreamland Barbuda: The Land Belongs to the People. A Study of the History and Development of Communal Land Ownership on the Island*. Signs and Impressions.

Frank, M. (2015, October 19). The Paradise Found Bill—A Response. *Barbudaful*. https://barbudaful.net/the-paradise-found-bill-a-response/

Fuller Marvel, L. (2008). *Listen to What they Say: Planning and community development in Puerto Rico*. La Editorial UPR.

García, I. (2022). Deemed Ineligible: Reasons Homeowners in Puerto Rico Were Denied Aid After Hurricane María. *Housing Policy Debate, 32*(1), 14–34. https://doi.org/10.1080/10511482.2021.1890633

Gaudry, A. J. P. (2011). Insurgent Research. *Wicazo Sa Review, 26*(1), 113–136. https://doi.org/10.5749/wicazosareview.26.1.0113

Geertz, C. (1998, October 22). Deep Hanging Out. *The New York Review*. https://www.nybooks.com/articles/1998/10/22/deep-hanging-out/

Ghosh, A. (2021). *The Nutmeg's Curse: Parables for a Planet in Crisis*. John Murray Publishers Ltd.

Gibson-Graham, J. K. (2006). *The End of Capitalism (As We Knew It): A Feminist Critique of Political Economy*. University of Minnesota Press.

Glassman, M., & Erdem, G. (2014). Participatory Action Research and Its Meanings: Vivencia, Praxis, Conscientization. *Adult Education Quarterly, 64*(3), 206–221.

Goldstein, M. (2017, December 16). The next crisis for Puerto Rico: A crush of foreclosures. *CBNC.* https://www.cnbc.com/2017/12/16/the-next-crisis-forpuerto-rico-a-crush-of-foreclosures.html

Government of Puerto Rico, & Department of Housing. (2018). *Community Development Block Grant Disaster Recovery Action Plan.*

Gramsci, A. (1995). *Further Selections from the Prison Notebooks* (D. Boothman, Ed.). University of Minnesota Press.

Graulau, B. (2021, December 28). *Are Puerto Ricans being pushed out?* [Video recording]. YouTube. https://youtu.be/YGXtWpCOiC8?si=aFabKWkTBhU2PyOA

Haas, P. M. (1992). Introduction: Epistemic Communities and International Policy Coordination. *International Organization, 46*(1), 1–35.

Haiti Lab. (2012). *Lakou Model.* Law & Housing in Haiti. https://sites.duke.edu/lawandhousinginhaiti/historical-background/lakou-model/

Handy, G. (2020, December 14). Barbudans "fight for survival" as resort project threatens islanders' way of life. *The Guardian.*

Haraway, D. (1988). Situated Knowledges: The Science Question in Feminism and the Privilege of Partial Perspective. In *Feminist Studies* (Vol. 14, Issue 3). http://www.jstor.org/about/terms.html

Hardin, G. (1968). The Tragedy of the Commons. In *Source: Science, New Series* (Vol. 162, Issue 3859).

Harjo, S. S. (1991). "My Turn: I won't be Celebrating Columbus Day." *Newsweek, Fall Winter 32.*

Harris, C. I. (1993). Whiteness As Property. *Harvard Law Review, 106*(8).

Harvey, D. (2003). *The New Imperialism.* Oxford University Press.

Harvey, D. (2004). The 'New' Imperialism: Accumulation by Dispossession. *Socialist Register.*

Hassan, A. (2018, September 13). Hurricane Florence and the Displacement of African Americans Along the Carolina Coast. *The New York Times.* https://www.nytimes.com/2018/09/13/us/african-americans-hurricane-florence-displacement.html

Hayes, T., & Murtinho, F. (2023). Diagnosing Participation and Inclusion in Collective Decision-Making in the Commons: Lessons from Ecuador. *International Journal of the Commons, 17*(1), 37–53. https://doi.org/10.5334/ijc.1200

Heath, T., & Newmyer, T. (2017, May 3). Puerto Rico, with $73 billion in debt, forced toward bankruptcy. *The Washington Post.* https://www.washingtonpost.com/business/economy/puerto-rico-with-73-billion-in-debt-forced-toward-bankruptcy/2017/05/03/92e39d76-3020-11e7-9534-00e4656c22aa_story.html

Hernández Torrales, M. E. (2007). "The Caño Martín Peña Community Land Trust: Corollary of a Model of Community Involvement, Progress." *Revista Del Colegio de Abogados de Puerto Rico, 68*(4), 794–817.

Hernández-Torrales, M. E., Rodríguez Del Valle, L., Algoed, L., & Torres Sueiro, K. (2020). *Seeding the CLT in Latin America and the Caribbean Origins, Achievements, and the Proof-of-Concept Example of the Caño Martín Peña Community Land Trust* (J. E. Davis, L. Algoed, & M. E. Hernández-Torrales, Eds.; On common ground). Terra Nostra Press.

Herrador Valencia, D., Mendizábal Riera, E., & Boada Juncà, M. (2012). Participatory Action

Research Applied to the Management of Natural Areas: The Case Study of Cinquera in El Salvador. *Journal of Latin American Geography, 11*(1), 45–65.

Hess, C., & Ostrom, E. (2007). Introduction: An Overview of the Knowledge Commons. In C. Hess & E. Ostrom (Eds.), *Understanding Knowledge as a Commons: From Theory to Practice* (pp. 3–26).

Hilhorst, D., & Bankoff, G. (2004). Introduction: Mapping Vulnerability. In G. Bankoff, G. Frerks, & D. Hilhorst (Eds.), *Mapping Vulnerability: Disasters, Displacements and People* (pp. 1–9). Taylor & Francis.

Human Rights Watch. (2018, July 12). *Antigua and Barbuda: Barbudans Fighting for Land Rights*. Human Rights Watch. https://www.hrw.org/news/2018/07/12/antigua-and-barbuda-barbudans-fighting-land-rights

Icaza Garza, R., & Salem, S. (2023). "A world in which many worlds can fit:" On Knowledge Production and Multiplicity. *Anticolonial Feminist Imaginaries, 9*(1).

Icaza, R., & Vasquez, R. (2013). Social Struggles as Epistemic Struggles. *Development and Change FORUM, 44*(3), 683–704.

James, C. (1938). *Black Jacobins*. Vintage.

Johnson, C., Jain, G., & Lavell, A. (2021). *Rethinking Urban Risk and Resettlement in the Global South*. UCL Press.

Johnson Lewis, J. (2019, July 13). *A Short History of Women's Property Rights in the United States*. ThoughtCo. https://www.thoughtco.com/property-rights-of-women-3529578

Johnson, M., & Luscombe, R. (2015, November 27). Robert De Niro's plan for Caribbean mega-resort opposed by island residents. *The Guardian*. https://www.theguardian.com/world/2015/nov/27/robert-de-niro-barbuda-island-resort-controversy

Judicial Committee of the Privy Council. (2022, June 13). *MacKenzie Frank and another (Appellants) v Attorney General of Antigua and Barbuda (Respondent) (Antigua and Barbuda)*. Judicial Committee of the Privy Council. https://www.jcpc.uk/cases/jcpc-2021-0070.html

Klein, N. (2007). *The Shock Doctrine: The Rise of Disaster Capitalism*. Metropolitan Books.

Klein, N., & Brown, A. (2018, January 23). Robert De Niro Accused of Exploiting Hurricane Irma to Build Resort in Barbuda. *The Intercept*. https://theintercept.com/2018/01/23/robert-de-niro-barbuda-hotel-hurricane-irma/

Kukh, A., Holemans, D., & Van den Broeck, P. (2018). *Op Grond Van Samenwerking*. EPO.

Lalji, A. F., & Hancheroff, J. (2023, April 28). The Vatican's historic repudiation of the Doctrine of Discovery – Now it's Canada's turn. *MLT Aikins*. https://www.mltaikins.com/indigenous/vaticans-historic-repudiation-of-the-doctrine-of-discovery-now-its-canadas-turn/#:~:text=The%20Vatican%20repudiates%20the%20Doctrine,year%2Dold%2-0Doctrine%20of%20Discovery.

Lawrence, J. (2015). *Barbuda and Betty's Hope: The Codrington Connection*. Sugarmill Tales.

Leckie, S. (2013). *Finding Land Solutions to Climate Displacement: A Challenge Like Few Others*. https://unfccc.int/files/adaptation/groups_committees/loss_and_damage_executive_committee/application/pdf/ds-report-finding-land-solutions-to-climate-displacement.pdf

Lightfoot, N. (2020). Disrepair, distress, and dispossession: Barbuda after Hurricane Irma. *Small Axe, 24*(2), 133–146. https://doi.org/10.1215/07990537-8604550

Lloréns, H., Santiago, R., Garcia-Quijano, C. G., & de Onís, C. M. (2018, January 22). *Hurricane Maria: Puerto Rico's Unnatural Disaster*. Social Justice: A Journal of Crime, Conflict & World Order.

Locke, J. (1690). *Two Treatises of Government.* Phoenix.

Lorde, A. (1981). *(1981) Audre Lorde, "The Uses of Anger: Women Responding to Racism."* Blackpast. https://www.blackpast.org/african-american-history/speeches-african-american-history/1981-audre-lorde-uses-anger-women-responding-racism/

Lugones, M. (2003). *Pilgrimages/Peregrinajes: Theorizing Coalition Against Multiple Oppressions.* Rowman & Littlefield Publishers.

Lugones, M. (2010). Toward a Decolonial Feminism. *Hypatia, 25*(4), 742–759. https://www.jstor.org/stable/40928654

Lugones, M. (2016). The Coloniality of Gender. In W. Harcourt (Ed.), *The Palgrave Handbook of Gender and Development Critical Engagements in Feminist Theory and Practice* (pp. 13–33). https://doi.org/https://doi.org/10.1007/978-1-137-38273-3

Lulich, J. (2018, June 25). Does Hurricane Damage Negatively Impact Your Real Estate Value? *Forbes.* https://www.nytimes.com/2022/01/31/us/puerto-rico-gentrification.html

Luxemburg, R. (1921). *The Accumulation of Capitalism: An Anti-Critique.* Marxists. https://www.marxists.org/archive/luxemburg/1915/anti-critique/ch06.htm

Luxemburg, R. (1925). *Introduction à l'économie politique.* Un Document Produit En Version Numérique Par Jean-Marie Tremblay.

Maldonado Torres, N. (2018). Fanon and Decolonial Thought. In M. A. Peters (Ed.), *Encyclopedia of Educational Philosophy and Theory.* Springer. https://doi.org/10.1007/978-981-287-588-4_506

Maldonado-Torres, N. (2007). On the Coloniality of Being: Contributions to the Development of a Concept. *Cultural Studies, 21*(2–3).

Marcos, C. M., & Mazzei, P. (2022, January 31). The Rush for a Slice of Paradise in Puerto Rico. *The New York Times.* https://www.nytimes.com/2022/01/31/us/puerto-rico-gentrification.html

Massey, D. (2011). A Counterhegemonic Relationality of Place. In E. McCann & K. Ward (Eds.), *Mobile Urbanism Cities and Policymaking in the Global Age* (pp. 1–14).

McCann, E. (2011). Urban policy mobilities and global circuits of knowledge: Toward a research agenda. *Annals of the Association of American Geographers, 101*(1), 107–130. https://doi.org/10.1080/00045608.2010.520219

McCann, E., & Ward, K. (2011). *Mobile Urbanism Cities and Policymaking in the Global Age* (E. McCann & K. Ward, Eds.). University of Minnesota.

Mehta, L., Allouche, J., Nicol, A., & Walnycki, A. (2014). Global environmental justice and the right to water: The case of peri-urban Cochabamba and Delhi. *Geoforum, 54,* 158–166. https://doi.org/10.1016/j.geoforum.2013.05.014

Meiskins Wood, E. (1999). *The Origin of Capitalism.* Verso.

Mignolo, W. D., & Escobar, A. (2010). *Globalization and the Decolonial Option* (W. D. Mignolo & A. Escobar, Eds.). Routledge.

Mora, M. (2017). *Kuxlejal Politics: Indigenous Autonomy, Race, and Decolonizing Research in Zapatista Communities.* University of Texas Press.

Mutter, J. C. (2015). *The Disaster Profiteers: How natural disasters make the rich richer and the poor even poorer.* St. Martin's Press.

National Oceanic and Atmospheric Administration (NOAA). (2017, November 30). *Extremely active 2017 Atlantic hurricane season finally ends.* NOAA. https://www.noaa.gov/media-release/extremely-active-2017-atlantic-hurricane-season-finally-ends

Negga Melchior, T. C. (2018, October 15). *#We The Peoples of the World… Except you: Disaster Capitalism in Barbuda*. Critical Legal Thinking.

Octifanny, Y., Norvyani, D. A., & Heriyani Pertiwi, S. A. (2022). Resistance to Formalisation in Informal Settlements: Evidence from Pontianak. In S. Roitman & D. Rukmana (Eds.), *Routledge Handbook of Urban Indonesia*. Routledge.

OHCHR. (2021, June 22). *OHCHR*. OHCHR. https://spcommreports.ohchr.org/TMResultsBase/DownLoadPublicCommunicationFile?gId=26336

O'Leary, L., & Chiriguayo, D. (2018, April 27). Puerto Rico governor says to people in informal housing "It's time to go." *Marketplace*. "https://www.marketplace.org/2018/04/27/economy/economics-disaster/sevenmonths- after-hurricane-María-uncertain-future-lies-ahead."

Oliver-Smith, A. (2003). Theorizing Vulnerability in a Globalized World: A Political Ecological Perspective. In G. Bankoff, G. Frerks, & D. Hilhorst (Eds.), *Mapping Vulnerability: Disasters, Displacements and People* (pp. 10–24). Taylor & Francis.

Oliver-Smith, A. (2005). Communities After Catastrophe. Reconstructing the Material, Reconstituting the Social. In S. E. Hyland (Ed.), *Community Building in the 21st Century* (pp. 45-70.). School of American Research Press.

Olsen, W. (2004). Triangulation in Social Research: Qualitative and Quantitative Methods Can Really Be Mixed. *Developments in Sociology, 20*.

Ong, A. (2011). Introduction: Worlding Cities, or the Art of being Global. In *Worlding Cities: Asian Experiments and the Art of Being Global* (pp. 1–26). Wiley-Blackwell. https://doi.org/10.1002/9781444346800

Oosterlynck, S., Beeckmans, L., Bassens, D., Derudder, B., Segaert, B., & Braeckmans, L. (2019). *The City as a Global Political Actor*. Routledge.

Orange, T. (2018). *There There*. Vintage.

Ortner, S. B. (2019, May). *Practicing engaged anthropology*. Anthropology of This Century. http://aotcpress.com/articles/practicing-engaged-anthropology/

Oxfam, International Land Coalition, & Rights and Resources Initiative. (2016). *Common Ground. Securing Land Rights and Safeguarding the Earth*. https://policy-practice.oxfam.org/resources/common-ground-securing-land-rights-and-safeguarding-the-earth-600459/

Patel, R., & Moore, J. W. (2018). *A History of the World in Seven Cheap Things: A Guide to Capitalism, Nature, and the Future of the Planet*. Black Inc.

Peck, J., & Theodore, N. (2010). Mobilizing policy: Models, methods, and mutations. *Geoforum, 41*(2), 169–174. https://doi.org/10.1016/j.geoforum.2010.01.002

Penados, F., Gahman, L., & Smith, S.-J. (2022). Land, race, and (slow) violence: Indigenous resistance to racial capitalism and the coloniality of development in the Caribbean. *Geoforum*. https://doi.org/10.1016/j.geoforum.2022.07.004

Penados, F., Gahman, L., & Smith, S.-J. (2023). Land, race, and (slow) violence: Indigenous resistance to racial capitalism and the coloniality of development in the Caribbean. *Geoforum, 145*.

Platteau, J. P. (1996). The evolutionary theory of land rights as applied to sub-saharan Africa: A critical assessment. *Development and Change, 27*(1), 29–86. https://doi.org/10.1111/j.1467-7660.1996.tb00578.x

Popke, J., & Rhiney, K. (2019). Introduction to Special Issue on The Caribbean after Irma and Maria: Climate, Development & the Post-Hurricane Context. *Journal of Extreme Events, 06*(01). https://doi.org/10.1142/S2345737619020019

Potter, A. E. (2011). *Transnational spaces and communal land tenure in a Caribbean place: "Barbuda is for Barbudans."* https://digitalcommons.lsu.edu/gradschool_dissertations/2575

Pradilla Cobos, E. (1983). *El problema de la vivienda en América Latina.* Centro de Investigaciones CIUDAD.

Pritz, A. (2022). *The Territory* [Video recording]. National Geographic.

Quijano, A. (1998). La Colonialidad del poder y la experiencia cultural latinoamericana. In R. Briceño-León & H. Sonntag (Eds.), *Pueblo, época y desarrollo: la sociología de América Latina.* Nueva Sociedad.

Quijano, A. & Ennis, M. (2000). Coloniality of Power, Eurocentrism, and Latin America. *Nepantla: Views from South,* 1(3), 533-580. Project MUSE. https://muse.jhu.edu/article/23906.

Rakodi, C., Durand-Lasserve, A., & Payne, G. (2009). The limits of land titling and home ownership. *Environment & Urbanization, 21*(2), 443–462. https://doi.org/10.1177/0956247809344364

Rights and Resources Initiative. (2015a). *Who Owns the Land in Latin America? The status of indigenous and community land rights in Latin America.* https://rightsandresources.org/wp-content/uploads/FactSheet_English_WhoOwnstheLandinLatinAmerica_web.pdf

Rights and Resources Initiative. (2015b). *Who Owns the World's Land? A Global Baseline of Formally Recognized Indigenous and Community Land Rights.*

Rights and Resources Initiative. (2016). *Toward a Global Baseline of Carbon Storage in Collective Lands: An Updated Analysis of Indigenous Peoples' and Local Communities' Contributions to Climate Change Mitigations.*

Robbins, P. (2012). *Political Ecology: A Critical Introduction.* John Wiley & Sons.

Robinson, J. (2002). Global and World Cities: A View from off the Map. *International Journal of Urban and Regional Research, 26.3,* 531–554.

Rogowska-Stangret, M. (2018, March 18). *Situated Knowledges.* New Materialism. https://newmaterialism.eu/almanac/s/situated-knowledges.html

Rolnik, R. (2019). *Urban Warfare: Housing under the Empire of Finance.* Verso.

Rosa Rosa, M. E., Rodríguez Del Valle, L. N., & Cotté Morales, A. (2023). *Propuestas para reducir el impacto de los arrendamientos de corto plazo en el desplazamiento de comunidades.* Hispanic Federation.

Roy, Ananya., & Ong, Aihwa. (2011). *Worlding cities: Asian experiments and the art of being global.* Wiley-Blackwell.

Santiago-Bartolomei, R., Lamba-Nieves, D., & Figueroa, E. A. (2022). *Tracking Neighborhood Change in Geographies of Opportunity for Post-Disaster Legacy Cities A Case Study of San Juan, Puerto Rico.* Lincoln Institute of Land Policy.

Santiago-Bartolomei, R., Lamba-Nieves, D., Figueroa, E. A., & Santiago Venegas, Y. A. (2022). *The impact of Short-Term Rentals in Puerto Rico: 2014-2020.* https://grupocne.org/wp-content/uploads/2022/12/2022.12.12-The-Impact-of-Short-Term-Rentals-in-Puerto-Rico-2014-2020.pdf.

Sefa Dei, G. J., Karanja, W., & Erger, G. (2022). *Elders' Cultural Knowledges and the Question of Black/African Indigeneity in Education.* Critical Studies of Education 16.

Seipp, D. J. (1994). The Concept of Property in the Early Common Law. *Law and History Review American Society for Legal History, 12*(1), 29–91. https://www.jstor.org/stable/30042821

Shi, L., Lamb, Z., Qiu, X. (Colleen), Cai, H., & Vale, L. (2018). Promises and perils of collective land tenure in promoting urban resilience: Learning from China's urban villages. *Habitat International, 77,* 1–11. https://doi.org/10.1016/j.habitatint.2018.04.006

Sholder, H., & Hasan, A. (2020). The Origins and Evolution of the CLT Model in South Asia. In J. E. Davis, L. Algoed, & M. E. Hernández Torrales (Eds.), *On Common Ground: International Perspectives on the Community Land Trust*. Terra Nostra Press.

Sieff, K. (2019, September 12). When Hurricane Dorian blew through the Bahamas, it exposed one of the world's great faultlines of inequality. *The Washington Post*. https://www.washingtonpost.com/world/the_americas/when-hurricane-dorian-blew-through-the-bahamas-it-exposed-one-of-the-worlds-great-faultlines-of-inequality/2019/09/12/9485f8ae-d415-11e9-8924-1db-7dac797fb_story.html

Sikkink, K. (2005). Patterns of Dynamic Multilevel Governance and the Insider-Outsider Coalition. In D. Della Porta & S. Tarrow (Eds.), *Transnational Protest and Global Activism* (pp. 151–173). Rowman and Littlefield.

Simonneau, C. (2019). Le Community Land Trust aux États-Unis, au Kenya et en Belgique. Canaux de circulation d'un modèle alternatif et jeu d'intertextualité. *Revue Internationale d'Urbanisme, 6*, 1–15. http://riurba.net/Revue/le-community-land-trust-aux-etats-unis-au-kenya-et-en-belgique-canaux-de-circulation-dun-modele-alternatif-et-jeu-dintertextualite/

Sin Comillas. (2018, February 14). Un 55% de las viviendas eran de construcción informal…y entonces llegó María. *Sin Comillas*. http://sincomillas.com/un-55-de-lasviviendas-eran-de-construccion-informal-y-entonces-llego-María/

Sorentino, S.-M. (2022). Expecting Blows: Sylvia Wynter, Sociogeny, and Exceeding Marxist Social Form. *Emancipations: A Journal of Critical Social Analysis. Vol 1(2), 1*(2).

Stronger Caribbean Together for Food, Land and Climate Justice (2020, May 1). *Hunger, Covid-19, Resistance and Farmer Based Solutions* [Video recording]. Stronger Caribbean Together for Food, Land, and Climate Justice. https://strongercaribbeantogether.org/workshops

Sutter, J. D., & Sosa Pascual, O. (2018, July 3). CPI+CNN Investigation: Records suggest Puerto Rico saw a leptospirosis outbreak after Hurricane Maria — but officials won't call it that. *Centro de Periodismo Investigativo*. https://periodismoinvestigativo.com/2018/07/records-suggest-puerto-rico-saw-a-leptospirosis-outbreak-after-hurricane-maria-but-officials-wont-call-it-that/

Sweeney, J. L. (2007). Caribs, Maroons, Jacobins, Brigands, and Sugar Barons: The Last Stand of the Black Caribs on St. Vincent. *African Diaspora Archeology Network, 10*(1). https://scholarworks.umass.edu/adan/vol10/iss1/7

Swyngedouw, E., & Heynen, N. (2003). Urban Political Ecology, Justice and the Politics of Scale. *Antipode, 35*(5), 898–918.

Temenos, C. (2015). Mobilizing drug policy activism: conferences, convergence spaces and ephemeral fixtures in social movement mobilization. *Space and Polity, 20*(1), 2–18. https://doi.org/10.1080/13562576.2015.1072913

Temenos, C., & Baker, T. (2015). Enriching Urban Policy Mobilities Research. *International Journal of Urban and Regional Research, 39*(4), 841–843. https://doi.org/10.1111/1468-2427.12258

Temper, L., & Del Bene, D. (2016). Transforming knowledge creation for environmental and epistemic justice. In *Current Opinion in Environmental Sustainability* (Vol. 20, pp. 41–49). Elsevier B.V. https://doi.org/10.1016/j.cosust.2016.05.004

Termo Territorial Coletivo. (n.d.). *Termo Territorial Coletivo*. Retrieved September 5, 2022, from https://www.termoterritorialcoletivo.org/

The Ramsar Convention Secretariat. (n.d.). *Antigua and Barbuda*. Ramsar. Retrieved August 9, 2022, from https://www.ramsar.org/wetland/antigua-and-barbuda

Theodore, N. (2019). Policy Mobilities. *Geography*. https://doi.org/10.1093/OBO/9780199874002-0205

Thompson, M. (2020). From Co-Ops to Community Land Trusts: Tracing the Historical Evolution and Policy Mobilities of Collaborative Housing Movements. *Housing, Theory and Society, 37*(1), 82–100. https://doi.org/10.1080/14036096.2018.1517822

Tokarczuk, O. (2023). *Empusion*. de Geus.

Torres Nieves, V. M., & Todas. (n.d.). La gentrificación desplaza a las sobrevivientes de violencia doméstica. *Centro de Periodismo Investigativo*. Retrieved May 11, 2022, from https://periodismoinvestigativo.com/2022/04/la-gentrificacion-desplaza-a-las-sobrevivientes-de-violencia-domestica/

Transnational Institute (TNI). (2013). *The Global Land Grab: A Primer*.

Tsing, A. (2015). *The Mushroom at the End of the World: On the Possibility of Life in Capitalist Ruins*. Princeton University Press.

Tuck, E., & Yang, K. W. (2012). Decolonization is not a metaphor. *Decolonization: Indigeneity, Education & Society., 01*(01), 1-40.

Tuhiwai Smith, L. (1999). *Decolonizing Methodologies: Research and Indigenous Peoples*. Zed Books.

UNC University of North Carolina School of Media and Journalism. (2018). *Rooted in el Caño* [Video recording]. https://vimeo.com/264156328

UN-Habitat. (2019). *A World in Which Everyone Enjoys Secure Land Rights. Land Tenure and Climate Vulnerability*. www.unhabitat.org

University of Nottingham. (n.d.). *Property Ownership*. University of Nottingham. Retrieved April 12, 2024, from https://www.nottingham.ac.uk/manuscriptsandspecialcollections/learning/medievalwomen/theme3/propertyownership.aspx

Valentín Ortiz, L. J., & Minet, C. (2019, July 13). Las 889 páginas de Telegram entre Rosselló Nevares y sus allegados. *CPI*. https://periodismoinvestigativo.com/2019/07/las-889-paginas-de-telegram-entre-rossello-nevares-y-sus-allegados/

van der Kolk, B. (2015). *The Body Keeps the Score*. Penguin.

Varley, A. (2017). Property titles and the urban poor: from informality to displacement? *Planning Theory and Practice, 18*(3), 385–404. https://doi.org/10.1080/14649357.2016.1235223

Vergès, F. (2021). *A Decolonial Feminism*. Pluto Press.

Verschuur, C., & Destremau, B. (2012). Decolonial Feminisms, Gender, and Development: History and Narratives of Southern Feminisms and Women's Movements. *Revue Tiers Monde, 209*(1), 7–18.

Vieira Junior, I. (2023). *Crooked Plow*. Verso.

Viguié Film Productions, Inc. (1950). Puerto Rico elimina el arrabal. *Puerto Rico: Laboratorio Viguié*.

Vincens, A. (2017, October 5). *Puerto Rico's Poorest Communities Are Doing the Rebuilding the Trump Administration Won't*. Mother Jones. https://www.motherjones.com/politics/2017/10/puerto-ricos-poorest-communities-are-doing-the-rebuilding-the-trump-administration-wont/

Volandes, S. (2020, December 6). Robert De Niro Is Creating a New Caribbean Getaway. *Town & Country Magazine*. https://www.townandcountrymag.com/leisure/a34687974/robert-de-niro-nobu-beach-inn-barbuda/

Wattles, J., & Harlow, P. (2017, September 15). Robert De Niro wants to help rebuild Barbuda after Hurricane Irma. *CNN Money*. https://money.cnn.com/2017/09/15/news/robert-de-niro-barbuda/index.html

Weiner, M. F., & Carmona Báez, A. (2018). *Smash the Pillars: Decoloniality and the Imaginary of Color in the Dutch Kingdom*. Lexington Books.

Whalen, C. T. (2005). Colonialism, Citizenship, and the Making of the Puerto Rican Diaspora: An Introduction. In C. T. Whalen & V. Vázquez-Hernández (Eds.), *The Puerto Rican Diaspora: Historical Perspectives* (pp. 1–42). Temple University Press.

Williams, O., & George, E. (2022, May 3). Barbudans one step closer to justice in fight for land ownership. *Antigua Observer*. https://antiguaobserver.com/barbuda-council-one-step-closer-to-justice-in-fight-for-land-ownership/

Willner, D. (1965). Politics and Change in Israel: The Case of Land Settlement. Human Organization, *Society for Applied Anthropology, 24*(1). https://www.jstor.org/stable/44124202

Wilson, J., & Swyngedouw, E. (2014). *The Post-Political and its Discontents. Spaces of Depoliticisations and Spectres of Radical Politics*. Edinburgh University Press.

Woellert, L. (2017, December 31). " 'We have a big problem': Puerto Rico seeks aid for tens of thousands of squatters. ". *Politico*. https://www.politico.com/story/2017/12/31/puerto-rico-squatters-hurricane-261495.

Wolfe, P. (2006). Settler colonialism and the elimination of the native. *Journal of Genocide Research, 8*(4), 387–409.

Wynter, S. (1971). Novel and History, Plot and Plantation. *Savacou*.

Wynter, S. (1982). Beyond Liberal and Marxist Leninist Feminisms: Towards an Autonomous Frame of Reference. *"Feminist Theory at the Cross Roads" Annual Conference of the American Sociological Association*.

Wynter, S. (1995). 1492: A New World View. In V. Lawrence Hyatt & R. Nettleford (Eds.), *Race, Discourse, and the Origin of the Americas*.

Wynter, S. (2003). Unsettling the coloniality of being/power/truth/freedom: Towards the human, after man, its overrepresentation—An argument. In *New Centennial Review* (Vol. 3, Issue 3, pp. 257–337). Michigan State University, Department of English. https://doi.org/10.1353/ncr.2004.0015

Wyss, J. (2020, January 15). Puerto Rico: Former education secretary indicted in bribery and fraud scheme. *Miami Herald*. https://www.miamiherald.com/news/nation-world/world/americas/article239319133.html

Z33. (2021). *In the Eye of the Storm*. Z33. https://www.z33.be/en/programma/in-the-eye-of-the-storm/

ACKNOWLEDGEMENTS

This book is based on my doctoral dissertation, itself the product of a collaborative journey that began well before my doctoral studies. Many have contributed—some so profoundly their names could be on the cover, others simply through their presence.

First and foremost, this work exists thanks to the unyielding spirit of the warriors from Barbuda and from the Caño Martín Peña communities and organizations, who embraced me and trusted me with their experiences, insights, and theories. The ideas presented here are theirs, and they deserve the credit. In Puerto Rico, I am especially grateful to José Caraballo Pagán, Evelyn Quiñones, Carmen Febres Alméstica, Lucy Cruz Rivera, Mario Nuñez Mercado, Rafael Ocasio, Doris Pizarro, Lucilla Fuller Marvel, and Alejandro Cotté Morales, all of whom contributed significantly to this research. Special thanks go to my colleague and friend Mariolga Juliá Pacheco who supported this research from its onset, and from whom I have learned so much about social struggles in Puerto Rico. In Barbuda, I owe everything to John Mussington, an endless source of inspiration and knowledge for a better world. I also extend my heartfelt gratitude to Jackie Frank, Gulliver Johnson, Devon Warner, Trevor Walker, Diane, Jacquee and Darlene Beazer, and everyone else involved in the Barbuda resistance. Thank you for showing me your beautiful island, I will continue to help protect it. Thanks also to everyone involved in the struggle for land and climate justice in Barbuda at the Global Legal Action Network.

Secondly, I want to acknowledge my co-authors. Primarily, María E. Hernández Torrales, with whom I have written two articles that serve as chapters of this book, as well as multiple other publications. María, I owe you immensely, not only for the work on these publications and the indispensable practical support you provided during my time in Puerto Rico, but also for sharing your sharp insights, especially on what it means to be an engaged researcher, that have influenced my worldview and deeply impacted this work. I also want to thank my co-author Lyvia N. Rodríguez Del Valle. Meeting you in your role as Executive Director of the Caño Martín Peña CLT profoundly shaped my understanding of urban planning, housing, and community participation. So much of what is written here derives from conversations with you. I also extend my sincere gratitude to my other co-authors Ellen M. Bassett and Antonio Carmona Báez, for their time and dedication. I also thank John Mussington for contributing to and editing the articles on Barbuda.

Sincere thanks also go to my supervisors Bas van Heur and David Bassens, for their support throughout this process, and to the jury members who reviewed the first version of the dissertation and enhanced it with their critical input: Prof. Dr. Michael Ryckewaert, Prof. Dr. Nele Aernouts, Prof. Dr. Brenna Bhandar, Prof. Dr. Érika Fontánez Torres, Prof. Dr. Rosalba Icaza Garza, and Dr. Adriana Moreno Cely. To John E. Davis, Greg Rosenberg, Brenda Torpy, Geert De Pauw, and everyone else at the International Center for Community Land Trusts for facilitating the publication of this book and for their support throughout the years. To my friends and comrades in Puerto Rico, Raúl Santiago Bartolomei, Sarah Molinari, Maritza Stanchich, Pete Becerra, Patricia Noboa Ortega, Carlos Claussell Velez, David Auerbach, Sean Doherty, Beto Talanehzar, Isabel Talanehzar. To my colleagues at VUB, Laura Deruytter, Hala El Moussawi, Nele Aernouts, Lena Imeraj, Mariana Santos, Céline Drieskens, and specifically Anna Plyushteva, Deborah Lambert, Arshia Ali Azmat, Amy Phillips, and René Kreichauf. To the VUB students, especially those who stood up for justice and liberation, when the world needed it most. Thanks also to Enrique Silva and the Lincoln Institute of Land Policy, to Tarcyla Fidalgo Ribeiro and Theresa Williamson at Catalytic Communities, and to Liz Alden Wily and Claire Simonneau. To the Stronger Caribbean Together for Land, Food, and Climate Justice network. To the University of St. Martin, and the Institute for Public Architecture and the Luskin Institute on Inequality and Democracy at UCLA.

Infinite thanks to Antonio Carmona Báez for inspiring this work, and thanks to my family for their support—my parents, my siblings, their partners, my niblings, my goddaughters and their brothers, and my chosen family. Special thanks to Maartje Alders for the beautiful cover art and the graphic design, and to Parastou Saberi for the copy-editing. Special thanks to my gifted nibling, Raven, for acting as my research assistant. This work, and all future work, is dedicated to all of you.

ABOUT THE AUTHORS

Line Algoed is an urban anthropologist and human geographer with expertise in communal land tenure, participatory urban planning, and affordable housing. She is a lecturer and postdoctoral researcher at the Cosmopolis Center for Urban Research, Department of Geography, Vrije Universiteit Brussel, Belgium. Her research explores the role of communal land tenure in the face of climate change in the Caribbean. She collaborates with the Caño Martín Peña Community Land Trust in Puerto Rico on international exchange projects, serves on the Board of Directors of the International Center for Community Land Trusts, and is co-editor of the book *On Common Ground: International Perspectives on the Community Land Trust*.

Ellen M. Bassett is Dean and John Portman Chair of the College of Design at the Georgia Institute of Technology. Trained as an urban planner, her areas of research interest and expertise are land tenure, land use planning and law, climate change planning, health and the built environment, and international development. She worked on one of the first land tenure projects in the Global South, namely the community land trust established in an informal settlement upgrading project in Voi, Kenya in the 1990s.

Antonio Carmona Báez is professor of International Relations and the Political Economy of Development, currently serving as President of the University of St. Martin in Philipsburg. Completing his doctoral degree from the University of Amsterdam in 2002, he has designed and taught graduate and undergraduate courses at the same university and at the University of Puerto Rico in Río Piedras and Bayamón. Carmona Báez is Co-PI of the 5-year multidisciplinary research programme Island(er)s at the Helm which studies climate challenges and is funded by the Dutch Research Council NWO. His publication record covers themes ranging from Caribbean socio-economic development, Decolonial Thought and political constellations, to public policies related to energy privatisation, gender and post-hurricane recovery.

María E. Hernández Torrales earned her Juris Doctor from the University of Puerto Rico and is a licensed attorney. She holds a master's degree in education from New York University, a master's degree in environmental law from the Vermont Law School, and certifications in mediation from the Supreme Court of Puerto Rico; in bioethics from the Medical Sciences Campus of the University of Puerto Rico; and a master's in land policy and sustainable urban development from the Lincoln Institute of Land Policy and the National University of Distance Education in Spain. She is currently pursuing a professional doctorate in organizational systems management. For 16 years, she has served as an adjunct clinical professor at the Legal Aid Clinic of the University of Puerto Rico Law School, where she teaches the Community Economic Development Clinic. Alongside her students, she advises and collaborates with organized or organizing communities on issues related to community economic development.

Lyvia N. Rodríguez Del Valle is an urban and regional planner with extensive executive experience, specializing in the right to the city, collective land tenure, community development, participatory action-planning and governance, particularly in self-built settlements. Lyvia served as founding executive director of the Proyecto ENLACE del Caño Martín Peña and the World Habitat Award recipient Fideicomiso de la Tierra del Caño Martín Peña. She cofounded El Enjambre Colectivo, a non-profit focused on collective land tenure, displacement, and grassroots organizing in Puerto Rico and Latin America, as well as the consultancy firm El Enjambre. She also serves in the boards of Catalytic Communities and the International Center for Community Land Trusts, and is an adjuct professor at the Graduate School of Planning, University of Puerto Rico.

www.ingramcontent.com/pod-product-compliance
Lightning Source LLC
Chambersburg PA
CBHW020540030426
42337CB00013B/917